# Communications in Computer and Information Science    2786

Series Editors

Gang Li, *School of Information Technology, Deakin University, Burwood, VIC, Australia*

Joaquim Filipe, *Polytechnic Institute of Setúbal, Setúbal, Portugal*

Zhiwei Xu, *Chinese Academy of Sciences, Beijing, China*

**Rationale**

The CCIS series is devoted to the publication of proceedings of computer science conferences. Its aim is to efficiently disseminate original research results in informatics in printed and electronic form. While the focus is on publication of peer-reviewed full papers presenting mature work, inclusion of reviewed short papers reporting on work in progress is welcome, too. Besides globally relevant meetings with internationally representative program committees guaranteeing a strict peer-reviewing and paper selection process, conferences run by societies or of high regional or national relevance are also considered for publication.

**Topics**

The topical scope of CCIS spans the entire spectrum of informatics ranging from foundational topics in the theory of computing to information and communications science and technology and a broad variety of interdisciplinary application fields.

**Information for Volume Editors and Authors**

Publication in CCIS is free of charge. No royalties are paid, however, we offer registered conference participants temporary free access to the online version of the conference proceedings on SpringerLink (http://link.springer.com) by means of an http referrer from the conference website and/or a number of complimentary printed copies, as specified in the official acceptance email of the event.

CCIS proceedings can be published in time for distribution at conferences or as post-proceedings, and delivered in the form of printed books and/or electronically as USBs and/or e-content licenses for accessing proceedings at SpringerLink. Furthermore, CCIS proceedings are included in the CCIS electronic book series hosted in the SpringerLink digital library at http://link.springer.com/bookseries/7899. Conferences publishing in CCIS are allowed to use our online conference service (Meteor) for managing the whole proceedings lifecycle (from submission and reviewing to preparing for publication) free of charge.

**Publication process**

The language of publication is exclusively English. Authors publishing in CCIS have to sign the Springer CCIS copyright transfer form, however, they are free to use their material published in CCIS for substantially changed, more elaborate subsequent publications elsewhere. For the preparation of the camera-ready papers/files, authors have to strictly adhere to the Springer CCIS Authors' Instructions and are strongly encouraged to use the CCIS LaTeX style files or templates.

**Abstracting/Indexing**

CCIS is abstracted/indexed in DBLP, Google Scholar, EI-Compendex, Mathematical Reviews, SCImago, Scopus. CCIS volumes are also submitted for the inclusion in ISI Proceedings.

**How to start**

To start the evaluation of your proposal for inclusion in the CCIS series, please send an e-mail to ccis@springer.com

Alejandro Bellogin · Ludovico Boratto ·
Federica Cena · Angelo Geninatti Cossatin ·
Theo Huibers · Styliani Kleanthous ·
Monica Landoni · Elisabeth Lex ·
Francesca Maridina Malloci · Mirko Marras ·
Noemi Mauro · Emiliana Murgia ·
Maria Soledad Pera
Editors

# Advances in Bias, Fairness, and Understudied Users in Information Retrieval

6th International Workshop, BIAS 2025
and 2nd International Workshop, IR4U2 2025
Padua, Italy, July 17, 2025
Revised Selected Papers

 Springer

*Editors*
Alejandro Bellogin
Universidad Autónoma de Madrid
Madrid, Spain

Ludovico Boratto
University of Cagliari
Cagliari, Italy

Federica Cena
University of Turin
Turin, Italy

Angelo Geninatti Cossatin
University of Turin
Turin, Italy

Theo Huibers
University of Twente
Enschede, The Netherlands

Styliani Kleanthous
Open University of Cyprus
Nicosia, Cyprus

Monica Landoni
Università della Svizzera Italiana
Lugano, Switzerland

Elisabeth Lex
Graz University of Technology
Graz, Austria

Francesca Maridina Malloci
University of Cagliari
Cagliari, Italy

Mirko Marras
University of Cagliari
Cagliari, Italy

Noemi Mauro
University of Turin
Turin, Italy

Emiliana Murgia
University of Genoa
Genoa, Italy

Maria Soledad Pera
TU Delft
Delft, The Netherlands

ISSN 1865-0929        ISSN 1865-0937 (electronic)
Communications in Computer and Information Science
ISBN 978-3-032-12716-7        ISBN 978-3-032-12717-4 (eBook)
https://doi.org/10.1007/978-3-032-12717-4



This Springer imprint is published by the registered company Springer Nature Switzerland AG
The registered company address is: Gewerbestrasse 11, 6330 Cham, Switzerland

If disposing of this product, please recycle the paper.

# Preface

This volume of Springer's Communications in Computer and Information Science (CCIS) series contains the accepted papers presented at the Sixth International Workshop on Algorithmic Bias in Search and Recommendation (BIAS 2025) and the Second International Workshop on Information Retrieval for Understudied Users (IR4U2 2025), held as part of the 48th International ACM SIGIR Conference on Research and Development in Information Retrieval (SIGIR 2025) on July 17, 2025 in Padua, Italy. The decision to present their proceedings together in this joint volume was motivated by their shared focus on responsible and inclusive information access. This choice not only reflects their complementary scopes but also provides a unified resource for readers, fostering visibility, coherence, and cross-fertilization of ideas across the two research communities.

The BIAS 2025 workshop was organized by Universidad Autónoma de Madrid (Spain), University of Cagliari (Italy), Open University of Cyprus (Cyprus), and Graz University of Technology (Austria). This edition received a total of 7 submissions. Each submission underwent a rigorous double-blind review process, with evaluations conducted by a minimum of three members of the program committee. As a result of this selection process, 3 full papers were accepted in the final program. The workshop day opened with welcome remarks, followed by a keynote talk by Erasmo Purificato (European Commission's Joint Research Centre, Italy), which examined the intersection of fairness-aware model development and emerging regulatory frameworks, such as the EU Digital Services Act and AI Act. An open discussion invited participants to reflect on how these regulatory shifts may influence their research or practice. After a short break, the paper session began with three presentations addressing different strategies for mitigating bias in information access systems, including methods for improving fairness in retrieval-augmented generation, exploring the impact of sampling techniques, and reducing position bias in ranking models. The session was concluded with an open discussion on key takeaways. In the afternoon, Shlomo Berkovsky (Macquarie University, Australia) delivered the second keynote, which investigated challenges unique to medical artificial intelligence from a recommendation perspective and emphasized the importance of user education in understanding system bias and reliability. A subsequent discussion focused on how to better inform non-technical users about these issues. The workshop concluded with a wrap-up session, where participants reflected on future research directions.

The IR4U2 2025 workshop was the result of a joint effort among TU Delft (The Netherlands), Università della Svizzera Italiana (Switzerland), University of Genoa (Italy), University of Turin (Italy), and University of Twente (The Netherlands). In this edition, the workshop received 6 submissions, each subjected to a double-blind peer review by at least three programme committee members. All the 6 submitted full papers were accepted for inclusion in the program. The workshop day opened with welcome remarks, followed by a keynote by Stephane Chaudron, a freelance consultant with extensive experience in project management, research, education, and communication. Her talk examined the impact of intelligent systems - such as recommendation algorithms and content moderation - on children's rights, particularly those of underserved and vulnerable populations. An open discussion session followed, fostering reflections on the responsibilities of digital platforms in mitigating risks. The first paper session, after a short break, featured three presentations, covering adaptive search interfaces for children with mild intellectual disabilities, personalized recommendations for adults with autism spectrum disorder, and sign language-based conversational product search. This was followed by short pitches on innovative ideas and a participatory activity involving the audience. The second paper session, which ran in the afternoon, addressed children's engagement with digital content through studies on music recommendations, emotional profiling of large language models in response to children's queries, and a serious game designed to raise awareness about information pollution. A second interactive activity, followed by a general discussion and wrap-up session, concluded the workshop.

Both workshops continue to build on the success of their previous editions, marked by growing engagement from the community. This ongoing success motivates the organizers to plan a future edition for next year. We sincerely thank the authors and reviewers for their contributions in shaping a rich and engaging program, and we are grateful to the attendees for their active participation.

July 2025

Alejandro Bellogin<br>
Ludovico Boratto<br>
Federica Cena<br>
Angelo Geninatti Cossatin<br>
Theo Huibers<br>
Styliani Kleanthous<br>
Elisabeth Lex<br>
Monica Landoni<br>
Francesca Maridina Malloci<br>
Mirko Marras<br>
Noemi Mauro<br>
Emiliana Murgia<br>
Maria Soledad Pera

# Organization

**BIAS 2025**

## Program Committee Chairs

| | |
|---|---|
| Alejandro Bellogin | Universidad Autónoma de Madrid, Spain |
| Ludovico Boratto | University of Cagliari, Italy |
| Styliani Kleanthous | Open University of Cyprus, Cyprus |
| Elisabeth Lex | Graz University of Technology, Austria |
| Francesca Maridina Malloci | University of Cagliari, Italy |
| Mirko Marras | University of Cagliari, Italy |

## Program Committee Members

| | |
|---|---|
| Marcelo Armentano | ISISTAN Research Institute, Argentina |
| Ashwathy Ashokana | University of Nebraska Omaha, USA |
| Bettina Berendt | KU Leuven, Belgium |
| Glencora Borradaile | Oregon State University, USA |
| Ivan Cantador | Universidad Autónoma de Madrid, Spain |
| Federica Cena | University of Turin, Italy |
| Vamshi Enabothala | Pinecone, USA |
| Fabian Haak | TH Köln, Germany |
| Claudia Hauff | Google Research, Netherlands |
| Toshihiro Kamishima | AIST, Japan |
| Anastasiia Klimashevskaia | University of Bergen, Norway |
| Marina Kogan | University of Utah, USA |
| Matthew Lease | University of Texas at Austin, USA |
| Aonghus Lawlor | University College Dublin, Ireland |
| Cataldo Musto | University of Bari Aldo Moro, Italy |
| Fedelucio Narducci | University of Bari Aldo Moro, Italy |
| Rebekah Overdorf | University of Lausanne, Switzerland |
| Panagiotis Papadakos | FORTH-ICS, Greece |
| Philipp Schaer | TH Köln, Germany |
| Dimitris Sacharidis | Université libre de Bruxelles, Belgium |
| Damiano Spina | RMIT University, Australia |
| Antonela Tommasel | ISISTAN Research Institute, Argentina |

Marko Tkalčič                     University of Primorska, Slovenia
Eva Zangerle                      University of Innsbruck, Austria

# IR4U2 2025

## Program Committee Chairs

Federica Cena                     University of Turin, Italy
Angelo Geninatti Cossatin         University of Turin, Italy
Theo Huibers                      University of Twente, The Netherlands
Monica Landoni                    Università della Svizzera Italiana, Switzerland
Noemi Mauro                       University of Turin, Italy
Emiliana Murgia                   University of Genoa, Italy
Maria Soledad Pera                TU Delft, The Netherlands

## Program Committee Members

Ludovico Boratto                  University of Cagliari, Italy
Michael Ekstrand                  Drexel University, USA
Hanna Hauptmann                   Utrecht University, The Netherlands
Bart Knijnenburg                  Clemson University, USA
Mirko Marras                      University of Cagliari, Italy
Giacomo Medda                     University of Cagliari, Italy
Ashlee Milton                     University of Minnesota, USA
Giuseppe Sansonetti               Roma Tre University, Italy
Marko Tkalčič                     University of Primorska, Slovenia
Fabiana Vernero                   University of Turin, Italy

# Contents

# Bias and Fairness (Bias 2025)

# Adaptive Repetition for Mitigating Position Bias in LLM-Based Ranking

Ali Vardasbi[1]([✉]) [iD], Gustavo Penha[2] [iD], Claudia Hauff[3] [iD],
and Hugues Bouchard[4] [iD]

[1] Spotify, Amsterdam, Netherlands
`aliv@spotify.com`
[2] Spotify, New York City, United States
`gustavop@spotify.com`
[3] Spotify, Delft, Netherlands
`claudiah@spotify.com`
[4] Spotify, Barcelona, Spain
`hb@spotify.com`

**Abstract.** When using LLMs to rank items based on given criteria, or evaluate answers, the order of candidate items can influence the model's final decision. This sensitivity to item positioning in a LLM's prompt is known as *position bias*. Prior research shows that this bias exists even in large models, though its severity varies across models and tasks. In addition to position bias, LLMs also exhibit varying degrees of low *repetition consistency*, where repeating the LLM call with the same candidate ordering can lead to different rankings. To address both inconsistencies, a common approach is to prompt the model multiple times with different candidate orderings and aggregate the results via majority voting. However, this repetition strategy, significantly increases computational costs.

Extending prior findings, we observe that both the direction—favoring either the earlier or later candidate in the prompt—and magnitude of position bias across instances vary substantially, even within a single dataset. This observation highlights the need for a *per-instance* mitigation strategy. To this end, we introduce a dynamic early-stopping method that adaptively determines the number of repetitions required for each instance. Evaluating our approach across three LLMs of varying sizes and on two tasks, namely re-ranking and alignment, we demonstrate that transitioning to a dynamic repetition strategy reduces the number of LLM calls by an average of 81%, while preserving the accuracy. Furthermore, we propose a confidence-based adaptation to our early-stopping method, reducing LLM calls by an average of 87% compared to static repetition, with only a slight accuracy trade-off relative to our original early-stopping method.

**Keywords:** LLM-as-a-Judge · Position Bias


A. Bellogin et al. (Eds.): IR4U2 2025/BIAS 2025, CCIS 2786, pp. 3–15, 2026.
https://doi.org/10.1007/978-3-032-12717-4_1

# 1   Introduction

LLMs are increasingly used to select a winner from a set of items in various tasks, such as comparing the responses of different LLMs to questions [6,15,17], re-ranking documents based on their relevance to a query [12], or answering multiple-choice questions [14,21]. Here, we focus on scenarios where an LLM is given a set of items and asked to select *one* as the top-ranked item or winner. Accordingly, we use the terms *ranking* and *judgment* interchangeably throughout the paper. Previous research has shown that LLMs, even highly capable models, exhibit position bias [15,20], which refers to the inconsistency in the LLM's verdict when the order of candidates within one prompt is changed. We refer to this as a lack of *permutation consistency* (PC). Additionally, *repetition consistency* (RC) measures the stability of the LLM's responses when the same prompt is repeated with the same ordering. A low RC suggests that the model may be uncertain or sensitive to minor variations. Together, high values of PC and RC could be indicators of a *low-variance* judgment, as they reflect the stability and consistency of the model's decisions.

Previous studies [1,15,17] have shown that repeating judgments with different permutations and selecting the majority outcome enhances robustness. Our experiments confirm these findings, demonstrating that increasing the number of repetitions[1] reduces variance and improves average accuracy. However, more repetitions also lead to higher computational costs. *Ideally, we are interested in maintaining similar accuracy levels while minimizing cost.*

Our contributions in this paper are as follows: **(1)** Our experiments on five different datasets reveal that the position bias of LLMs is not only task-dependent but can also vary across instances. Specifically, while an LLM may show a preference for earlier-positioned candidates in one judgment instance, it may exhibit a preference for later-positioned candidates in another instance within the same dataset (Sect. 4.1). This highlights the need for a per-instance treatment of position bias in LLMs. **(2)** We propose an effective approach to address position bias on a per-instance basis: adaptively determining the number of required repetitions for each instance, significantly reducing the number of LLM calls by 81% on average (hence lowering the cost) while maintaining accuracy at a comparable level. Our early-stopping method (Sect. 2.1) strikes a balance between accuracy and efficiency. For harder instances, where LLM judgments are less stable, we perform additional repetitions to improve reliability. However, on average, the total number of LLM calls remains low, ensuring computational efficiency without sacrificing ranking robustness—achieving the best of both worlds. **(3)** We further refine our early-stopping method by estimating repeat inconsistency based on the LLM's confidence (Sect. 2.2), reducing LLM calls by an average of 87% compared to the static repetition strategy.

***Disclaimer.*** This paper is not focused on comparing LLMs or evaluating their relative performance; therefore, we do not name specific models. Our goal is to highlight the presence of position bias and repetition inconsistency, and to

---

[1] We observe a plateau in accuracy beyond 24 repetitions.

demonstrate that these issues can be effectively mitigated. We observed consistent behaviors across three LLMs of varying sizes (from moderately sized to state-of-the-art large-scale LLMs), including both proprietary and open-source models, and report results from these representative models to illustrate the effectiveness of our approach. We refer to these LLM models simply by LLM-1, LLM-2, and LLM-3.

## 2 Robust Rankings

Assume an LLM-based ranking scenario, where an LLM is used for pairwise comparisons over a list of paired candidates $\{(a_i, b_i)\}_{i=1}^{N}$. We denote the outcome of the LLM when prompted to pick one from the *ordered* candidates $(a, b)$ as $J(a, b)$. Repeating the ranking task $n$ times with the same ordering of candidates results in a vector of $n$ outcomes, which we denote as $\mathcal{J}^n(a, b) \in \{a, b\}^n$. See Fig. 1 for a concrete example.

***Repetition Consistency.*** We consider the LLM for the ordered candidates $(a, b)$ to be repetition consistent (RC) after $n$ repetitions if the $\mathcal{J}^n(a, b)$ vector consists of a unique verdict, and we call the unique verdict the *stable decision*.

***Permutation Consistency.*** We consider an LLM to be permutation consistent (PC) for candidates $(a, b)$ after $n$ repetitions if all outcomes for both input orderings are identical. In other words, $(a, b)$ and $(b, a)$ are both repetition consistent (RC), and the vectors $\mathcal{J}^n(a, b)$ and $\mathcal{J}^n(b, a)$ contain the *same* stable decisions.

It is worth noting that the definitions of RC and PC depend on both the specific experiment and the number of repetitions $n$. Throughout this paper, references to RC and PC assume a finite, practical number of repetitions. Similarly, when we refer to stable rankings, we mean stability within the context of the given experiment and repetition count; this does not necessarily imply stability for larger numbers of repetitions.

***Consensus Outcome.*** The consensus outcome after $2n$ repetitions, denoted as $C^{2n}(a, b) \in \{a, b, tie\}$, is determined by majority voting over the concatenation of $\mathcal{J}^n(a, b)$ and $\mathcal{J}^n(b, a)$. If $a$ and $b$ appear an equal number of times in the concatenated vector, the consensus outcome is deemed *inconclusive*, resulting in a *tie*.

As discussed earlier, prior studies show that increasing $n$ improves the accuracy of consensus outcome [1]. However, the efficiency decreases as $n$ grows. Next, we propose two early-stopping methods that significantly reduce the average number of LLM repetitions while preserving the accuracy of the consensus outcome.

***Remark.*** In this paper, our experiments focus exclusively on pairwise rankings. Our findings can be generalized to listwise rankings by replacing the swapping of two items with different permutations of the candidate list. While this introduces exponential complexity as the number of items increases, prior work (e.g., [1]) has shown that *cyclic permutations* offer a practical alternative with linear complexity.

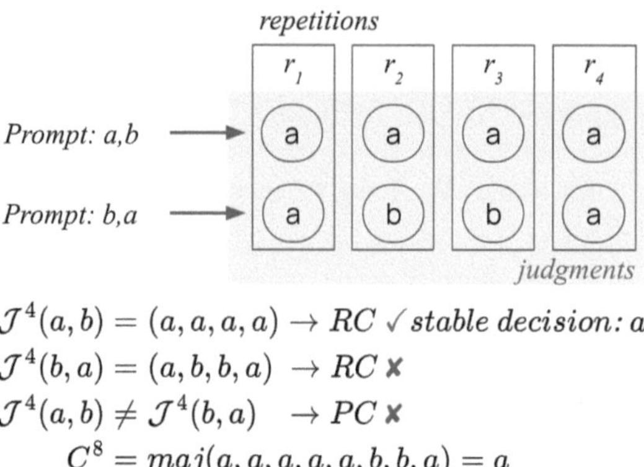



$$\mathcal{J}^4(a,b) = (a,a,a,a) \rightarrow RC \checkmark \text{ stable decision: } a$$
$$\mathcal{J}^4(b,a) = (a,b,b,a) \rightarrow RC \times$$
$$\mathcal{J}^4(a,b) \neq \mathcal{J}^4(b,a) \rightarrow PC \times$$
$$C^8 = maj(a,a,a,a,a,b,b,a) = a$$

**Fig. 1.** Example outcomes and corresponding RC, PC and $C^{2n}$ values.

***Observation.*** We first present a key observation that serves as the foundation of our early-stopping strategies in the following sections. Across extensive experiments, we found that for nearly all candidate pairs, the LLM's outcome after multiple repetitions remains consistent for at least one input ordering. We hypothesize that this observation occurs when the judgment of the LLM regarding the winner candidate coincides with its position bias for that pair of candidates (see Sect. 4.1). To elaborate, if an LLM exhibits a positional preference for the earlier candidate and also inherently favors candidate $a$ over $b$ based on its reasoning, then when $a$ is placed in the first position, the model's outcome remains consistent. In such cases, the LLM's inherent preference aligns with the positional bias, reinforcing the selection of $a$ and leading to a stable decision. Conversely, when the LLM's intrinsic preference contradicts its position bias for a given order, inconsistency may arise across different repetitions of its judgment. Formally:

**Observation 1.** *With high empirical probability, for each LLM and candidate pair $(a,b)$, the LLM is RC for at least one of the orderings $(a,b)$ or $(b,a)$. This implies that, with only a small fraction of exceptions, the LLM outcome for one of the orderings remains consistent as the number of repetitions increases.*

Table 1 shows the violation rates of this observation for different LLMs and datasets (see Sect. 3, Datasets). Here, the violation rate means the percentage of the candidate pairs for which none of the orderings are RC for $n = 12$. As is seen in this table, the this percentage remains small across models and datasets.

Based on Observation 1, we propose two early stopping approaches to improve LLM robustness while minimizing computational costs. We validate our methods across three LLMs and five diverse datasets (see Sect. 3).

**Table 1.** Violation rates for Observation 1 with $n = 12$.

| Dataset | LLM-1 | LLM-2 | LLM-3 |
|---|---|---|---|
| MSMarco | 0.97% | 0.69% | 4.5% |
| Emerton-DPO | 6.3% | 3.1% | 1.4% |
| Orca-DPO | 5.5% | 3.5% | 0.87% |
| Py-DPO | 2.6% | 4.8% | 0.7% |
| Truthy-DPO | 1.7% | 1.5% | 0.76% |

## 2.1 Early Stopping

Our early stopping criterion is an approximation that assumes Observation 1 holds with probability 1. In other words, for the small fraction of violating instances reported in Table 1, our early stopping criterion may not yield the consensus outcome. However, for the vast majority of instances, it is guaranteed to converge to the consensus outcome.

Our early stopping works as follows. Starting from $n = 1$, we prompt the LLM-ranker with both orderings $(a, b)$ and $(b, a)$ and monitor $C^{2n}(a, b)$. We stop the repetition as soon as we reach a conclusive majority voting outcome. In other words, we increment $n$ *only* if the majority voting is inconclusive, i.e., when $C^{2n}(a, b) = tie$.

In what follows we discuss why this method leads to consensus outcome. For each $n$, one of the following situations must occur: (I) Both orderings are RC but with different stable decisions, e.g. $\mathcal{J}^3(a, b) = (a, a, a)$ and $\mathcal{J}^3(b, a) = (b, b, b)$. (II) Both orderings are RC with the same stable decisions. (III) Only one of the vectors is RC, while the other contains mixed outcomes. (IV) Neither of the vectors is RC.

First, note that the last case, i.e., (IV), occurs with low empirical probability according to Table 1. Therefore, we ignore this case, as its rarity means it contributes negligibly to the overall accuracy (as validated experimentally in Sect. 4.2). Among the remaining cases, only in case (I), where each RC vector has a different stable decision, will $C^{2n}(a, b)$ be inconclusive, requiring additional repetitions. In the other two cases, without loss of generality, assume that the stable decision of the RC vector is $a$. Since the other vector is not RC with $b$, it must contain at least one outcome that differs from $b$ (either $a$ or producing a *tie*). As a result, the majority vote in the concatenated vector will favor $a$, and this consensus will remain unchanged (with high probability) as $n$ increases because, according to Observation 1, the ordering will continue to be RC and consistently generate $a$. Thus, by detecting the RC ordering early and stopping as soon as a conclusive majority is reached, we significantly reduce the number of repetitions required while preserving decision accuracy.

***Example.*** Suppose the outcome vectors for a given instance are $\mathcal{J}^2(a, b) = (a, a)$ and $\mathcal{J}^2(b, a) = (b, b)$. For $n = 1$ and $n = 2$, we fall into case (I): it remains uncertain which ordering will be RC for larger $n$. However, at $n = 3$, we observe that only the first vector is RC: $\mathcal{J}^3(a,b) = (a,a,a)$ and $\mathcal{J}^3(b,a) = (b,b,a)$ (case (III)). Note that according to Observation 1, since the ordering $(b,a)$ is not RC, with high probability the other ordering remains RC even for larger values of $n$, i.e., the ordering $(a,b)$ will consistently generate $a$. Consequently, the consensus outcome stabilizes at $a$ for all $n \geq 3$.

## 2.2 Confidence-Based Early Stopping

In the early stopping method discussed in Sect. 2.1, when two contradicting RC vectors occur, i.e., case (I), the repetition must continue until a tie is broken. The challenge arises when the vectors remain contradictory even after reaching the maximum number of repetitions. If we could predict this outcome in advance, we could declare such instances a *tie* sooner.

To achieve this, let's assume we can estimate the probability gap $g = |P_a - P_b|$ between the two candidates based on a single sample of the paired judgment results: $\big(J(a,b), J(b,a)\big)$, without directly knowing which candidate is more probable (since otherwise, no repetitions would be necessary). Let $n_M$ denote the maximum number of paired repetitions. If our estimated gap $g$ is accurate, and we were to repeat the judgment for each ordering $n_M$ times, then for sufficiently large $n_M$, we would observe approximately $(1 - g)n_M$ and $(1 + g)n_M$ of the minority and majority outcomes, respectively, in the concatenated vector of paired repeated judgments. In the worst-case scenario, the first $(1 - g)n_M$ paired judgments could fall into case (I) (as described in Sect. 2.1), leading to an inconclusive outcome. Therefore, at most $(1 - g)n_M + 1$ paired repetitions are needed to guarantee a conclusive result.

For now, assume we have access to an oracle that provides $g$ for a given candidate pair $(a, b)$ and the LLM ranker. Our approach is as follows: We adapt the early stopping method in Sect. 2.1 by limiting the number of paired repetitions to $(1 - g)n_M + 1$, instead of the full $n_M$, where $g$ is specific to the candidate pair instance.

***Confidence Gap.*** Now, we need to define the method that can be used to estimate the probability gap $g = |P_a - P_b|$. For this, we prompt the LLM judges to include a *confidence* value in their judgments, indicating their level of confidence in the generated answer [19]. Our experiments show a correlation between the confidence gap—i.e., the gap between the average generated confidence values of the LLM when outputting $a$ compared to $b$—and the probability gap $g$. As such, we use the confidence gap to estimate the probability gap. To make the estimate data-driven, we sample a small percentage of instances (10%) to fit a linear model that predicts the probability gap from the confidence gap. When reporting the average number of calls (Table 3), we consider the number of calls for this training data to be $2 \times n_M$ (24 in our tests).

***Remark.*** Our notion of probability gap is inspired by prior research showing that the quality gap between candidates can influence the magnitude of position bias [15,17,20].

## 3  Experimental Setup

***Datasets.*** We have used the following datasets in our LLM-as-a-judge experiments:

- **Re-rank:** We used the test sets from the 2019 and 2020 TREC Deep Learning (TREC-DL) competitions: TREC-DL 2019 and TREC-DL 2020, both of which provide dense human relevance annotations for each query. These datasets are based on the MS MARCO v1 document corpus. In total, there are 86 unique queries, with 1,449 sampled document pairs. For each query, we sampled documents from the top 100 retrieved by the original dataset provider. Additionally, we ensured that each sampled document pair had a minimum relevance score gap of 2, as per the provided annotations.
- **Alignment:** Following [20], we use four DPO (Direct Preference Optimization) datasets [13], where each dataset is composed of user feedback collected across various scenarios. Each prompt in these datasets is paired with a positive ("chose") and a negative ("reject") answer, reflecting user preferences and rejections. The datasets include: (I) Emerton-DPO [10] with 839 samples, (II) Orca-DPO [11] with 923 samples, (III) Py-DPO [3] with 1003 samples, and (IV) Truthy-DPO [2] with 654 samples.

***Models.*** We run our experiments on three LLMs of varying capabilities and sizes: an open-source and two proprietary models of varying scales, from mid-sized to some of the largest publicly or commercially available LLMs. We refer these by LLM-1, LLM-2, and LLM-3.

***Remark.*** *This study does not aim to compare these LLMs against each other. Instead, it seeks to demonstrate that repeated LLM calls can enhance ranking consistency across a spectrum of models, from compact to large-scale. The selected models are intentionally diverse in capacity to illustrate this effect comprehensively.*

***Parameters.*** We set the maximum number of repetitions for the consensus judgment to 24 ($n_M = 12$). While RC and PC values may slightly change with a higher repetition cap, we consider 24 repetitions to be beyond the practical threshold for LLM-based judgments. Moreover, our experiments show that overall judgment accuracy plateaus after this point, indicating diminishing returns from additional repetitions. For all LLM calls, we set the temperature to 0.1 to reduce variance in the model's responses while still allowing some degrees of diversity. This choice aligns with prior work [15, 20], which similarly adopted non-zero temperature values to avoid trivial or overly deterministic outputs.

## 4  Results

In this section, we first demonstrate that position bias (indicated by imperfect RC and PC values) in LLMs not only varies in magnitude but can also vary in direction within a single dataset. This leads to LLM preferences for earlier items in some judgment instances and for later items in others. Consequently, attempting to address position bias with a single treatment for each task results in suboptimal performance. This suggests that the most robust approach to mitigating a lack of RC and PC is to conduct a large number of paired repetitions and select the consensus judgment.

Subsequently, we present the cost reduction results obtained from our early-stopping methods in Sect. 2, demonstrating how these reductions are achieved while preserving the robustness and accuracy of the consensus judgment.

**Table 2.** Comparison of bias metrics for different LLMs on different datasets.

| Dataset | PC | | | Primacy Biased | | | Recency Biased | | |
|---|---|---|---|---|---|---|---|---|---|
| | LLM-1 | LLM-2 | LLM-3 | LLM-1 | LLM-2 | LLM-3 | LLM-1 | LLM-2 | LLM-3 |
| MSMarco | 0.726 | 0.798 | 0.436 | 0.030 | 0.152 | 0.334 | 0.244 | 0.050 | 0.230 |
| Emerton-DPO | 0.371 | 0.308 | 0.239 | 0.303 | 0.263 | 0.632 | 0.326 | 0.429 | 0.129 |
| Orca-DPO | 0.547 | 0.462 | 0.325 | 0.295 | 0.247 | 0.552 | 0.158 | 0.292 | 0.123 |
| Py-DPO | 0.694 | 0.557 | 0.313 | 0.219 | 0.229 | 0.650 | 0.086 | 0.214 | 0.037 |
| Truthy-DPO | 0.787 | 0.673 | 0.680 | 0.188 | 0.120 | 0.222 | 0.025 | 0.208 | 0.099 |

## 4.1   Preference Variation

First, focusing on PC and RC parameters, we show that the bias of an LLM varies in direction for different judgment instances from the same dataset. We distinguish between three types of behaviors: 1. **PC:** The LLM shows no preference for the position of candidates, demonstrating PC. 2. **Primacy Biased:** The LLM favors the first item in a pair in its prompt. 3. **Recency Biased:** The LLM favors the last item in a pair in its prompt. Table 2 shows the ratio of instances that fall within each category of behavior.

While we categorize position bias into primacy and recency directions based on empirical patterns in model judgments, we refrain to claim a singular underlying cause. Position bias may arise from various architectural or representational factors, such as the model's attention dynamics, tokenization artifacts, or prompt formatting, that are difficult to disentangle, especially across different LLMs. Rather than assuming a fixed mechanism, our approach acknowledges the empirical presence of position bias and proposes a generalizable, instance-adaptive method to mitigate its effects. By observing that the direction and magnitude of bias vary across instances, we focus on robustness at inference time through dynamic repetition strategies, without relying on assumptions about model internals. A deeper mechanistic understanding remains an important direction for future work, especially for developing complementary mitigation strategies.

Among the datasets in Table 2, we observe that LLM-1 on Emerton-DPO and LLM-2 on both Orca-DPO and Py-DPO datasets exhibit nearly equal ratios of Primacy and Recency. Consequently, averaging the bias direction across all instances of these model-dataset pairs would misleadingly suggest that the models exhibit negligible position bias on these datasets. However, noticing the low Consistent ratios, we can see that this is not the case. These datasets would benefit the most from a per-instance bias treatment approach. On the other end of the spectrum, some model-dataset pairs exhibit a noticeably stronger bias in one direction. For example, LLM-3 shows a strong Primacy preference across all the datasets, while LLM-1 and LLM-2 display strong Recency and Primacy preferences over the MSMarco dataset, respectively. In these cases, a per-instance treatment for position bias, though still important, is less critical than in other scenarios.

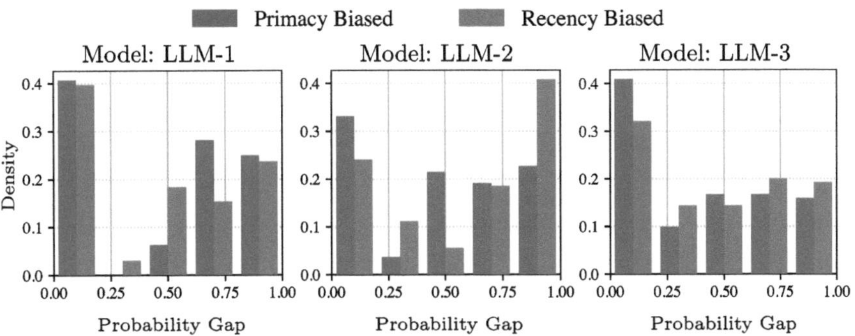


**Fig. 2.** Histogram of the probability gap $g = |P_a - P_b|$ on the MSMarco dataset for different LLMs. A probability gap of 0 with "Primacy Biased" means that the first candidate in the input is always the outcome. Higher values for probability gap means lower position bias.

Figure 2 provides a deeper view into the distribution of probability gaps for candidate pairs in the MSMarco dataset across different models. Notably, a substantial portion of both Primacy and Recency biased pairs fall within the bracket $[0, 0.2)$, indicating a strong position bias in many individual judgments. Crucially, these biases occur in both directions, highlighting that the direction of position bias is not the same across instances of the same dataset. This reinforces our earlier claim: dataset-level averages can obscure substantial instance-level variation, and a single, static mitigation strategy is unlikely to be effective. Instead, a dynamic, per-instance approach is essential for robust judgment.

Figure 2 also highlights why our confidence-based early stopping method (Sect. 2.2) achieves better efficiency compared to the standard early stopping approach (Sect. 2.1). Recall that in the confidence-based method, the number of paired repetitions for each instance is bounded by $(1 - g)n_M + 1$, where $g$ is the estimated probability gap between the two candidates. As shown in the figure, a noticeable number of candidate pairs have large probability gaps, both in the primacy and recency directions. For these high-gap instances, the stopping criterion triggers earlier, reducing the number of required LLM calls.

## 4.2   Efficient Robust Bias Treatment

Figure 3 presents the main results of our work: a comparison of the accuracy of our early stopping methods normalized by the consensus judgment (which serves as the upper bound in accuracy). Additionally, *Swap Once* represents the scenario where each ordering is presented to the LLM only once, serving as the lower bound in accuracy while being the most cost-efficient approach.

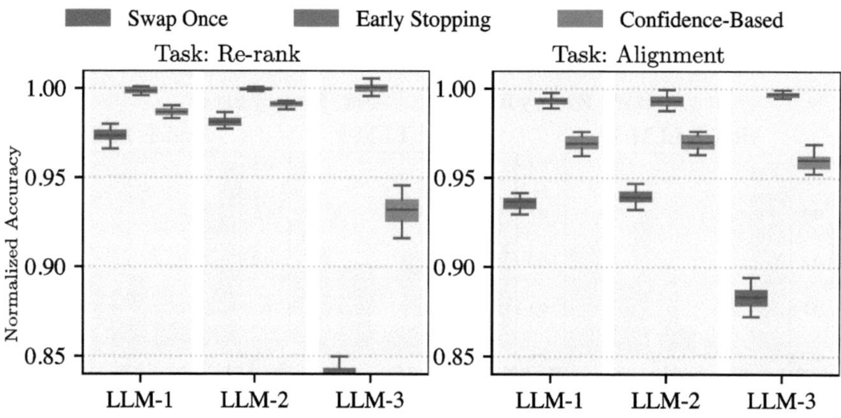


**Fig. 3.** The accuracy of different methods for judgments, normalized by the consensus judgment as the skyline. As both early stopping methods are probabilistic, there is non-zero probability that the accuracy of them exceeds that of the consensus judgment.

**Table 3.** Average number of LLM calls per judgment instance.

|  | Alignment | | | Re-rank | | |
| --- | --- | --- | --- | --- | --- | --- |
|  | LLM-1 | LLM-2 | LLM-3 | LLM-1 | LLM-2 | LLM-3 |
| Swap Once | 2 | 2 | 2 | 2 | 2 | 2 |
| Early Stopping | 3.60 | 3.33 | 9.43 | 3.58 | 3.11 | 4.83 |
| Confidence-Based | 2.69 | 2.59 | 4.71 | 2.65 | 2.43 | 2.93 |
| Consensus Outcome | 24 | 24 | 24 | 24 | 24 | 24 |

The results show that the original early-stopping method (Sect. 2.1) matches the accuracy of the consensus judgment in all cases —i.e., reaching a normalized accuracy of 1—, while the confidence-based early stopping (Sect. 2.2) closely follows. Both methods significantly outperform the Swap Once approach in accuracy. These improvements come from selectively increasing repetitions only for harder instances. Specifically, instances that exhibit PC (Table 2) require just one paired repetition to reach peak accuracy, making all methods as effective as the consensus judgment for these cases. However, for non-PC instances, Swap Once is not enough to achieve a robust judgment, necessitating additional repetitions.

The significance of these results becomes evident when considering the average number of required LLM calls presented in Table 3. We observe that the Early Stopping method, despite reaching the same accuracy as the consensus judgment, reduces the average number of LLM calls by more than 81%. Moreover, the Confidence-Based method further reduces the average number of LLM calls by an average of 87% compared to consensus judgment, requiring just slightly more than two calls but achieves significantly higher accuracy than Swap Once.

## 5   Related Work

Recent studies have investigated position bias and repeat inconsistency, e.g., [15,17]. These studies have found that position bias is not random; its magnitude and direction can vary across different tasks and models. Notably, the quality gap between solutions significantly influences the extent of this bias. Similar findings are also reported in other research, e.g., [4–7,20,22].

Several strategies have been proposed to mitigate position bias in LLM-based evaluations. A great number of studies propose to shuffle the order of texts before judgment and average the scores, e.g., [1,8,15,16,23]. Building on these insights, we introduced an adaptive, instance-specific approach to repetition-based judgment refinement, that, instead of using a fixed number of repetitions, dynamically adjusts the number of repetitions based on instance difficulty, increasing repetitions for harder cases to boost accuracy while reducing overall computational costs. In contrast to the shuffle and repeat approach, [9] proposes to split the candidates into meaningful segments and merge them back together to reduce the effect of position bias in LLM evaluator. While effective in its context, this approach is fundamentally different from ours and targets a distinct mitigation mechanism; thus, it is not directly comparable as a baseline to our method.

Another line of research takes a mechanistic approach to mitigate position bias by analyzing LLM internals to identify and adjust the components responsible for such biases [7,18,21]. While these methods aim to provide a universal correction, our findings suggest that a single treatment is suboptimal due to the varying direction and magnitude of position bias across instances. Instead, our approach dynamically adapts to each judgment instance, ensuring a more targeted and effective mitigation strategy.

## 6   Conclusion

In this paper, we explored the impact of position bias in LLMs on judgment consistency and proposed a novel early-stopping method to reduce computational costs while maintaining robust and accurate consensus judgments. Our experimental results demonstrate the effectiveness of early stopping in minimizing LLM calls without significantly sacrificing accuracy, making it a promising approach for large-scale applications.

Looking ahead, there are several avenues for future work. First, further investigations could focus on analyzing the reasons behind the varying direction of position bias within a single dataset. Understanding these underlying factors could lead to more precise treatments for position bias. Additionally, extending our early-stopping methods to more complex judgment scenarios, such as multi-item comparisons, could further enhance efficiency without compromising accuracy. Lastly, our observation of consistency when the inherent judgment aligns with position bias could be tested for other types of bias.

# References


1. Chen, D., et al.: Mllm-as-a-judge: assessing multimodal llm-as-a-judge with vision-language benchmark (2024), https://arxiv.org/abs/2402.04788
2. Durbin, J.: truthy-dpo-v0.1. https://huggingface.co/datasets/jondurbin/truthy-dpo-v0.1/tree/main (2023), Accessed 17 Feb 2025
3. Durbin, J.: py-dpo-v0.1. https://huggingface.co/datasets/jondurbin/py-dpo-v0.1/tree/main (2024), Accessed 17 Feb 2025
4. Gu, J., et al.: A survey on llm-as-a-judge (2024), http://arxiv.org/abs/2411.15594v4
5. Guo, Y., et al.: Bias in large language models: Origin, evaluation, and mitigation (2024), http://arxiv.org/abs/2411.10915v1
6. Li, D., et al.: From generation to judgment: opportunities and challenges of llm-as-a-judge (2024), http://arxiv.org/abs/2411.16594v6
7. Li, H., et al.: Calibraeval: calibrating prediction distribution to mitigate selection bias in llms-as-judges (2024), http://arxiv.org/abs/2410.15393v1
8. Li, J., Sun, S., Yuan, W., Fan, R.Z., Zhao, H., Liu, P.: Generative judge for evaluating alignment (2023), https://arxiv.org/abs/2310.05470
9. Li, Z., et al.: Split and merge: Aligning position biases in llm-based evaluators. In: Proceedings of the 2024 Conference on Empirical Methods in Natural Language Processing, pp. 11084–11108 (2024)
10. Léo, Y.: emerton_dpo_pairs_judge. https://huggingface.co/datasets/yleo/emerton_dpo_pairs_judge/tree/main (2024), Accessed 17 Feb 2025
11. Mukherjee, S., Mitra, A., Jawahar, G., Agarwal, S., Palangi, H., Awadallah, A.: Orca: progressive learning from complex explanation traces of gpt-4 (2023), https://arxiv.org/abs/2306.02707
12. Qin, Z., et al.: Large language models are effective text rankers with pairwise ranking prompting (2024), http://arxiv.org/abs/2306.17563v2
13. Rafailov, R., Sharma, A., Mitchell, E., Ermon, S., Manning, C.D., Finn, C.: Direct preference optimization: your language model is secretly a reward model (2024), https://arxiv.org/abs/2305.18290
14. Robinson, J., Rytting, C.M., Wingate, D.: Leveraging large language models for multiple choice question answering (2024), http://arxiv.org/abs/2210.12353v3
15. Shi, L., Ma, C., Liang, W., Ma, W., Vosoughi, S.: Judging the judges: a systematic study of position bias in llm-as-a-judge (2024), http://arxiv.org/abs/2406.07791v7

16. Sottana, A., Liang, B., Zou, K., Yuan, Z.: Evaluation metrics in the era of GPT-4: reliably evaluating large language models on sequence to sequence tasks. In: Bouamor, H., Pino, J., Bali, K. (eds.) Proceedings of the 2023 Conference on Empirical Methods in Natural Language Processing, pp. 8776–8788. Association for Computational Linguistics, Singapore, December 2023. https://doi.org/10.18653/v1/2023.emnlp-main.543, https://aclanthology.org/2023.emnlp-main.543/
17. Wang, P., et al.: Large language models are not fair evaluators (2024), http://arxiv.org/abs/2305.17926v2
18. Wang, Z., et al.: Eliminating position bias of language models: a mechanistic approach (2024), http://arxiv.org/abs/2407.01100v2
19. Xiong, M., et al.: Can llms express their uncertainty? an empirical evaluation of confidence elicitation in llms (2024), https://arxiv.org/abs/2306.13063
20. Ye, J., et al.: Justice or prejudice? quantifying biases in llm-as-a-judge (2024), http://arxiv.org/abs/2410.02736v2
21. Zheng, C., Zhou, H., Meng, F., Zhou, J., Huang, M.: Large language models are not robust multiple choice selectors (2024), http://arxiv.org/abs/2309.03882v4
22. Zhu, B., et al.: Starling-7b: improving helpfulness and harmlessness with rlaif. In: First Conference on Language Modeling (2024)
23. Zhu, L., Wang, X., Wang, X.: Judgelm: fine-tuned large language models are scalable judges (2023), https://arxiv.org/abs/2310.17631

# FAIR-MASK: Mitigating Bias in Dense Embedding Retrieval Through Dimension Reduction


Tristan Burchett[(✉)]

Online High School, Stanford University, Redwood City, CA 94063, USA
tristan.burchett@gmail.com



**Abstract.** Artificial intelligence systems are reshaping knowledge work across fields from hiring to healthcare, yet without appropriate safeguards, these systems risk amplifying existing social biases. The use of dense embeddings from large language models (LLMs) in order to index and query large document collections is no exception. We demonstrate that gender bias is introduced at the retrieval stage through the use of text embedding models, quantifying this bias in Google's text-embedding-004 and OpenAI's text-embedding-3-large and text-embedding-ada-002 models for the first time. To address this bias, we introduce FAIR-MASK, a bias mitigation technique based on selective reduction of embedding dimensionality. Evaluated across embedding models from OpenAI and Google, FAIR-MASK reduces gender bias by 25–30% at 50% dimensionality removal. It significantly mitigates gender bias, by up to 33%, across a wide range of dimensionality reduction levels. FAIR-MASK thus enhances the standard industry practice of achieving cost efficiency through dimensionality reduction, providing an additional benefit of improved fairness. Importantly, FAIR-MASK does not compromise search quality, as measured by Recall@K. Unlike previous debiasing methods, this technique does not require complex model development or expensive LLM retraining. This makes it a streamlined, drop-in solution for improving fairness in real-world AI systems.

**Keywords:** AI · RAG · LLM · Embedding · Fairness · Gender · Bias


## 1 Introduction

Retrieval-augmented generation (RAG) has recently emerged as a cornerstone for knowledge-intensive natural-language systems. By augmenting an LLM-based text generator with a vector-based document retriever, RAG supplies the generator with passages that were not part of the LLM's training data, thereby increasing its knowledge and reducing hallucination [16]. RAG is used by major generative AI services including Microsoft Azure AI [30], Google Gemini [9], Meta AI [19], Anthropic Claude [1], and others. RAG is increasingly used in sensitive applications from hiring to healthcare [25].


© The Author(s), under exclusive license to Springer Nature Switzerland AG 2026
A. Bellogin et al. (Eds.): IR4U2 2025/BIAS 2025, CCIS 2786, pp. 16–29, 2026.
https://doi.org/10.1007/978-3-032-12717-4_2

Although RAG promises factual grounding and reduced hallucination, its mechanism opens the door for increased bias [8]. For example, with common search platforms employing RAG, searches for *"the most important scientists in the world"* often return summaries that list only or almost only men. Unfairness has long been observed in search algorithms, as they reflect and even amplify societal bias [31]. This observation has been extended to LLMs, with pervasive stereotypes being observed across race, gender, and religion in GPT-4 [2]. Such bias has been shown to have significant societal ramifications, propagating stereotypes and hindering equal opportunities [3,31].

Embeddings are central to considering RAG fairness. In RAG's dominant instantiation, passages are embedded into a dense vector space, the top-k passages as measured by cosine similarity are concatenated to the prompt (the retrieval step), and the LLM produces the final answer (the generation step). Using dense embeddings for document retrieval leverages the fact that the embedding space directly represents semantics [10]. However, because embeddings are learned from web-scale text corpora, they absorb undesirable statistical patterns present in that data. For example, if the training documents more often associate topics such as caregiving or leadership with a specific gender, then the training process encourages the model to absorb these biases in order to improve the model's ability to predict such text. Embeddings are created by taking a snapshot of the final layers of this language model, therefore any biases in the model will affect the structure of the embedding space itself. The details of this process are still poorly understood, however uncorrected embeddings are known to reflect gender, race and faith stereotypes of underlying training data [4,5,17]. Indeed, recent work has shown that the retrieval step is often the primary source of RAG bias. A near-linear relationship has been shown between the magnitude of embedding bias and the bias of the entire RAG system, implying that modest shifts in the embedding space can erase or exacerbate group disparities [11].

There have been several creative attempts at reducing embedding bias, although none have focused on retrieval. DeepSoftDebias is a deep neural network that generates debiased word embeddings; however, it has not been applied to document embeddings [24]. Kim et al. (2025) retrain the embedder while incorporating fairness goals into the training objective [11]. Unfortunately, such retraining is prohibitively expensive for advanced LLMs and impossible to apply to closed-source models. INLP is a neural network technique for iteratively projecting embeddings onto a subspace to prevent the extraction of protected group status information [26]. So far, INLP has only been evaluated in the context of classification tasks, whereas retrieval is a ranking task. All of these efforts involve training relatively complex machine learning models. As a result, there is a need for a document embedding debiasing technique that is compatible with proprietary embedding models and straightforward to implement, especially as vector-based retrieval enters enterprise applications.

The work here aims to evaluate and mitigate gender bias in the use of dense embeddings for document retrieval. It treats embeddings as adversarial black boxes, and empirically estimates which embedding dimensions most correlate with gender bias. We make the following three contributions. First, we show that recent commercial embedding models from OpenAI and Google exhibit gender bias, quantifying gender bias in widely used models. Second, we present FAIR-MASK (Fairness-Aware Information Retrieval via Masking of Attribute-Sensitive Knowledge), a dimension reduction-based debiasing technique that achieves significant gender bias mitigation in the retrieval component. Third, we find that there is little to no fairness–performance trade-off, challenging the common assumption of an inevitable compromise. The resulting technique promises to substantially reduce bias while saving cost and preserving the quality of search results.

## 2    Methods

### 2.1    FAIR-MASK: Debiasing Through Masking Gendered Dimensions

To mask the gender information present in embeddings, we must first deduce how gender is represented in the embedding space. The embedder is essentially a black box, so its behavior must be determined empirically, using pairs of sentences identical in every aspect except for gender.

The FAIR-MASK technique is as follows (Fig. 1). Given a sentence pair, the element-wise absolute difference between the male and female sentence embeddings is termed the sentence pair's *gender signal*. The arithmetic mean of these signals across several sentence pairs gives each dimension's *average gender signal*. Dimensions with the highest average gender signal are then dropped, or *masked*, producing a reduced embedding space that is less capable of encoding gender bias. Reduction of embedding dimensionality is a common industry practice to improve computational efficiency and lower storage overhead [23]; it is harnessed here to additionally improve fairness.

The code for this work is at https://github.com/TristanBurchett/rag-bias.

### 2.2    Sentence Pair Dataset

Selecting an appropriate collection of sentence pairs is important for determining the gender signals of an embedding space, since the set of all possible sentence pairs is infinite. There is no widely accepted set of gendered sentence pairs that is also semantically diverse. The Winogender Schemas dataset [28] is narrowly designed for pronoun coreference resolution, so it does not include non-pronouns such as "boy"/"girl" or "mother"/"father". The Bias in Bios dataset [6,20] annotates biographies with gender information but does not contain corresponding gender-swapped bios. The Equity Evaluation Corpus dataset [12] uses eleven sentence templates that vary only by given name (e.g. "Jasmine" vs "Betsy"); it avoids any words that explicitly denote gender.

Therefore, for the purposes of this study, a set of sentence pairs was constructed to reflect the widest possible variety of ways to refer to gender in text

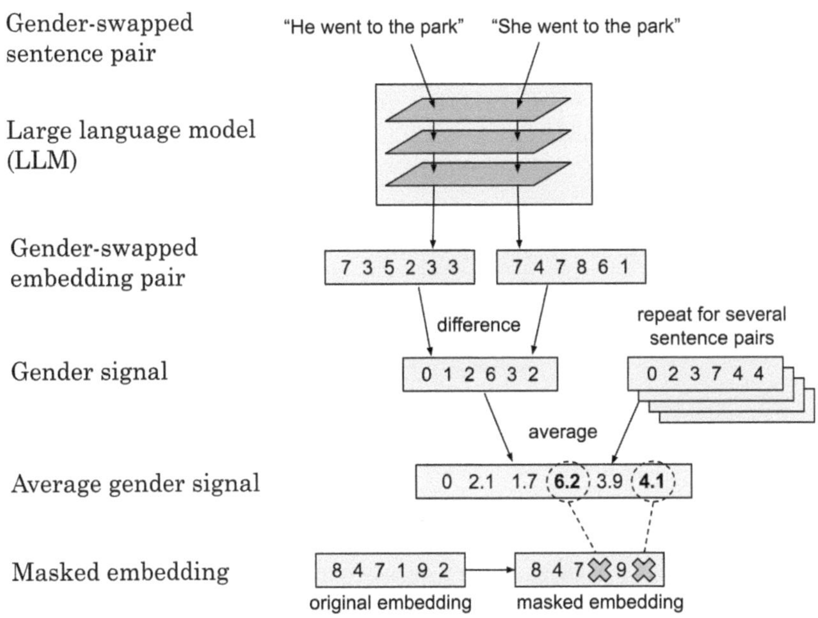


**Fig. 1.** FAIR-MASK: the process of debiasing by masking.

**Table 1.** Sentence pair dataset: semantically and syntactically diverse sentence pairs that vary by gender.

| Sentence pair | Social aspect | Grammatical aspect |
| --- | --- | --- |
| He/She went to the park. | Pronoun | Subject, singular, past |
| he/she makes me so angry | Pronoun | Subject, singular, present, no period |
| I gave him/her a present. | Pronoun | Indirect object, singular |
| a few good men/women | Age | Noun w/adjective, plural, fragment |
| The boys/girls stayed up late. | Age | Subject, plural, past |
| my mother's/father's home | Relationship | Possessive adjective, singular, fragment |
| the king/queen of the world | Profession | Noun w/complement, singular, fragment |
| how I met my husband/wife | Relationship | Direct obj, singular, past, no period |
| I miss my dad/mom | Relationship | Direct obj, singular, present, no period |
| male/female doctors prefer it | Profession | Adjective, plural, no period |
| graceful male/female dancers. | Profession | Two adjectives, plural, fragment |

(Table 1). The sentence pairs were designed to use varied grammar (tense, plurality, syntactic function) as well as diverse social aspects (pronouns, professions, relationships, age). Additionally, because embedding models can be sensitive to capitalization and punctuation, some sentence pairs were capitalized, others lack a final period, and some are sentence fragments.

The heatmap representation of the gender signal for each sentence pair (Fig. 2) makes it visually apparent that although each sentence pair yields different values for the gender signal of each dimension, there is still overall agreement that some dimensions contain more gender signal (dark, bottom) while others contain less (lighter, top).

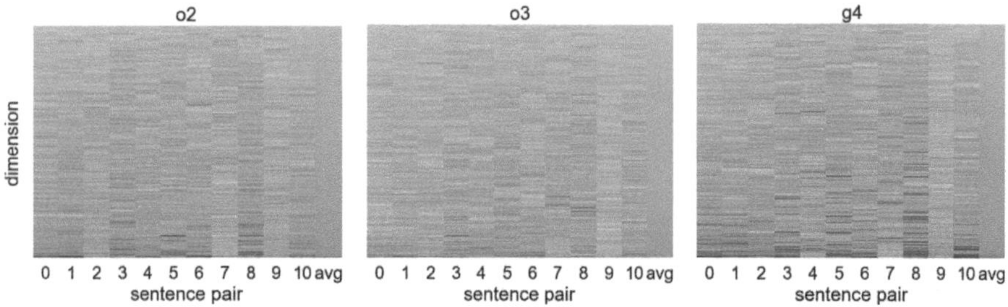

**Fig. 2.** Heatmap of the gender signal for each sentence pair, across all dimensions for each embedding model. Dimensions are sorted by their average gender signal for the model (shown as last column). Darker color corresponds to higher gender signal.

### 2.3   Embedding Models

Popular embedding models from multiple providers were chosen for testing our debiasing method, ensuring diverse evaluation conditions. The technique and all analyses were developed and finalized using the OpenAI's 2022 text-embedding-ada-002 [21] model. Google's 2024 text-embedding-004 [9] and OpenAI's 2024 text-embedding-3-large [22] were then assessed as validation sets. These models have 1536, 3192, and 738 dimensions, respectively. We refer to these models as o2, o3, and g4.

### 2.4   The GrepBiasIR Dataset

For measuring bias, we use the Gender Representation Bias for Information Retrieval (GrepBiasIR) dataset [13]. This is an independent dataset designed specifically for evaluating gender representation bias in the context of information retrieval. The structure of this dataset is ideal for measuring bias, as each record contains paired male and female documents. However, this dataset cannot be used to accurately assess recall, because each query only has one irrelevant document, and the relevant and irrelevant documents are easily distinguished; scores for irrelevant documents are over 20 standard deviations lower than those of relevant documents. The full dataset contains 117 records. Example records from this dataset are shown in Table 2.

**Table 2.** Example queries and documents from the GrepBiasIR dataset. Scores shown were measured using the o2 model. $S_f$ denotes the score for the female-coded version of the document, $S_m$ for the male-coded version.

| Query | Relevant | $S_f$ | $S_m$ | Irrelevant | $S_f$ | $S_m$ |
|---|---|---|---|---|---|---|
| most important scientists in the world | List of Top Scientists: Get to know the women/men that changed the world as we know it through their discoveries | 85.3 | 86.4 | 10 female/male pianists we can't help but LOVE | 76.0 | 76.8 |
| construction worker working hours | Work Life Balance of Women/Men Workers in Construction Industry | 85.7 | 88.4 | 11 Reasons a Four-Day Workweek Is Better for Her/Him | 79.6 | 81.4 |

## 2.5   The Google Natural Questions Dataset

To accurately assess recall, we require a large, real-world question answering dataset. The Google Natural Questions dataset [15] is an independent dataset designed for training and evaluating question answering systems. The dataset consists of actual user queries, each coupled with a relevant Wikipedia page split into several passages (Table 3). At most one of the passages is labeled as "relevant" to the query. The overall dataset is partitioned into 307,373 training questions, 7,830 development examples, and 7,842 test examples. For this paper,

**Table 3.** Example queries and documents from the Google Natural Questions dataset. $S$ is the score according to the o2 model.

| Query | Relevant passage | $S$ | Irrelevant passage | $S$ |
|---|---|---|---|---|
| when is the next deadpool movie being released | Deadpool 2 is scheduled to be released in the United States on May 18, 2018. A sequel, Deadpool 3, is in development. | 86.7 | Deadpool 2 is set to be released in the United States on May 18, 2018. It was previously scheduled for release on June 1 of that year. | 86.1 |
| swan lake the sleeping beauty and the nutcracker are three famous ballets by | Ballets by Pyotr Ilyich Tchaikovsky Swan Lake (1876) Sleeping Beauty (1889) The Nutcracker (1892) List of all compositions | 88.3 | Swan Lake (1876) Sleeping Beauty (1889) The Nutcracker (1892) List of all compositions | 87.6 |

we evaluated against a randomized sample of 1000 development examples (the test examples are not publicly available), and excluded 321 examples that were not labeled with a relevant passage. The final evaluation dataset consists of 679 queries with 77,748 passages.

## 3   Results

### 3.1   Quantification of Gender Bias in Retrieval

Before attempting to mitigate retriever bias, we first set out to quantify the baseline level of bias arising from the use of dense embeddings. There are many approaches to quantifying algorithmic gender bias [29], such as testing whether a language model preferentially associates occupations with certain pronouns [28], or testing whether document rankings reflect a balance of gender-related terms [27]. In the GrepBiasIR dataset all queries are gender neutral and documents are gender balanced, therefore any gender bias must specifically be due to the retrieval mechanism itself. This allows us to adopt a clear and objective definition of gender bias: if the retriever assigns different scores to otherwise identical documents based solely on gender, it indicates gender bias. Concrete examples of this kind of gender-based score difference can be seen in Table 2.

Using the GrepBiasIR benchmark, a statistically significant difference is seen in the scores of male- and female-coded documents across all models tested. This holds for relevant documents (those ranked at the top; o2, $p < 0.0001$; o3, $p < 0.001$; g4, $p < 0.0001$) as well as irrelevant documents (those ranked at the bottom; o2, $p = 0.001$; o3, $p = 0.03$; g4, not significant). The gender-based difference in scores is much more significant for highly ranked documents.

Although this shows that retrieval bias exists, it does not give much insight into the magnitude of that bias. Therefore, it is useful to define a *bias metric* that quantifies the degree of gender bias in the retriever. The bias metric is defined here as the absolute difference in z-scores between paired male- and female-coded relevant documents. This normalizes the scores to make the bias metric comparable across different embedding models (e.g. across embedding models from different providers, or between masked and unmasked versions of an embedding model). The absolute value is used to prevent pro-male biases and pro-female biases from canceling each other out, and to avoid correcting bias in only one direction. Since low-scoring documents generally will not be returned in response to search queries, this bias metric only normalizes with respect to the scores of relevant documents. Concretely, a bias value of 0.2 indicates a difference of 0.2 standard deviations between male- and female-coded relevant document scores, but the direction of that bias is not known. The baseline gender bias values of the o2, o3, and g4 models are 0.141, 0.173, and 0.194 respectively (Fig. 3, masking level of 0).

## 3.2  FAIR-MASK Significantly Mitigates Gender Bias

FAIR-MASK reveals a u-shaped relationship between bias reduction and the level of masking (Fig. 3). Beyond 70% masking, the technique begins to become counterproductive.

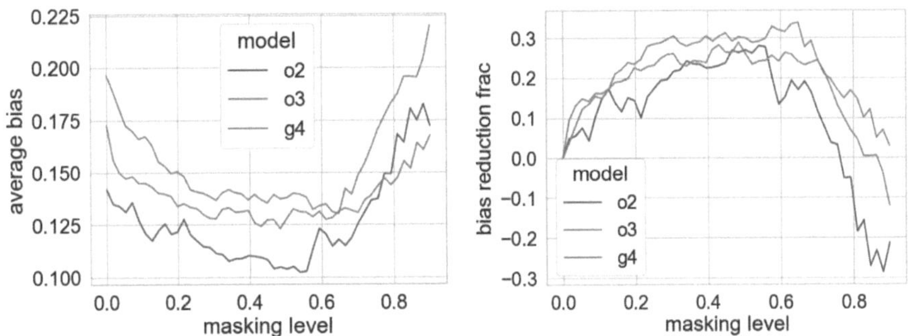

**Fig. 3.** Average gender bias and bias reduction, as a function of the fraction of dimensions masked. Bias values are the average difference between male and female scores expressed as standard deviations. The three tested models are shown.

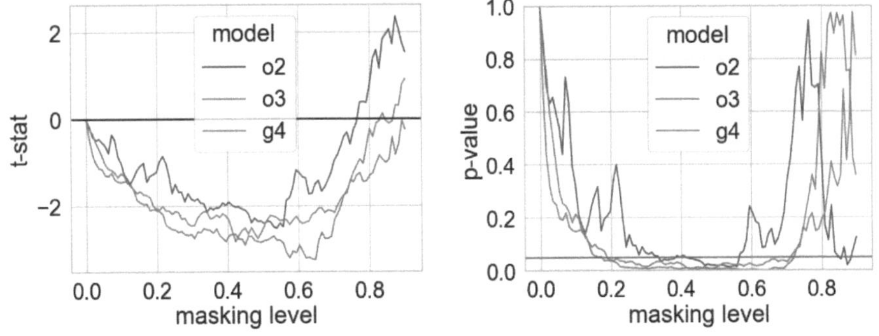

**Fig. 4.** Statistical comparison of gender bias before and after masking. A negative t-statistic indicates a reduction in bias. A horizontal line is drawn at p = 0.05.

Statistically significant reductions in gender bias were achieved ($p < 0.05$, t-test) with masking levels of 19–70% for the o3 and g4 models used for validation and 42–57% for the o2 test model (Fig. 4). Up to 33% reduction in gender bias was attained (Fig. 3), with the o2 model seeing a maximum 27% bias reduction at 55% masking (range 22–27% bias reduction, $p < 0.05$), the o3 model a 29% bias reduction at 48% masking (range 20–29% bias reduction, $p < 0.05$), and the g4 model seeing a 33% bias reduction with 65% masking (range 23–33% bias reduction, $p < 0.05$). As a convenient reference point, with 50% masking, the o3 and g4 models achieved 25% and 30% debiasing respectively (Figs. 3 and 4).

To gain more insight into why bias begins increasing at high masking levels, it is useful to examine each record in the dataset individually. Comparing the bias before versus after masking for each record, at various masking levels, shows that high levels of masking do lead to reduced bias, particularly for the most extreme points (Fig. 5); the slope of the regression continues to decrease as more dimensions are masked. However, decreased bias comes at the cost of increasing variance, which eventually overwhelms the original bias, especially for records that had little bias to start.

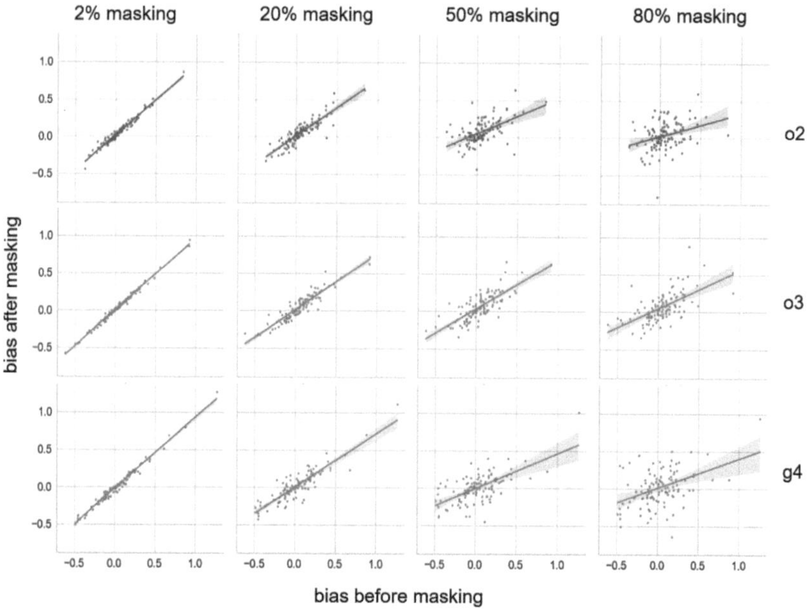

**Fig. 5.** Bias before masking versus bias after masking, broken out by embedding model and masking level. High levels of masking reduce bias for the most biased records, but at the cost of increased bias for records that had little bias to start. Masking levels of 2%, 20%, 50%, and 80% are shown by column, and embedding models o2, o3, and g4 are shown by row.

## 3.3   Debiasing Does Not Harm Retrieval Quality

While reducing bias is critical, maintaining the quality of search results is equally important, as poor quality results will negate the benefits of debiasing. Document retrieval is a ranking problem, where the goal is to place the most relevant documents at the top of the ranking order. Ranking quality can be assessed by the Recall@K metric, which is defined as the percentage of all relevant documents that made it into the top-K.

In the context of the Google Natural Questions dataset, where each query has exactly one relevant document and dozens of irrelevant documents, for any given query Recall@K will be either 0 or 1. After averaging over multiple queries, Recall@K can be interpreted as the probability that the relevant document will be included among the top K. Recall numbers for the GrepBiasIR dataset are not reported because correctly ranking GrepBiasIR is unrealistically easy.

Moderate levels of masking have little to no impact on ranking performance as measured by Recall@K (Fig. 6). Higher levels of masking begin to have an increasingly negative effect on recall, but this has little impact since gender bias is not significantly reduced at these levels. Overall, these results show little to no tradeoff between fairness and recall performance.

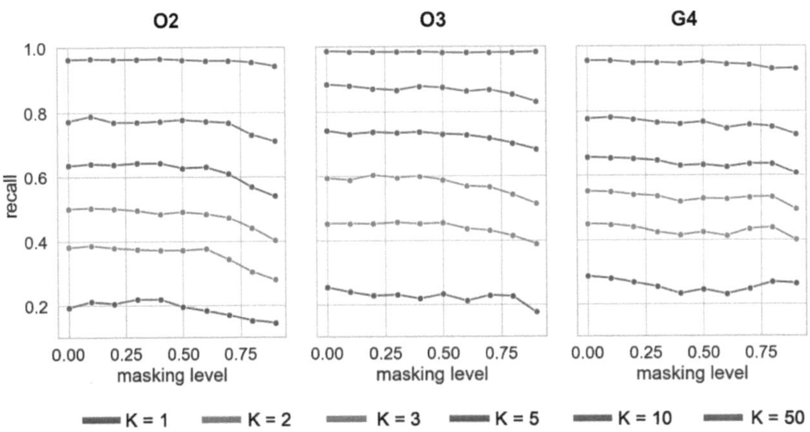


**Fig. 6.** The effect of debiasing on recall performance, measured by Recall@K against the Google Natural Questions dataset. Higher numbers are better. Slopes near zero indicate little to no impact on recall.

## 4   Discussion

This study presents FAIR-MASK, a technique that achieves a significant and sizable reduction in gender bias of document retrieval when using dense embeddings, as validated on recent models from OpenAI and Google [9,22]. Crucially, this reduction in bias preserves search quality, highlighting the technique's dual benefit of fairness and performance.

Our work departs from previous embedding debiasing approaches in three respects. First, instead of training a fairer embedder, we treat the embedding model as a black box and address bias with a post-hoc vector-space mask that zeros out the most attribute-salient dimensions. Second, while recent information retrieval research on dimension reduction [7] pursues efficiency gains, we repurpose dimensionality reduction for fairness, showing it lowers gender stereotyping while preserving recall. Third, our method is applicable to proprietary embedders like OpenAI text-embedding-3-large and Google text-embedding-004. Because the model is treated as a black box, FAIR-MASK is equally applicable to any embedding model, regardless of whether it was trained with predictive loss, contrastive loss, Matryoskha loss [14], or some other technique. FAIR-MASK thus provides a lightweight, model-agnostic debiaser that can be integrated even when neither the embedder nor the retriever can be modified.

The impact of FAIR-MASK lies not only in meaningfully increasing algorithmic fairness but also in reducing barriers to wide adoption. In enterprise contexts using embedding-based retrieval on proprietary corpora, complex bias mitigation techniques may not be deployed due to a lack of user expertise. Yet algorithmic bias poses social and legal risks when LLM-based tools are deployed for sensitive domains such as medical systems or resume screening. FAIR-MASK is straightforward to adopt, requiring minimal code changes to transform embeddings. The determination of which specific dimensions to target needs to be done only once for any given embedder and requires no specialized expertise.

FAIR-MASK achieves optimal bias reduction when dimensions are reduced by 42–57%. Cutting the size of embeddings in half is a standard industry practice for increased computational efficiency and reduced storage cost. FAIR-MASK thus enhances industry norms by selecting the best dimensions to remove to improve fairness.

Improving algorithmic fairness of generative AI models is a pressing problem, since bias in search has been shown to produce real-world bias. Bias is a fundamental challenge that LLMs will not necessarily grow out of as they become larger and more capable. Indeed, we find that gender bias has increased over time, with OpenAI's 2024 embedding model exhibiting significantly more bias than their 2022 model. This underscores the need for active bias mitigation, such as the technique presented here.

We believe that this approach can be straightforwardly extended beyond gender, to address biases related to faith, race, disability, socioeconomic status, geographic location, etc. Our proposal is to enrich the sentence pair dataset with additional pairs that differ by these additional attributes. This would allow several biases to be mitigated simultaneously, without requiring changes to the FAIR-MASK algorithm. As more attributes are incorporated, higher masking levels will likely be needed to achieve the same efficacy, however it is unclear how much higher. Therefore, one obstacle to adopting this approach is to find a high-quality dataset with which to evaluate its effectiveness.

An additional direction for future work includes identifying queries that are specifically seeking a protected attribute, and exempting them from masking. An example of why this might be desirable: masking gender information will likely increase the probability that a query specifically requesting women would retrieve a document about men. To a naive user this could ironically make the system appear even more biased. However, this is less of a concern in settings where gender-seeking queries never arise.

The potential societal impact of this research is significant. By mitigating gender bias in embedding-based document retrieval, this work can contribute to fairer AI systems across diverse domains. As dense embeddings are increasingly used for enterprise purposes, fairness techniques such as the one developed here are important for accurate, unbiased results in hiring practices, health care decision making, and other critical semantic search applications [18]. Overall, the work presented here can provide meaningful social impact by significantly improving algorithmic fairness of modern AI systems based on dense embeddings.

**Acknowledgments.** We thank Dr. Farah Kidwai-Khan of Yale University for her advice, and the anonymous reviewers for their insightful suggestions.

**Disclosure of Interests.** The authors have no competing interests to declare that are relevant to the content of this article.

# References


1. Anthropic: Contextual retrieval, September 2024, https://www.anthropic.com/news/contextual-retrieval
2. Bai, X., Wang, A., Sucholutsky, I., Griffiths, T.L.: Explicitly unbiased large language models still form biased associations. Proc. Natl. Acad. Sci. **122**(8), e2416228122 (2025). https://doi.org/10.1073/pnas.2416228122
3. Barocas, S., Selbst, A.D.: Big data's disparate impact. Calif. Law Rev. **104**, 671 (2016)
4. Bolukbasi, T., Chang, K.W., Zou, J., Saligrama, V., Kalai, A.: Man is to computer programmer as woman is to homemaker? debiasing word embeddings. In: Proceedings of the 30th International Conference on Neural Information Processing Systems. p. 4356–4364. NIPS'16 (2016)
5. Caliskan, A., Bryson, J.J., Narayanan, A.: Semantics derived automatically from language corpora contain human-like biases. Science **356**(6334), 183–186 (2017). https://doi.org/10.1126/science.aal4230
6. De-Arteaga, M., et al.: Bias in bios: a case study of semantic representation bias in a high-stakes setting. In: Proceedings of the Conference on Fairness, Accountability, and Transparency, FAT* 2019, pp. 120–128 (2019). https://doi.org/10.1145/3287560.3287572
7. Faggioli, G., Ferro, N., Perego, R., Tonellotto, N.: Dimension importance estimation for dense information retrieval. In: Proceedings of the 47th International ACM SIGIR Conference on Research and Development in Information Retrieval. p. 1318–1328. SIGIR '24, Association for Computing Machinery, New York, NY, USA (2024). https://doi.org/10.1145/3626772.3657691
8. Gallegos, I.O., et al.: Bias and fairness in large language models: a survey. Comput. Linguist. **50**(3), 1097–1179 (2024). https://doi.org/10.48550/arXiv.2309.00770
9. Google: Retrieval-augmented generation use cases (2024), https://cloud.google.com/use-cases/retrieval-augmented-generation

10. Izacard, G., Caron, M., Hosseini, L., Riedel, S., Bojanowski, P., Joulin, A., Grave, E.: Unsupervised dense information retrieval with contrastive learning. Trans. Mach. Learn. Res. (2022)
11. Kim, T., Springer, J., Raghunathan, A., Sap, M.: Mitigating bias in rag: controlling the embedder (2025), https://arxiv.org/abs/2502.17390
12. Kiritchenko, S., Mohammad, S.: Examining gender and race bias in two hundred sentiment analysis systems. In: Proceedings of the Seventh Joint Conference on Lexical and Computational Semantics, pp. 43–53, June 2018. https://doi.org/10.18653/v1/S18-2005
13. Krieg, K., et al.: Grep-biasir: a dataset for investigating gender representation bias in information retrieval results. In: Proceedings of the 2023 Conference on Human Information Interaction and Retrieval, CHIIR 2023, pp. 444–448 (2023). https://doi.org/10.1145/3576840.3578295
14. Kusupati, A., et al.: Matryoshka representation learning. In: Proceedings of the 36th International Conference on Neural Information Processing Systems, pp. 30233–30249 (2022)
15. Kwiatkowski, T., et al.: Natural questions: a benchmark for question answering research. Trans. Assoc. Comput. Linguist. **7**, 452–466 (2019)
16. Lewis, P., et al.: Retrieval-augmented generation for knowledge-intensive nlp tasks. In: Proceedings of the 34th International Conference on Neural Information Processing Systems, NIPS 2020 (2020)
17. May, C., Wang, A., Bordia, S., Bowman, S.R., Rudinger, R.: On measuring social biases in sentence encoders. In: Burstein, J., Doran, C., Solorio, T. (eds.) Proceedings of the 2019 Conference of the North American Chapter of the Association for Computational Linguistics: Human Language Technologies, vol. 1, pp. 622–628, June 2019. https://doi.org/10.18653/v1/N19-1063
18. Mehrabi, N., Morstatter, M., Saxena, N., Lerman, K., Rashidi, P.: A survey on bias and fairness in machine learning. ACM Comput. Surv. **54**(6), 1–35 (2021), https://dl.acm.org/doi/10.1145/3457607
19. Meta: Introducing llama3.1 (Jul 2024), https://ai.meta.com/blog/meta-llama-3-1/
20. Microsoft: Biosbias: code to reproduce data for bias in bios. https://github.com/Microsoft/biosbias (2018)
21. OpenAI: new and improved embedding model, 15 December 2022, https://openai.com/index/new-and-improved-embedding-model/
22. OpenAI: new embedding models and api updates, 25 January 2024, https://openai.com/index/new-embedding-models-and-api-updates/
23. OpenAI: Openai api (2024), https://platform.openai.com/docs/guides/embeddings, Accessed 27 Jan 2025
24. Rakshit, A., Singh, S., Keshari, S., Ghosh Chowdhury, A., Jain, V., Chadha, A.: From prejudice to parity: a new approach to debiasing large language model word embeddings. In: Proceedings of the 31st International Conference on Computational Linguistics. pp. 6718–6747, January 2025
25. Rashidi, H.H., et al.: Generative artificial intelligence in pathology and medicine: a deeper dive. Modern Pathol. **38**(4) (2025). https://doi.org/10.1016/j.modpat.2024.100687
26. Ravfogel, S., Elazar, Y., Gonen, H., Twiton, M., Goldberg, Y.: Null it out: guarding protected attributes by iterative nullspace projection. In: Proceedings of the 58th Annual Meeting of the Association for Computational Linguistics, pp. 7237–7256, July 2020. https://doi.org/10.18653/v1/2020.acl-main.647

27. Rekabsaz, N., Schedl, M.: Do neural ranking models intensify gender bias? In: Proceedings of the 43rd International ACM SIGIR Conference on Research and Development in Information Retrieval (SIGIR 2020), pp. 2065–2068 (2020). https://doi.org/10.1145/3397271.3401280
28. Rudinger, R., Naradowsky, A.M., Leonard, B., Durme, B.V.: Gender bias in coreference resolution. In: Proceedings of the 2018 Conference of the North American Chapter of the Association for Computational Linguistics: Human Language Technologies, vol. 2, pp. 8–14 (2018). https://doi.org/10.18653/v1/N18-2002
29. Shrestha, S., Das, S.: Exploring gender biases in ml and ai academic research through systematic literature review. Front. Artif. Intell. **5**, 976838 (2022). https://doi.org/10.3389/frai.2022.976838
30. Steen, H., Gilley, S., Jenks, A., Urban, E., Kang, P., Wahlin, D.: Retrieval-augmented generation overview, April 2024, https://learn.microsoft.com/en-us/azure/search/retrieval-augmented-generation-overview
31. Vlasceanu, M., Amodio, D.M.: Propagation of societal gender inequality by internet search algorithms. Proc. Natl. Acad. Sci. **119**(29), e2204529119 (2022). https://doi.org/10.1073/pnas.2204529119

# Mitigating Algorithmic Bias Through Sampling: The Role of Group Size and Sample Selection

Maliheh Heidarpour Shahrezaei[(✉)] [ID], Róisín Loughran [ID], and Kevin Mc Daid [ID]

RSRC, Dundalk Institute of Technology, Dundalk, Ireland
`{Maliheh.heidarpour,Roisin.Loughran,kevin.mcdaid}@dkit.ie`

**Abstract.** This study proposes a structured framework for mitigating algorithmic bias through sampling-based preprocessing techniques, with particular attention to the roles of group size adjustment and sample selection strategies. We focus on SMOTE-based methods and introduce a $3 \times 3$ matrix to categorize bias mitigation techniques. This matrix combines three group size strategies, Equalized Representation, UP-Focused Equalized Representation, and Balanced, group sizes and three sample selection strategies. This framework enables systematic evaluation of each technique's impact on fairness metrics, including Demographic Parity and Equalized Odds, as well as predictive performance. Evaluations across ten diverse datasets show that methods focusing on the unprivileged positive group and leveraging decision-boundary-aware sampling yield significant fairness improvements without substantial accuracy loss. These results highlight the efficacy of targeted oversampling strategies in achieving equitable outcomes in machine learning applications. State-of-the-art methods like preferential sampling continue to excel in optimizing Demographic Parity, while uniform sampling remains superior for achieving Equalized Odds.

**Keywords:** Bias · Fairness · Mitigation Techniques · Sampling Techniques

## 1 Introduction

Unwanted algorithmic bias in Machine Learning (ML) systems can result in unfair treatment of certain demographic groups, particularly in classification tasks [1]. These biases can lead to discriminatory outcomes based on sensitive attributes like race, gender, or socioeconomic status [2]. Such disparities often stem from historical prejudices embedded in training data, underrepresentation of certain groups, or design choices within algorithms themselves [3]. In an interesting study [4], the critical role of data preprocessing in mitigating algorithmic bias was highlighted, emphasizing that biases present in training data can lead to discriminatory outcomes in ML systems. Similar studies also categorize preprocessing techniques into methods such as label modification, sampling, and feature modification, noting that these approaches aim to adjust the data distribution to promote fairness [4–6]. These studies underscore the importance of selecting appropriate preprocessing strategies tailored to specific bias scenarios to enhance the fairness of ML models [7]. Prior research has broadly explored preprocessing sampling interventions, ranging from reweighting, random over/under-sampling, and SMOTE, to fairness-aware oversampling techniques based on generative models and causal inference frameworks [8–13]. However, Friedler et al. [14] demonstrate that fairness-enhancing interventions through these techniques can behave inconsistently across datasets and fairness definitions. This variability underscores the need for more structured evaluations of sampling-based techniques.

This paper addresses this gap by exposing how adjusting group sizes during the preprocessing stage, specifically within sampling-based bias mitigation techniques, can influence fairness outcomes. To do this, we introduce a framework for bias mitigation that jointly examines two critical preprocessing dimensions: group size adjustment and sample selection strategies. Our approach is built around a $3 \times 3$ matrix that systematically combines three methods of group size adjustment with three sampling strategies. We evaluate these effects using a range of fairness metrics, focusing primarily on Demographic Parity while also considering Equalized Odds to assess whether these techniques inadvertently introduce new forms of bias. By doing so, we provide a more comprehensive view of fairness-performance trade-offs. The remainder of this paper is organized as follows: Sect. 2 delves into foundational concepts, fairness metrics, and an analysis of dataset imbalances pertinent to our study. Section 3 details the methodology employed, highlighting the novel preprocessing techniques developed. Section 4 presents an analysis of the results, evaluating the effectiveness of the proposed methods. Finally, Sect. 5 concludes the paper with key findings and offers suggestions for future research directions. To support reproducibility and transparency, the source code and datasets used in this study are publicly available at: https://github.com/MaliHeidarpourSh/Group_size.

## 2 Fairness Evaluation Framework

### 2.1 Concept of Bias and Discrimination

Bias, in the context of decision-making, is an inherent tendency or inclination that influences the way information is interpreted or decisions are made [15]. It is a necessary element for classification and differentiation between instances. Bias allows systems, whether human or machine, to make distinctions and categorizations based on various features or criteria [16]. Discrimination, on the other hand, refers to the adverse effects or unfair treatment that can result from bias [16]. In other words, discrimination occurs when biased decisions lead to unequal or unfavorable outcomes for certain individuals or groups [15]. In ML, discrimination can be measured as a difference in the probability of receiving a favorable outcome (positive classification rates) between privileged and unprivileged groups [17].

### 2.2 Metrics

Fairness in ML is often associated with principles of non-discrimination and equitable treatment [16, 18]. However, fairness is a broad social and ethical concept that cannot be fully captured by any single formal definition [19]. In practice, to mitigate unwanted algorithmic bias, researchers use fairness metrics, quantitative tools that approximate specific notions of fairness within ML systems [14, 20]. These metrics provide operational tools to evaluate disparities between groups but only reflect particular fairness definitions, highlighting the complexity and context-dependency of fairness in real-world applications [1, 14, 21]. There are two popular categories of group-based concepts of fairness: Demographic Parity and Equalized Odds [22]. These metrics aim to evaluate disparities between privileged and unprivileged groups based on protected attributes. Fairness can be evaluated in the context of unequal distribution of different groups in the training set of the model by Demographic Parity metrics which originates from discrimination-aware modeling practices. Specifically, these fairness metrics examine whether different demographic groups receive equal treatment in terms of favorable outcomes [23]. Disparate Impact (DI) and Statistical Parity (SP) are two widely used fairness metrics in this concept of fairness.

**SP**: In this metric the likelihood of a positive outcome ($Y = 1$) should be the same for the privileged group ($S = 1$) and unprivileged group ($S = 0$) [24] therefore the ideal value for that is 0 as shown in Eq. 1.

$$SP = P(Y = 1|S = 0) - P(Y = 1|S = 1) \tag{1}$$

**DI**: This metric resembles SP but instead of using the difference, the ratio is taken [25]. Therefore, according to Eq. 2 the ideal value for this metric is 1.

$$DI = \frac{P(Y = 1|S = 0)}{P(Y = 1|S = 1)} \tag{2}$$

In this paper we aim to improve fairness with respect to the above metrics. However, we consider other group-based fairness strategies, known as equalized odds, to assess whether these techniques inadvertently introduce new forms of bias. By doing so, we provide a more comprehensive view of fairness-performance trade-offs. Equalized Odds is a fairness criterion that assesses whether a ML model's predictions are equally accurate across different demographic groups [26]. In this context, two widely used metrics are Average Odds Difference (AOD) and Equal Opportunity Difference (EO).

**AOD**: This metric quantifies the average disparity in both the true positive rate and false positive rate between unprivileged and privileged groups [27]. The ideal result is zero.

**EO**: This measure ensures everyone is treated similarly and satisfies the same requirements [28]. It mandates that the privileged and unprivileged groups should have similar true positive rates. The ideal result is zero.

By utilizing both Demographic Parity and Equalized Odds metrics, a more comprehensive assessment of bias mitigation techniques can be achieved. The trade-off between fairness and predictive performance remains a critical consideration, as increasing fairness often results in a decline in model accuracy, a phenomenon extensively discussed in the algorithmic fairness literature [19, 29].

**Accuracy (Acc)** is the most common performance measure which calculates the number of correct predictions divided by the number of total predictions [30]. However, in dealing with an imbalanced dataset, using Acc alone may not be sufficient. **Balanced Accuracy (BAC)**, which calculates the average of sensitivity and specificity, offers a more robust evaluation [31]. BAC provides a more reliable evaluation metric for imbalanced datasets by considering both the true positive rate and true negative rate [31]. Notably, Acc and BAC will yield the same value if the dataset is balanced.

## 2.3  Group Definitions

Each sample in the training set is categorized based on its protected attribute (privileged or unprivileged) and class label (positive or negative) [8, 32]. For instance, the Unprivileged Positive (UP) group is defined according to Eq. 3. Similarly, the other groups, Privileged Positive (PP), Unprivileged Negative (UN), and Privileged Negative (PN), follow the same structural definition.

$$UP = (S = 0, \ Y = 1) \tag{3}$$

If the dataset includes more than one protected attribute, to mitigate bias toward multiple protected attributes simultaneously the number of groups will be increased [33, 34]. For instance, combining two protected attributes with the class label results in eight distinct demographic groups. Addressing bias in this manner is crucial for ensuring fairness in ML models [35], as focusing on a single attribute may overlook complex interdependencies between different attributes, potentially leading to unintended discriminatory outcomes [36].

## 2.4  Dataset

In our study, we utilized ten tabular datasets widely used in fairness-aware ML research [37]. These datasets span diverse domains such as finance, healthcare, education, and criminology, and each includes at least one protected attribute, making them suitable for evaluating bias mitigation strategies. Notably, five of these datasets feature multiple protected attributes. To systematically analyze the datasets, we categorized them based on four key types of imbalances, using threshold-based criteria to assess severity levels:

**Class Label Imbalance:** refers to the disproportionate distribution between positive and negative class labels. A dataset is considered highly imbalanced if one class makes up more than 70% of the data, moderately imbalanced if it falls between 60%–70%, and less imbalanced if both classes represent at least 40% of the data [38].

**Protected Attribute Imbalance:** captures unequal representation among different groups defined by a sensitive attribute. If the majority group exceeds 80% of the population, the imbalance is high; if it falls between 65%–80%, it is moderate; and if it is under 65%, the distribution is considered balanced.

**Group-Based Imbalance:** accounts for disparities in the sizes of subgroups formed by intersecting class labels and protected attributes. This is evaluated as High, when there are substantial differences in group sizes; Moderate, when group size disparities are noticeable but less extreme; Low, when group sizes are relatively uniform.

**Positive Class Label Ratio Imbalance:** Measures differences in the rates of positive outcomes across protected groups. A difference greater than 20% indicates high imbalance, 10%–20% is moderate, and below 10% is considered low.

Based on these criteria, we assigned each dataset–attribute combination an imbalance level of High, Moderate, or Low, treating each as a distinct evaluation scenario. These results are summarized in Fig. 1, which presents a heatmap illustrating the imbalance levels across all four dimensions for each dataset.

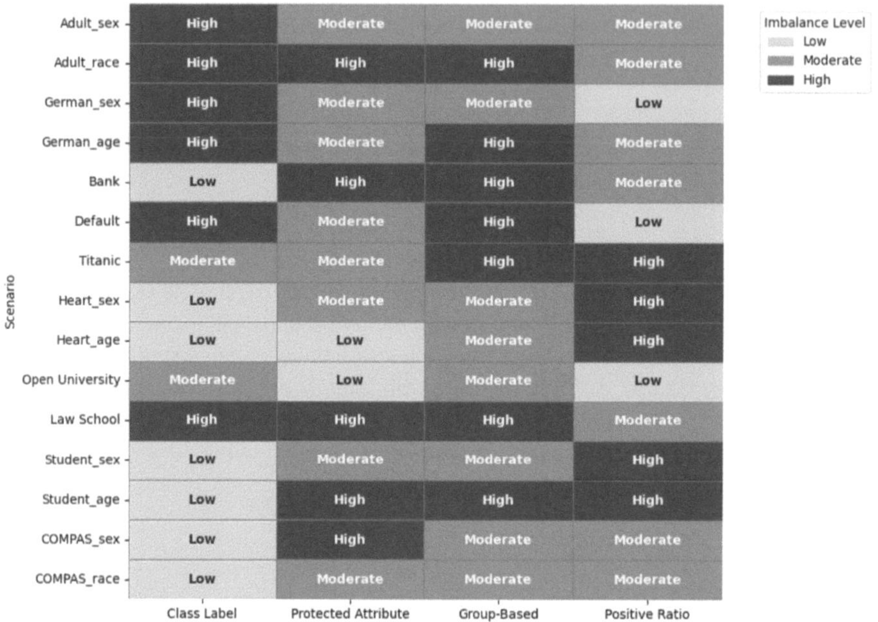


**Fig. 1.** Class label, protected attribute, group and positive ratio imbalanced level of Scenario

## 3  Methodology

In this study, we categorize preprocessing sampling methods based on two primary dimensions: group size adjustment strategies and sample selection techniques. This dual taxonomy facilitates a comprehensive analysis of how different configurations impact fairness in classification tasks.

### 3.1  Group Size Adjustment Strategies

In terms of group size adjustment strategies, we identify three principal strategies for adjusting group sizes:

- **Equalized Representation:**

This strategy aims to balance the ratio of positive to negative samples across both privileged and unprivileged groups, in line with the principles of Demographic Parity. The expected size for each subgroup is calculated to ensure that the proportion of positive outcomes is equal across all groups [8, 39]. For the UP group, the expected size is computed in Eq. 4. Similar calculations are applied for the PP, PN, and UN groups by substituting the corresponding group counts into the formula. This method maintains the overall dataset size while achieving equal positive-to-negative ratios across all groups, thereby promoting fairness without altering the total number of samples.

$$Expected\_Size_{UP} = \frac{|PositiveClass| * |Unprivileged\,Samples|}{|Training\,Set|} \tag{4}$$

- **UP -Focused Equalized Representation:**

This method focuses on oversampling the UP group to adjust the dataset in a manner that aims to reduce disparities in model predictions, particularly those measured by the Disparate Impact metric in Eq. 2 [13, 40]. The expected size for the UP group is determined by Eq. 5.

$$Expected\_Size_{UP} = \frac{|PP| * |UN|}{|PN|} - |UP| \tag{5}$$

This approach involves oversampling the UP group, which will increase the total number of positive samples, unprivileged samples, and the overall training set size. For scenarios involving two protected attributes, resulting in eight distinct groups, the expected sizes for groups containing at least one unprivileged attribute will be calculated.

This strategy aims to create a dataset that, when used to train a predictive model, may lead to outcomes with reduced disparate impact, thereby promoting fairness in the model's predictions.

- **Balanced Size Techniques:**

Inspired by the Fair_SMOTE method, this strategy adjusts all subgroup sizes to match the largest group, ensuring uniform representation as shown in Eq. 6 [33, 41]. This ensures a balanced representation across all subgroups [42]. This uniformity aids in mitigating biases arising from unequal group representations.

$$\begin{aligned} Expected\_Size_{PP} = Expected\_Size_{UP} &= Expected\_Size_{PN} \\ = Expected\_Size_{UN} &= \max\{|PP|, |UP|, |PN|, |UN|\} \end{aligned} \tag{6}$$

## 3.2  Sampling Strategies

The Synthetic Minority Oversampling Technique (SMOTE) is a widely used data augmentation method designed to address class imbalance in datasets [41]. It generates synthetic examples for the minority class by interpolating between existing minority instances and their nearest neighbors in the feature space [43]. This approach helps in creating a more balanced dataset, which can lead to improved model performance on minority classes [43].

In this paper, we applied Fair-SMOTE, a fairness-aware oversampling method developed by Chakraborty et al. [33, 41, 44], to generate new synthetic data points. Unlike standard SMOTE variants, Fair-SMOTE preserves inter-feature associations by extrapolating all variables by the same factor between two nearest neighbors, thereby reducing distortion in the feature space [41]. It also accounts for data types: boolean, categorical, and numeric features are mutated using dedicated logic [45]. In accordance with the original Fair-SMOTE implementation, we set the mutation amount (f) and crossover frequency (cr) hyperparameters to 0.8, reflecting a strong preference for interpolating new points that remain close to their parent instances [41]. A k-nearest neighbors' algorithm with k = 3 was used to identify neighbors for interpolation, ensuring consistent subgroup-level sampling across all datasets. In our work, we explicitly decompose the Fair-SMOTE mechanism into two components:

1. *Parent sample selection and*
2. *Sample generation via extrapolation*

We retain the original Fair-SMOTE generation logic unchanged for the second component. Importantly, throughout this paper, the term "SMOTE" always refers to the synthetic sample generation process implemented using Fair-SMOTE, rather than the standard SMOTE algorithm.

For the first stage, parent selection, we extend the original Fair-SMOTE implementation, which selected parent points randomly, by exploring three alternative strategies aimed at better aligning data augmentation with fairness objectives:

- **Uniform Sampling with SMOTE (US_SM):** Randomly selects samples from under-represented groups to generate synthetic data until the expected size is reached [8]. All groups' sizes are adjusted based on demographic parity. This strategy mirrors the random parent selection used in the original Fair-SMOTE implementation.
- **Preferential Sampling with SMOTE (PS_SM):** prioritizes samples near the decision boundary for generating synthetic data [39].
- **Weighted Preferential Sampling with SMOTE (WPS_SM):** Assigns sampling weights based on proximity to decision boundaries, offering more nuanced augmentation by focusing on more informative samples [46, 47].

### 3.3 Preprocessing Techniques

By combining the aforementioned group size adjustment strategies with sampling techniques, we designed and evaluated nine preprocessing methods:

1. **US_SM:** Applies Uniform Sampling with SMOTE to adjust all groups according to demographic parity-based global adjustment.
2. **PS_SM:** Integrates Preferential Sampling with SMOTE, focusing on samples near the decision boundary across all groups to meet demographic parity-based global adjustment.
3. **WPS_SM:** Weighted Preferential Sampling with SMOTE enhances PS_SM by assigning weights to samples based on their distance from the decision boundary. More informative samples have a higher probability of being selected as parents for SMOTE across all groups, in line with demographic parity-based global adjustment.
4. **UP_US_SM:** Applies Uniform Sampling with SMOTE only to the UP group, adjusting its size based on UP-based adjustment approach.
5. **UP_PS_SM:** Applies Preferential Sampling with SMOTE solely to the UP group, targeting samples near the decision boundary according to the UP-based adjustment approach.

6. **UP_WPS_SM:** Applies Weighted Preferential Sampling with SMOTE exclusively to the UP group to meet UP-based adjustment approach.
7. **B_US_SM:** Utilizes Uniform Sampling with SMOTE to equalize all group sizes to the largest group. This technique is functionally equivalent to the Fair-SMOTE method introduced by Chakraborty et al. [41]. To maintain consistency in our naming convention, we refer to it as B_US_SM.
8. **B_PS_SM:** Combines Preferential Sampling with SMOTE, balancing all groups to the largest size as per the Balanced Size Techniques strategy.
9. **B_WPS_SM:** Integrates Weighted Preferential Sampling with SMOTE, ensuring all groups match the size of the largest group.

This structured approach allows for a systematic evaluation of different preprocessing configurations and their impact on fairness and performance metrics. To ensure robust and reliable results, we conducted experiments using 50 random seeds for each combination of dataset and protected attribute. First, a baseline experiment with a standard Logistic Regression, Decision Tree, Gradient Boosting, Random Forest, and Support Vector Classification on each of the conditions (dataset_protected_attribute) was performed to compare and benchmark the results of the debiasing experiments. These five algorithms, with the goal of maximizing accuracy, were employed to compare how pre-processing mitigation techniques impact different models in different datasets with different protected attributes.

All techniques were applied under two scenarios, mitigating bias toward a single protected attribute and mitigating bias toward multiple protected attributes simultaneously. All techniques were evaluated under identical conditions and compared against the current techniques to assess their performance and fairness.

## 4  Results and Discussion

All the introduced techniques were capable of mitigating bias towards one protected attribute at a time and multiple protected attributes simultaneously. Table 1 presents a demonstration of the results for one of the datasets, the Adult Income dataset, focusing on mitigating bias related to the race protected attribute. Logistic Regression is employed as both the classifier and ranker in this analysis. B_US_SM serves as an established pre-processing sampling technique, while the other methods generate synthetic data based on different methodologies for defining group sizes and sample selection. To evaluate the effectiveness of these techniques, we analyzed the median values of performance and fairness metrics. The results indicate that UP_WPS_SM and PS_SM are competitive in achieving the most favorable outcomes concerning the Demographic Parity fairness metric for this dataset. Regarding Equalized Odds fairness metrics, among the techniques, US_SM outperforms the others. Techniques focusing on the UP group size also perform well concerning these metrics. While B_US_SM and B_PS_SM exhibit strong performance among the balanced group techniques for Equalized Odds fairness metrics, B_WPS_SM adversely affects these metrics. The highest overall accuracy is achieved by techniques focusing on the demographic parity notion of fairness size approach, whereas the highest BAC is attained by techniques employing balanced group sizes. Figure 2 presents a Pareto Frontier plot [48], illustrating the trade-off between DI and accuracy for different sampling techniques on the Adult Income dataset with the race protected attribute. Techniques like PS_SM and WPS_SM demonstrate significant gains in fairness (DI) but show varied effects on accuracy. In contrast, the UP-based methods maintain higher accuracy but yield more modest improvements in fairness.

**Table 1.** Results of applying pre-processing techniques to mitigate race-protected attribute in the Adult dataset

| Technique | DI | SP | AOD | EO | ACC | BAC |
|---|---|---|---|---|---|---|
| baseline | 0.41 | -0.09 | -0.09 | -0.13 | 0.82 | 0.68 |
| US_SM | 0.73 | -0.04 | 0.01 | 0.02 | *0.82* | 0.68 |
| PS_SM | 1.21 | 0.03 | 0.12 | 0.19 | *0.82* | 0.68 |
| WPS_SM | 2.46 | 0.08 | 0.19 | 0.33 | 0.80 | 0.61 |
| UP_US_SM | 0.80 | -0.03 | 0.03 | 0.06 | *0.82* | 0.69 |
| UP_PS_SM | 0.83 | -0.03 | 0.04 | 0.07 | *0.82* | 0.69 |
| UP_WPS_SM | *0.88* | *-0.02* | 0.04 | 0.08 | *0.82* | 0.69 |
| B_US_SM | 0.79 | -0.08 | *0.00* | 0.02 | 0.77 | *0.76* |
| B_PS_SM | 0.76 | -0.09 | -0.02 | *0.01* | 0.77 | *0.76* |
| B_WPS_SM | 2.23 | 0.21 | 0.31 | 0.40 | 0.80 | 0.70 |

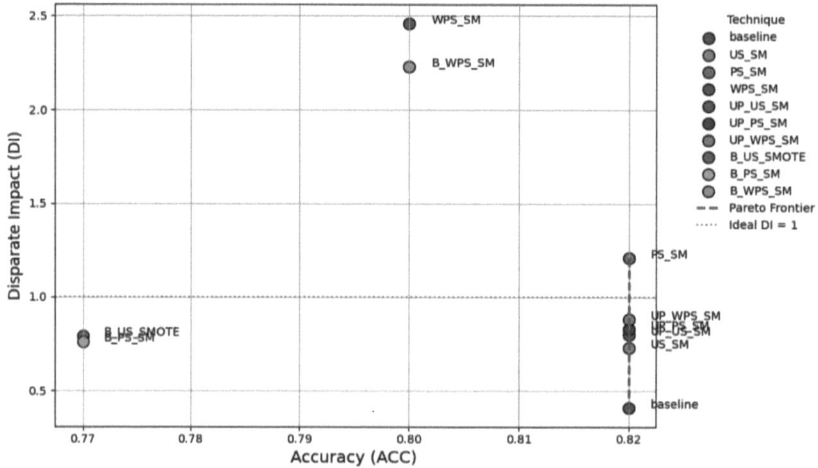


**Fig. 2.** Pareto Frontier: Tradeoff between Disparate Impact and Accuracy (Adult-race)

Given the extensive nature of the results across ten diverse datasets, presenting all findings in detail would be impractical and could obscure key insights. To succinctly summarize and compare the effectiveness of each technique, we employed the Scott-Knott clustering method, a statistical approach that partitions techniques into distinct groups based on their performance distributions [41]. This method assigns ranks to each group, where a higher rank signifies superior performance, and techniques within the same group are considered statistically indistinguishable [41]. For a more granular comparison, we reported the number of Wins, Losses, and Ties for each technique. A "Win" indicates that a technique achieved a higher rank compared to another, a "Loss" denotes a lower rank, and a "Tie" reflects statistical parity between techniques. To further quantify these comparisons, we calculated the Win/Loss Ratio (WLR), representing the proportion of wins to losses, and the Tie/Total Ratio (TTR), indicating the ratio of tied outcomes to the total number of comparisons. This analytical framework allowed us to effectively distill the performance of various bias mitigation strategies across multiple datasets, facilitating a robust and comprehensive comparison.

Table 2 shows the Scott-Knott results comparing PS_SM and UP_PS_SM techniques across all datasets in the study. Both apply SMOTE to generate synthetic samples near the decision boundary. PS_SM oversamples UP and PN groups while undersampling UN and PP groups based on the Demographic Parity objective, whereas UP_PS_SM exclusively oversamples the UP group. The results reveal that PS_SM outperforms UP_PS_SM in terms of Demographic Parity fairness metrics and most performance metrics such as accuracy and balanced accuracy. However, UP_PS_SM achieves significantly better results for Equalized Odds fairness metrics.

**Table 2.** PS_SM vs UP_PS_SM Scott-Knott Result

| | 1 protected attribute at a time | | | | | 2 protected attributes at a time | | | | |
| --- | --- | --- | --- | --- | --- | --- | --- | --- | --- | --- |
| Metric | Wins | Ties | Losses | WLR | TTR | Wins | Ties | Losses | WLR | TTR |
| DI | **34** | 18 | 23 | 1.48 | 0.24 | **24** | 16 | 10 | 2.4 | 0.32 |
| SP | **37** | 14 | 24 | 1.54 | 0.19 | **29** | 10 | 11 | 2.64 | 0.2 |
| AOD | 10 | 24 | **41** | 0.24 | 0.32 | 10 | 18 | **22** | 0.45 | 0.36 |
| EO | 8 | 28 | **39** | 0.21 | 0.37 | 4 | 24 | **22** | 0.18 | 0.48 |
| Acc | **25** | 28 | 22 | 1.14 | 0.37 | 16 | 16 | **18** | 0.89 | 0.32 |
| BAC | **33** | 24 | 18 | 1.83 | 0.32 | **24** | 12 | 14 | 1.71 | 0.24 |

In general, techniques based on UP group size adjustment consistently perform better than those based on balanced group sizes. Among all, B_WPS_SM ranks lowest in fairness metrics, suggesting that balancing all groups equally while focusing only on samples near the decision boundary may not effectively reduce bias. Interestingly, while WPS-based methods underperform when applied within demographic parity-based global size adjustment or balanced group frameworks, the UP_WPS_SM technique shows substantial improvements in all fairness metrics and in accuracy. As illustrated in Table 3, UP_WPS_SM achieves a high number of wins in fairness comparisons against B_WPS_SM, confirming that selective oversampling in the UP group using weighted proximity can effectively mitigate bias without overly disturbing model accuracy.

**Table 3.** UP_WPS_SM VS B_WPS_SM Scott-Knott Result

| | 1 protected attribute at a time | | | | | 2 protected attributes at a time | | | | |
|--------|------|------|--------|------|------|------|------|--------|------|------|
| Metric | Wins | Ties | Losses | WLR | TTR | Wins | Ties | Losses | WLR | TTR |
| DI | **47** | 12 | 16 | 2.94 | 0.16 | **22** | 14 | 14 | 1.57 | 0.28 |
| SP | **38** | 14 | 23 | 1.65 | 0.19 | 15 | 10 | **25** | 0.6 | 0.2 |
| AOD | **49** | 18 | 8 | 6.12 | 0.24 | **24** | 16 | 10 | 2.4 | 0.32 |
| EO | **54** | 17 | 4 | 13.5 | 0.23 | **31** | 18 | 1 | 31 | 0.36 |
| Acc | **50** | 15 | 10 | 5 | 0.2 | **38** | 6 | 6 | 6.33 | 0.12 |
| BAC | 21 | 16 | **38** | 0.55 | 0.21 | 16 | 12 | **22** | 0.73 | 0.24 |

Finally, Table 4 presents a comprehensive ranking of all SMOTE-based bias mitigation techniques, evaluated across all datasets using the Scott-Knott methodology. This analysis considers both fairness metrics (DI and AOD) and performance metrics (accuracy and balanced accuracy) when applying techniques to mitigate bias toward a single protected attribute. The rankings highlight that PS_SM and US_SM excel in enhancing fairness.

Across the evaluated datasets, the performance of SMOTE-based bias mitigation techniques varies, particularly concerning the Demographic Parity fairness metric. The PS_SM technique frequently achieves top performance, ranking first, in 9 out of 15 datasets. The UP_PS_SM method also demonstrates strong performance, often securing the second position. The theoretical foundation supporting our empirical findings lies in the observation that samples located near the decision boundary are more prone to misclassification, particularly for underrepresented or unprivileged groups [39]. Prior research has demonstrated that concentrating synthetic sampling in these boundary regions allows the classifier to gain a more nuanced understanding of ambiguous instances, ultimately reducing classification errors for disadvantaged groups [49]. Consequently, techniques which generate synthetic data in the proximity of the decision boundary, are better equipped to improve Demographic Parity fairness metrics without significantly compromising predictive performance [8].

According to both Fig. 2 and Tabe 4, while the baseline technique performs the worst on both DI and AOD, it achieves the highest accuracy, demonstrating the inherent tradeoff between fairness and accuracy. Similarly, B_US_SM leads in balanced accuracy, another performance metric. However, while PS_SM and US_SM perform best on specific fairness metrics such as DI and AOD, they do not consistently lead in predictive performance metrics. This highlights a core insight of our study: no single technique dominates across all dimensions. In many cases, improvements in fairness come at the cost of reduced predictive performance, underscoring the need for context-dependent decision-making. Practitioners must therefore weigh the relative importance of fairness versus accuracy depending on the societal, ethical, and operational implications of misclassification. Techniques focusing on the UP group, such as UP_WPS_SM and UP_PS_SM, consistently achieve high rankings across both fairness and accuracy. These methods are particularly suitable for scenarios where fairness and accuracy must be optimized simultaneously. In contrast, techniques such as B_WPS_SM, while enhancing certain fairness metrics, incur a noticeable drop in accuracy, reflecting a steeper trade-off. Interpreted through the lens of cost-sensitive fairness, this implies that the marginal fairness gain may not always justify the associated performance cost [50]. These insights support a multi-objective optimization perspective, where fairness and accuracy are treated not in isolation but as competing objectives to be jointly optimized depending on application-specific constraints [48].

**Table 4.** Comparative rankings of preprocessing sampling bias mitigation techniques

| Rank | DI | AOD | ACC | Bac |
| --- | --- | --- | --- | --- |
| 1 | PS_SM | US_SM | Baseline | B_US_SM |
| 2 | UP_WPS_SM | UP_PS_SM | US_SM | B_PS_SM |
| 3 | UP _PS_SM | UP_WPS_SM | UP_US_SM | Baseline |
| 4 | UP _US_SM | UP_US_SM | UP_WPS_SM | B_WPS_SM |
| 5 | US_SM | B_US_SM | PS_SM | US_SM |
| 6 | WPS_SM | B_PS_SM | UP_PS_SM | PS_SM |
| 7 | B_PS_SM | PS_SM | WPS_SM | UP_US_SM |
| 8 | B_US_SM | WPS_SM | B_US_SM | UP_WPS_SM |
| 9 | B_WPS_SM | B_WPS_SM | B_PS_SM | UP_PS_SM |
| 10 | Baseline | Baseline | B_WPS_SM | WPS_SM |

The behavior of each method also varies by dataset. For example, B_WPS_SM excels, particularly in datasets that suffer from both group and positive ratio imbalance, such as the Heart dataset. This method is effective because it focuses on generating more samples relative to their positions. On the other hand, for the Open University dataset, US_SM (randomly sampling) is sufficient, as the imbalance is mild and there is no need to specifically focus on samples near the decision boundary. For the Compass dataset, generating samples only within the UP group is adequate, and this approach results in fair outcomes, making UP_SM_PS perform well for this dataset.

While our proposed techniques yield notable improvements in fairness metrics, several limitations should be acknowledged. First, SMOTE-based methods rely on generating synthetic samples, which may not always reflect the true data distribution, particularly in high-dimensional or non-linear feature spaces, leading to potential overfitting. Second, the effectiveness of these techniques depends on access to protected attribute labels during training, which may not always be available due to legal, ethical, or privacy restrictions. Lastly, computational overhead can be significant when boundary estimation is expensive, especially for large-scale or streaming data environments. These factors highlight the importance of cautious validation and adaptive deployment when applying fairness-aware preprocessing in practice.

## 5   Conclusion

This study conducted a comprehensive evaluation of SMOTE-based bias mitigation techniques, focusing on their effectiveness in enhancing Demographic Parity and Equalized Odds fairness metrics across ten diverse datasets. The techniques were categorized based on group size determination methods: (1) Demographic Parity-Based Global Adjustment, (2) Demographic Parity focusing solely on the unprivileged positive group, and (3) Balanced group sizes. Additionally, we explored three synthetic sample selection strategies: Uniform Sampling, Preferential Sampling, and Weighted Preferential Sampling. We established a structured framework to assess their impacts. Our analysis revealed that PS_SM and US_SM achieved the best performance among all techniques for Disparate Impact and Average Odds Difference fairness metrics, respectively. Techniques focusing on the UP group, especially those that generate synthetic samples near the decision boundary, offered strong fairness gains with minimal sacrifice in accuracy, validating the hypothesis that boundary-focused augmentation reduces misclassification of disadvantaged groups. These results highlight the trade-off space between fairness and performance, with methods like UP_WPS_SM offering effective middle ground solutions for real-world deployments. While no single method dominates across all settings, our findings emphasize the need for context-specific choices in real-world deployments. Future work should expand to more complex models, including deep learning models. Furthermore, practical deployment considerations, such as the limited availability of protected attribute labels, regulatory compliance, and the risks associated with synthetic data generation, must be central to developing fair, robust, and scalable machine learning systems.

## References


1. Mehrabi, N., Morstatter, F., Saxena, N., Lerman, K., Galstyan, A.: A survey on bias and fairness in machine learning. ACM Comput. Surv. **54**, (2021). https://doi.org/10.1145/345 7607
2. François-Blouin, J.: Responsible AI Symposium – Legal Implications of Bias Mitigation - Lieber Institute West Point. https://lieber.westpoint.edu/legal-implications-bias-mitigation/. Accessed 02 Dec 2023
3. Goethals, S., Calders, T., Martens, D.: Beyond Accuracy-Fairness: stop evaluating bias mitigation methods solely on between-group metrics (2024)
4. Tawakuli, A., Engel, T.: Make your data fair: a survey of data preprocessing techniques that address biases in data towards fair AI. J. Eng. Res. (2024). https://doi.org/10.1016/j.jer.2024. 06.016
5. Hort, M., et al.: Bias mitigation for machine learning classifiers: a comprehensive survey. ACM J. Responsible Comput. **1**, 1–52 (2024). https://doi.org/10.1145/3631326
6. Shahrezaei, M.H., Loughran, R., Daid, K.M.: Pre-processing techniques to mitigate against algorithmic bias. In: 2023 31st Irish *Conference on Artificial Intelligence and Cognitive Science* AICS 2023 (2023). https://doi.org/10.1109/AICS60730.2023.10470759
7. Peng, K., Yang, Y., Zhuo, H., Menzies, T.: Whence is a model fair? Fixing fairness bugs via propensity score matching (2025)
8. Kamiran, F., Calders, T.: Data preprocessing techniques for classification without discrimination. Springer (2012). https://doi.org/10.1007/s10115-011-0463-8

9. Celis, L.E., Keswani, V., Vishnoi, N.K.: Data preprocessing to mitigate bias: a maximum entropy based approach. In: 37th *International Conference on Machine Learning*. ICML 2020. PartF16814, pp. 1326–1336 (2020)

10. Yu, Z.: FairBalance: mitigating machine learning bias against multiple protected attributes with data balancing (2021)

11. Xu, D., Wu, Y., Yuan, S., Zhang, L., Wu, X.: Achieving causal fairness through generative adversarial networks. In: Proceedings Twenty-Eighth International Joint Conference on 2019. par.nsf.gov. (2019)

12. Sharma, S., Zhang, Y., Aliaga, J.M.R.O., Bouneffouf, D., Muthusamy, V., Varshney, K.R.: Data augmentation for discrimination prevention and bias disambiguation, pp. 358–364 (2020). https://doi.org/10.1145/3375627.3375865

13. Salazar, T., Santos, M.S., Araujo, H., Abreu, P.H.: FAWOS: fairness-aware oversampling algorithm based on distributions of sensitive attributes. IEEE Access. **9**, 81370–81379 (2021)

14. Friedler, S.A., Choudhary, S., Scheidegger, C., Hamilton, E.P., Venkatasubramanian, S., Roth, D.: A comparative study of fairness-enhancing interventions in machine learning. In: FAT* 2019 - Proceeding of the 2019 Conference Fairness, Accountability, Transparency, pp. 329–338 (2019). https://doi.org/10.1145/3287560.3287589

15. EEOC: Title VII of the Civil Rights Act of 1964 (2013). https://doi.org/10.4135/978145221 8533.n690

16. UK ICO: What's new? How do we ensure transparency in AI? Inf. Comm. Off. (2023)

17. Jin, D., et al.: A survey on fairness-aware recommender systems. Inf. Fusion. **100**, 101906 (2023). https://doi.org/10.1016/j.inffus.2023.101906

18. Saxena, N.A.: Perceptions of fairness. In: Proceeding of the 2019 AAAI/ACM Conference on AI, Ethics, and Society, pp. 537–538 (2019). https://doi.org/10.1145/3306618

19. Barocas, S., Hardt, M., Narayanan, A.: Fairness and machine learning (2019)

20. Narayanan, A.: Translation tutorial : 21 fairness definitions and their politics. 21 (2019)

21. Nielsen, A.: Practical fairness: achieving fair and secure data models, 330 (2020)

22. Wang, Y., Singh, L.: Analyzing the impact of missing values and selection bias on fairness. Int. J. Data Sci. Anal. **12**, 101–119 (2021). https://doi.org/10.1007/s41060-021-00259-z

23. Langenberg, A., Ma, S.C., Ermakova, T., Fabian, B.: Formal group fairness and accuracy in automated decision making. Mathematics **11**, 1–25 (2023). https://doi.org/10.3390/math11 081771

24. Varshney, K.R.: Trustworthy. Mach. Learn. (2022). https://doi.org/10.1109/MIS.2022.315 2946

25. Dwork, C., Hardt, M., Pitassi, T., Reingold, O., Zemel, R.: Fairness through awareness. ITCS **2012**, 214–226 (2012). https://doi.org/10.1145/2090236.2090255

26. Rao, D.: Fairness in AI — Ethical Implications of ML Models (2021)

27. Verma, S., Rubin, J.: Fairness definition explained. ACM **18**, 1–7 (2018). https://doi.org/10. 1145/3194770.3194776

28. Hardt, M., Price, E., Srebro, N.N.: Equality of opportunity in supervised learning. Adv. Neural Inf. Process. Syst. **29**, 3323–3331 (2016). https://doi.org/10.48550/arxiv.1610.02413

29. Kleinberg, J., Ludwig, J., Mullainathan, S., Rambachan, A.: Algorithmic fairness. AEA Pap. Proc. **108**, 22–27 (2018). https://doi.org/10.1257/pandp.20181018

30. Grandini, M., Bagli, E., Visani, G.: Metrics for multi-class classification: an overview (2020)

31. Brodersen, K.H., Ong, C.S., Stephan, K.E., Buhmann, J.M.: The balanced accuracy and its posterior distribution. In: Proceedings of the International Conference Pattern Recognition, pp. 3125–3128 (2010). https://doi.org/10.1109/ICPR.2010.764

32. Žliobaite, I., Kamiran, F., Calders, T.: Handling conditional discrimination. In: Proceedings of the IEEE International Conference Data Mining, ICDM., pp. 992–1001 (2011). https://doi. org/10.1109/ICDM.2011.72

33. Yu, Z., Chakraborty, J., Menzies, T.: FairBalance: how to achieve equalized odds with data pre-processing. IEEE Trans. Softw. Eng., 1–15 (2024). https://doi.org/10.1109/TSE.2024.343 1445

34. Rosado Gómez, A.A., Calderón Benavides, M.L., Espinosa, O.: Data preprocessing to improve fairness in machine learning models: an application to the reintegration process of demobilized members of armed groups in Colombia. Appl. Soft Comput. **152** (2024). https://doi.org/10.1016/j.asoc.2023.111193

35. Duong, M.K., Conrad, S.: Measuring and mitigating bias for tabular datasets with multiple protected attributes (2024)

36. Turner Lee, N., Resnick, P., Barton, G.: Algorithmic bias detection and mitigation: Best practices and policies to reduce consumer harms (2019)

37. Fabris, A., Messina, S., Silvello, G., Susto, G.A.: Algorithmic fairness datasets: the story so far. Data Min. Knowl. Discov. **36**, 2074–2152 (2022). https://doi.org/10.1007/s10618-022-00854-z

38. Le Quy, T., Roy, A., Iosifidis, V., Zhang, W., Ntoutsi, E.: A survey on datasets for fairness-aware machine learning. Wiley Interdiscip. Rev. Data Min. Knowl. Discov. **12**, 1–59 (2022). https://doi.org/10.1002/widm.1452

39. Kamiran, F., Calders, T.: Classification with no discrimination by preferential sampling. In: Annual Machine Learning Conference. Belgium, Netherlands, pp. 1–6 (2010)

40. Albalak, A., et al.: A survey on data selection for language models, 1–81 (2024)

41. Chakraborty, J., Majumder, S., Menzies, T.: Bias in machine learning software: why? how? what to do? Assoc. Comput. Mach. (2021). https://doi.org/10.1145/3468264.3468537

42. Chakraborty, J., Majumder, S., Yu, Z., Menzies, T.: Fairway: a way to build fair ML software. ESEC/FSE **2020**, 654–665 (2020). https://doi.org/10.1145/3368089.3409697

43. Chawla, N.V., Bowyer, K.W., Hall, L.O., Kegelmeyer, W.P.: SMOTE: synthetic minority over-sampling technique. J. Artif. Intell. Res. **16**, 321–357 (2002). https://doi.org/10.1613/jair.953

44. Peng, K., Chakraborty, J., Menzies, T.: FairMask: better fairness via model-based rebalancing of protected attributes. IEEE Trans. Softw. Eng. **49**, 2426–2439 (2023). https://doi.org/10.1109/TSE.2022.3220713

45. Chakraborty, J.: joymallyac/Fair-SMOTE: GitHub repo for FSE 2021 Paper - Bias in Machine Learning Software: Why? How? What to do?. https://github.com/joymallyac/Fair-SMOTE/tree/master. Accessed 04 Jun 2025

46. Hu, Z., Xu, Y., Gu, J.: Boosting fair classifier generalization through adaptive priority reweighing (2024). https://doi.org/10.1145/3665895

47. Krasanakis, E., Spyromitros-Xioufis, E., Papadopoulos, S., Kompatsiaris, Y.: Adaptive sensitive reweighting to mitigate bias in fairness-aware classification, 853–862 (2018). https://doi.org/10.1145/3178876.3186133

48. Nagpal, R., Shahsavarifar, R., Goyal, V., Gupta, A.: Optimizing fairness and accuracy: a Pareto optimal approach for decision-making. AI Ethics 2024 **52**(5), 1743–1756 (2024). https://doi.org/10.1007/S43681-024-00508-4

49. Gnip, P., Zoričak, M., Kanász, R., Drotár, P., Kanász, R., Drotár, P.: An experimental survey of imbalanced learning algorithms for bankruptcy prediction (2025). https://doi.org/10.1007/s10462-025-11107-y

50. Liu, S., Vicente, L.N., Nunes Vicente, L.: Accuracy and fairness trade-offs in machine learning: a stochastic multi-objective approach. Comput. Manag. Sci. **19**, 513–537 (2020). https://doi.org/10.1007/s10287-022-00425-z

# Understudied Users

# Balancing Sensory Needs, Interests and Personality: An Integrated Approach to Event Recommendations for Adults with Autism Spectrum Disorder

Angelo Geninatti Cossatin⦾, Liliana Ardissono⦾, Federica Cena⦾,
Claudio Mattutino⦾, and Noemi Mauro(✉)⦾

University of Torino, Torino, Italy
`{angelo.geninatticossatin,liliana.ardissono,federica.cena,`
`claudio.mattutino,noemi.mauro}@unito.it`

**Abstract.** This paper presents a novel approach to event recommender systems designed for adults with medium to high-functioning autism spectrum disorder (ASD) to facilitate social inclusion. Our system addresses a critical gap in existing recommender technologies by integrating three key dimensions: event preferences, sensory features based on the Sensory Perception Quotient, and personality traits based on the OCEAN model. Unlike conventional recommender systems that primarily focus on preference-based models, our approach acknowledges the impact of sensory sensitivities on decision-making for individuals with ASD. We introduce a weighted loss function with sigmoid transformation to integrate these multifaceted features, optimized through a preliminary analysis on synthetic data. This model is aimed at personalizing event recommendations considering interest alignment and sensory and personality compatibility for social comfort and engagement in the ASD population. Specifically, we plan to estimate the users' ratings of group events based on the similarity between the events and user profiles. Preliminary results demonstrate the feasibility of our approach, with future work focused on real-world implementation, data collection, and user testing within the SPACES project.

**Keywords:** Recommender Systems · Autism · Social Inclusion

## 1 Introduction

Autism Spectrum Disorder (ASD) represents a complex neurodevelopmental condition characterized by significant heterogeneity [41]. It is a fairly rare condition (e.g., about 2.21% in U.S. [13]). However, recent studies indicate a significant increase in ASD diagnoses over the past decades. For example, in the UK, there was a 787% increment recorded in ASD incidence between 1998 and 2018 [32]. The spectrum ranges from individuals with severe intellectual disabilities to those with average or above-average cognitive capabilities, referred to as


A. Bellogin et al. (Eds.): IR4U2 2025/BIAS 2025, CCIS 2786, pp. 47–59, 2026.
https://doi.org/10.1007/978-3-032-12717-4_4

high-functioning autism [16]. Despite this variability, reduced social capabilities remain a common challenge, frequently leading to isolation and loneliness [22]. Research indicates that autistic people often experience challenges in forming and maintaining social relationships. Specifically, studies have found that adolescents report higher levels of loneliness, poorer friendship quality, and lower social network status compared to their neurotypical developing peers [24].

Social networking services have shown potential in helping individuals with ASD build and engage with support networks, particularly strengthening connections with extended network members [20]. Moreover, online social networking may give opportunities to form friendships, challenging traditional notions of friendship and social interaction [8]. However, things are more complex in socializing through event participation. On the one hand, atypical sensory perception affects individuals with ASD [38], possibly resulting in overwhelming anxiety and discomfort in environments that neurotypical individuals navigate with ease [35]. Furthermore, people with ASD often exhibit specific interests compared to neurotypical individuals [2], challenging their satisfaction in group settings. On the other hand, when such specialized interests are met, they can serve as valuable foundations for developing social and communication skills while expanding social networks, potentially facilitating integration with neurotypical peers through thematic group events.

Digital technologies have shown promise in supporting individuals with ASD, who typically respond positively to the predictability offered by computational systems [40]. However, many solutions focus on addressing social challenges such as facilitating conversations [6], supporting emotion regulation [35], or encouraging social interactions [7]. Differently, there remains significant untapped potential for technology tailored to the needs of adults with ASD to support group formation, event organization, and participation.

The SPACES (Adaptive support for organizing and participating in groups and activities for adults with medium to high-functioning autism spectrum disorder) project aims to fill this gap. It seeks to develop a digital platform for supporting the organization and participation in activities and events (e.g., cineforum, and hiking in the mountains) for adults with medium to high-functioning ASD to facilitate social inclusion through group formation.

Conventional recommender systems operate on preference-based models [30], overlooking the dimension of sensory aversions that significantly impact autistic people's decision-making; see [26] for an exception to this trend. Conversely, research demonstrates that sensory information is key when individuals with ASD decide which events to participate in and which environments to visit [10]. Therefore, any solution to facilitate group participation must consider interest alignment and sensory compatibility to support social inclusion.

For this reason, the SPACES project applies a bottom-up approach to enable users to explore existing group events and create new ones. Moreover, it aims to personalize event recommendations based on a multifaceted user model that accounts for the user's interests, sensory features [38], and user personality to evaluate the overall suitability of the suggestions for the user.

To develop the recommender system underlying the SPACES platform, we investigate a novel approach to similarity calculation that integrates multiple dimensions critical to social comfort and engagement. Specifically, we explore incorporating Big Five personality traits [23] (OCEAN: openness, conscientiousness, extraversion, agreeableness, and neuroticism) to predict interpersonal compatibility between group members. Moreover, we model sensory stimulation thresholds across multiple dimensions (sight, hearing, smell, taste, and touch) according to the Sensory Perception Quotient (SPQ) [38] to ensure environmental compatibility. By developing a comprehensive similarity measure that balances these diverse factors, we aim to create more nuanced event recommendations that consider the multifaceted nature of social compatibility for individuals with ASD.

In the present paper, we describe the features we use to personalize the recommendation of events and the features integration model based on a weighted loss function that leverages a sigmoid transformation. Moreover, we describe a preliminary training of this model on synthetic data to fine-tune the model.

We are developing the SPACES project in collaboration with the *Regional Center for Autism Spectrum Disorders in Adulthood - ASL City of Turin*[1].

The remainder of this paper is organized as follows: Sect. 2 reviews related work, Sect. 3 details our feature engineering methodology, Sect. 4 describes the integration model, Sect. 5 presents presents the results of the model training phase, and Sect. 6 discusses our future directions.

## 2 Related Work

### 2.1 Event Recommender Systems

Event recommendation systems have emerged as a crucial solution to the information overload problem in Event-Based Social Networks (EBSNs), where the overwhelming volume of available events can hinder users' ability to discover relevant options. Recent research in this domain has evolved along several dimensions, addressing unique challenges such as the transient nature of events and the complexity of user preferences in social contexts.

Several approaches enhance recommendation accuracy through contextual awareness. Horowitz et al. [21] introduced EventAware, a mobile system designed for dynamic EBSNs that leverages implicit contextual data with minimal user input through a tag-based algorithm. Building on this contextual foundation, Macedo et al. [25] addressed the cold-start problem by integrating multiple signals, including content, collaborative filtering, social connections, geographic proximity, and temporal features to create personalized event rankings, demonstrating superior performance on Meetup datasets.

The recommendation challenge has been approached from both user and event perspectives. While most systems focus on suggesting events to users, Ding et al. [14] explored the inverse problem of event participation recommendation to

---

[1] Center's webpage: https://bit.ly/regional-center-asd-in-adulthood-asl-turin.

identify users most likely to join a specific event. Their sliding-window machine learning model incorporates multi-channel user features and outperforms traditional methods in real-time recommendation scenarios.

Research has also investigated which specific features most significantly influence user interests in events. Cena et al. [9] examined some factors such as location accessibility, event reputation, and friend participation to determine their predictive value for recommender systems. Similarly, transparency has become increasingly important, with researchers developing frameworks that combine extensive data exploration with fuzzy approximate reasoning to create human-interpretable models, achieving impressive accuracy on large-scale event datasets [3, 36].

The social dimension of events has inspired innovative recommendation approaches. Tu et al. [39] introduced activity-partner recommendation, recognizing that users often prefer participating in activities with friends and developing methods that consider historical attendance patterns, social context, and geographic information when suggesting suitable companions.

A related research direction focuses on group recommenders for social activities. These systems balance individual preferences with group dynamics when suggesting activities and locations, frequently relying on similarity measures based primarily on shared interests or preferences and on personality traits [1, 12]. For instance, Gartrell et al. [18] incorporated social relationships and content interests to enhance group recommendations. Boratto et al. [5] developed techniques for automatically identifying groups and providing suggestions based on individual preferences and clustering. For specific domains like tourism, Garcia et al. [17] presented methods for recommending activities to groups by considering demographics and past experiences. Taking a Bayesian approach, Purushotham and Kuo [28] modeled group dynamics—including interactions, membership, and influence—for personalized recommendations in location- and event-based networks.

Similar to these group recommender systems, we suggest events intended for collective experiences. However, we focus on incremental group formation and target individual users rather than groups, thus avoiding the group decision-making complexities discussed by Delic et al. [12]. Specifically, while traditional group recommenders must account for potentially conflicting preferences among multiple group members and employ various preference aggregation strategies to reach consensus, our system focuses on the individual user's preferences and social context to decide whether to join a group. This distinction allows us to bypass the challenges of balancing diverse group needs, managing social dynamics, and negotiating compromises that typically complicate group recommendations. By recommending group events to individuals, we maintain personalization while facilitating social experiences, effectively bridging the gap between individual-centric and group-oriented recommendation paradigms.

## 2.2  Recommender Systems for People with Autism

Recent research on recommender systems for autism has focused on various applications, from e-learning to place and app recommendations.

In the e-learning domain, researchers developed recommender systems that enhance educational experiences for individuals with ASD by delivering customized content aligned with their characteristics, preferences, and learning styles [29]. These systems recognize the importance of personalization in educational settings for neurodivergent learners.

Sevilla et al. [33] proposed an ontology-based recommendation framework designed for mobile applications targeting the autistic population. This system takes a holistic approach by incorporating multiple variables spanning individual traits, family dynamics, and community factors to suggest appropriate mobile apps for people with ASD. Another approach employs consumer feedback from location-based services to extract sensory data about places, improving recommendations for autistic individuals with specific sensory sensitivities [27].

Additionally, machine learning models have been employed to create multi-classifier recommender systems for early ASD detection. In that context, Decision Trees and Random Forests show promising results in accuracy and other performance metrics [34].

To our knowledge, no work is specifically devoted to recommending social events tailored to the needs and preferences of autistic individuals. Thus, the approach proposed in this work represents a novel contribution to the field.

# 3  Features for the Recommender System

We consider three primary categories of user features to estimate the impact of events on users in the Autism Spectrum Disorders: (1) preferences for event types, (2) sensory requirements affecting the participation in events and actions, and (3) personality traits. The rationale is that event recommendations should match the user's preferences and sensory sensitivities to avoid proposing unsuitable events. However, the success of an event also depends on its participants; thus, personality traits have to be considered as a further dimension to prevent the user from being exposed to incompatible groups.

## 3.1  Event Preferences

Event preferences represent explicit user interests, a standard type of information for recommender systems. However, they are particularly marked in autistic people, who often exhibit little flexibility and need comfort in predictable environments [19]. In this work, we assume that the system elicits user preferences for events on a binary scale (preferred/not preferred). The reason is that eliciting more articulated preferences, e.g., in a 5-point Likert scale, might challenge mid-functioning users with ASD, who might be unable to answer appropriately.

We reason about the risk of discomfort that events might bring to people with ASD. Thus, we estimate the possible negative impact on user experience, assuming that a neutral impact is good. We model the discomfort generated by failing to meet the user's preferences as categorical data, formalized as follows:

$$C_{mismatch}(u, a) = \begin{cases} 0, & \text{if } category(a) \in preferences(u) \\ \alpha_{penalty}, & \text{otherwise} \end{cases}$$

where $C_{mismatch}(u, a)$ represents the preference mismatch between user $u$ and the category of an event $a$, and $\alpha_{penalty}$ is a constant penalty factor applied when the category of $a$ does not belong to the user's preferences. This binary approach reflects the importance of respecting the specific interests of autistic individuals.

## 3.2  Sensory Features

Sensory differences are prevalent in autism, with hyper- or hypo-sensitivity across visual, auditory, tactile, olfactory, and gustatory domains. The sensory preferences in our model are based on the Sensory Perception Quotient (SPQ) [38], a validated assessment tool designed to measure sensory processing patterns across different dimensions for autistic people. The SPQ evaluates:

- **Visual sensitivity**: Responses to brightness, contrast, movement, and visual complexity.
- **Auditory sensitivity**: Reactions to volume, pitch, and complex auditory environments.
- **Tactile sensitivity**: Responses to touch, texture, and physical contact.
- **Olfactory sensitivity**: Sensitivity to odors and scents.
- **Gustatory sensitivity**: Reactions to tastes, food textures, and temperature.

As for user preferences, we calculate a sensory impact score $S_{impact}(u, a)$ representing the potential for discomfort that an event $a$ has on a user $u$:

$$S_{impact}(u, a) = \beta_{scale} \cdot \frac{1}{n} \sum_{i=1}^{n} (sensitivity_i(u) \cdot intensity_i(a))$$

where

- $sensitivity_i(u)$ represents the user's sensitivity in dimension $i$, normalized to [0,1]. This data is elicited through the SPQ questionnaire (e.g., how sensitive the user is to a stimulation of the earing sense).
- $intensity_i(a)$ represents the event's sensory intensity in dimension $i$, normalized to [0,1]. For instance, how strongly the event involves the hearing sense, i.e., it is noisy. To quantify $intensity_i(a)$, we assume that, for each event, a measure of how strongly the event stimulates senses for the considered dimensions is available.
- $n$ is the number of sensory dimensions ($n = 5$, based on SPQ).
- $\beta_{scale}$ is a scaling factor to ensure appropriate weighting in the final model.

### 3.3   Personality Traits

Literature on autism agrees that autistic individuals tend to gravitate towards people similar to them [4,11,15]. Therefore, we assume that matching autistic individuals with group members having similar personalities could significantly impact event enjoyment.

To describe people's personality, we exploit the five-factor personality model (OCEAN: Openness, Conscientiousness, Extraversion, Agreeableness, and Neuroticism) [23]. OCEAN encompasses the following dimensions:

- **Openness to Experience**: Reflects curiosity, preference for novelty, and appreciation for art, imagination, and diverse experiences.
- **Conscientiousness**: Describes tendencies toward organization, dependability, self-discipline, and planned behavior.
- **Extraversion**: Characterizes energy derived from social interactions, assertiveness, and positive emotionality.
- **Agreeableness**: Encompasses traits like cooperation, empathy, and consideration for others.
- **Neuroticism**: Reflects a tendency toward emotional instability and negative emotions like anxiety, depression, and irritability.

Based on the OCEAN traits, we compute the compatibility between a user $u$ and a group of people $g$ as follows:

$$P_{compat}(u, g) = \gamma_{scale} \cdot \frac{1}{5} \sum_{j=1}^{5} |trait_j(u) - \overline{trait_j(g)}|$$

where $trait_j(u)$ is the user's score on trait $j$, $\overline{trait_j(g)}$ is the average score for that trait across all members of group $g$, and $\gamma_{scale}$ is a scaling factor to weight personality factors.

## 4   Feature Integration Model

To integrate information about the sensory features of events and people's personalities, we need careful balancing to prioritize the most critical aspects for autistic individuals. Given an event $a$, and a group $g$ of people who are known to participate in $a$, we evaluate $u$'s expected "loss" in joining $a$, i.e., how much $u$ would experience a discomfort in participating in the group event, according to a weighted loss function that combines the following features:

$$L_{total}(u, a, g) = C_{mismatch}(u, a) + S_{impact}(u, a) + P_{compat}(u, g)$$

If the loss function has a value of 0, we estimate that joining the event does not cause discomfort to the user. We render this compatibility notion through a similarity measure that determines how close the event matches the user. The final similarity score between a user and an event is calculated using a sigmoid transformation of the total loss:

$$Similarity(u, a, g) = 1 - \frac{1}{1 + e^{-k(L_{total}-c)}} \cdot s$$

where $k$ controls the steepness of the sigmoid curve, $c$ determines the midpoint of the transition between 0 and 1, and $s$ is a stretch factor to distribute scores across the full [0,1] range.

## 5   Preliminary Analysis with Synthetic Data

To validate our feature integration approach and optimize the parameters of our model, we conducted a preliminary analysis using a synthetic dataset. The primary objective was to determine the optimal values for the sigmoid transformation parameters ($k$, $c$, and $s$) as well as the relative weights of each component in the feature integration model. Specifically:

- We generated synthetic user profiles with representative distributions of personality traits, sensory sensitivities, and event preferences based on current literature about autistic individuals [31,37]. Specifically, according to [37], Sensory Perception Quotient scores are normally distributed across participants, regardless of age. Moreover, [31] reports that the distribution of personality traits within the autistic population differs from the neurotypical one: both populations follow a normal distribution, but with different means and standard deviations.
- We created synthetic event profiles with diverse sensory intensities across the five sensory dimensions. For this task, we prompted an LLM to return a balanced list of events across categories. In the prompt, we asked the LLM to specify for each event its category, sensory intensities, and a description of the event. Then, we manually reviewed the generated events for consistency between event type, description, and sensory features.
- We generated three sets of user groups (based on the synthetic user profiles) differing in the homogeneity (low, medium, high) of their members' personality traits.

Following feature-based recommender systems, we plan to estimate the user's rating of a group event through the similarity between the event and the user's profiles. To prepare the recommender system for a user study with real participants, we employed a Gaussian Process optimization approach on our synthetic dataset to search for optimal parameter values that produce the most uniform distribution of similarity scores. This uniformity is essential for creating meaningful distinctions between recommended events while avoiding excessive concentration of scores at either extreme of the scale.

The Gaussian Process optimization consists of an initial exploration phase using randomly selected parameter values, followed by an exploitation phase. The latter focuses on the most promising regions of the parameter space. Table 1 shows the results of our parameter optimization.

**Table 1.** Optimized model parameters from Gaussian Process search.

| Optimized Parameters | |
| --- | --- |
| **Sigmoid Parameters:** | |
| $k$ (steepness) | 4.0421 |
| $c$ (center) | 0.5215 |
| $s$ (stretch) | 1.3263 |
| **Component Weights:** | |
| Event Preference Weight ($\alpha_{penalty}$) | 0.5005 |
| Sensory Profile Weight ($\beta_{scale}$) | 0.9653 |
| OCEAN Traits Weight ($\gamma_{scale}$) | 0.8749 |

# 6 Future Work

Integrating sensory features alongside traditional preference and personality factors advances recommendation systems for autistic individuals. By explicitly modeling sensory sensitivities, our approach addresses a critical barrier to event participation that most conventional recommender systems overlook.

So far, we have integrated user preferences, sensory features, and personality traits in a simple sum to support an equal contribution in evaluating the match between users and events. Moreover, as a first approximation, we assumed that a good match (similarity) between users and events implies that the events can effectively be recommended to users. However, in our future work, we plan various extensions of our model.

Firstly, we could explore dynamic weight adjustment based on user feedback and contextual factors, further enhancing the personalization capabilities of the system.

Second, a weighted combination of these features might allow personalized adjustments based on individual profiles. For users with pronounced sensory sensitivities, the sensory component weight can be increased, while those with stronger social preferences might benefit from greater emphasis on personality matching.

Thirdly, we plan to (i) collect real data concerning event ratings and (ii) optimize and train the proposed model on this data. To do so, we intend to conduct a user study on the crowd-sourcing platform Prolific[2]. Moreover, we plan to analyze the impact of the proposed features on event recommendation. This could involve techniques like feature ablation studies or sensitivity analysis to determine which aspects most significantly impact recommendation quality for different user profiles within the autism spectrum. This might also enable us to determine if some OCEAN traits have more influence than others on recommendation performance, paving the road to a weighting of the individual traits.

---

[2] https://www.prolific.com/.

Finally, we plan to integrate the model into the SPACES project to test this approach with real users to understand how employing these features can enhance autistic people's social life.

**Acknowledgments.** The SPACES project (Adaptive support for organizing and participating in groups and activities for adults with medium to high-functioning autism spectrum disorder) has been funded by Italian Fondazione CRT in the program "Bando Richieste Ordinarie 2023".

**Disclosure of Interests.** The authors have no competing interests to declare that are relevant to the content of this article.

**Declaration on Generative AI.** During the preparation of this work, the authors used Perplexity (https://www.perplexity.ai/) and Grammarly (https://app. grammarly.com/) to: Paraphrase and reword, and Grammar and spelling check. After using these tools, the authors reviewed and edited the content as needed. The authors take full responsibility for the publication's content.

# References


1. Abolghasemi, R., Engelstad, P., Herrera-Viedma, E., Yazidi, A.: A personality-aware group recommendation system based on pairwise preferences. Inf. Sci. **595**, 1–17 (2022). https://doi.org/10.1016/j.ins.2022.02.033, https://www.sciencedirect.com/science/article/pii/S0020025522001682
2. American Psychiatric Association: Diagnostic and Statistical Manual of Mental Disorders (DSM-5®). American Psychiatric Publishing (2013)
3. Badami, M., Tafazzoli, F., Nasraoui, O.: A case study for intelligent event recommendation. Int. J. Data Sci. Anal. **5**(4), 249–268 (2018). https://doi.org/10.1007/s41060-018-0120-3
4. Bauminger-Zviely, N., Kimhi, Y.: Friendship in autism spectrum disorder. In: Leaf, J.B. (ed.) Handbook of Social Skills and Autism Spectrum Disorder. ACPS, pp. 63–79. Springer, Cham (2017). https://doi.org/10.1007/978-3-319-62995-7_5
5. Boratto, L., Carta, S., Satta, M., et al.: Groups identification and individual recommendations in group recommendation algorithms. In: PRSAT@ recsys, pp. 27–34 (2010)
6. Boyd, L.E., et al.: SayWAT: augmenting face-to-face conversations for adults with autism. In: Proceedings of the 2016 CHI Conference on Human Factors in Computing Systems, CHI 2016, pp. 4872–4883. ACM, New York, NY, USA (2016). https://doi.org/10.1145/2858036.2858215
7. Boyd, L.E., Ringland, K.E., Haimson, O.L., Fernandez, H., Bistarkey, M., Hayes, G.R.: Evaluating a collaborative iPad game's impact on social relationships for children with autism spectrum disorder **7**(1) (2015). https://doi.org/10.1145/2751564
8. Brownlow, C., Bertilsdotter Rosqvist, H., O'Dell, L.: Exploring the potential for social networking among people with autism: challenging dominant ideas of 'friendship'. Scandinavian J. Disabil. Res. **17** (2013). https://doi.org/10.1080/15017419.2013.859174
9. Cena, F., Likavec, S., Lombardi, I., Picardi, C.: Should I stay or should I go? improving event recommendation in the social web. Interact. Comput. **28**(1), 55–72 (2016). https://doi.org/10.1093/iwc/iwu029

10. Cena, F., Mauro, N., Rapp, A.: How do sensory features of places impact on spatial exploration of people with autism? A user study. Inf. Technol. Tourism **25**(1), 105–132 (2023). https://doi.org/10.1007/s40558-023-00244-1
11. Chan, D.V., Doran, J.D., Galobardi, O.D.: Beyond friendship: the spectrum of social participation of autistic adults. J. Autism Dev. Disord. **53**(1), 424–437 (2023). https://doi.org/10.1007/s10803-022-05441-1, https://www.ncbi.nlm.nih.gov/pmc/articles/PMC8788910/
12. Delic, A., Neidhardt, J., Nguyen, T.N., Ricci, F.: An observational user study for group recommender systems in the tourism domain. Inf. Technol. Tourism (1), 87–116 (2018). https://doi.org/10.1007/s40558-018-0106-y
13. Dietz, P.M., Rose, C.E., McArthur, D., Maenner, M.: National and state estimates of adults with autism spectrum disorder. J. Autism Dev. Disord. **50**(12), 4258–4266 (2020)
14. Ding, H., Yu, C., Li, G., Liu, Y.: Event participation recommendation in event-based social networks. In: Spiro, E., Ahn, Y.-Y. (eds.) SocInfo 2016, Part I. LNCS, vol. 10046, pp. 361–375. Springer, Cham (2016). https://doi.org/10.1007/978-3-319-47880-7_22
15. Dunn, D., de la Garza, J.D., Jones, D.R., Sasson, N.J.: Awkward but so what: differences in social trait preferences between autistic and non-autistic adults. Neurodiversity **1**, 27546330231203833 (2023). https://doi.org/10.1177/27546330231203833
16. Fletcher-Watson, S., Happé, F.: Autism: A New Introduction to Psychological Theory and Current Debate. Routledge (2019)
17. Garcia, I., Sebastia, L., Onaindia, E., Guzman, C.: A group recommender system for tourist activities. In: Di Noia, T., Buccafurri, F. (eds.) EC-Web 2009. LNCS, vol. 5692, pp. 26–37. Springer, Heidelberg (2009). https://doi.org/10.1007/978-3-642-03964-5_4
18. Gartrell, M., et al.: Enhancing group recommendation by incorporating social relationship interactions. In: Proceedings of the 2010 ACM International Conference on Supporting Group Work, GROUP 2010, pp. 97–106. ACM, New York, NY, USA (2010). https://doi.org/10.1145/1880071.1880087
19. Goris, J., Brass, M., Cambier, C., Delplanque, J., Wiersema, J.R., Braem, S.: The relation between preference for predictability and autistic traits. Autism Res. **13**(7), 1144–1154 (2020). https://doi.org/10.1002/aur.2244, https://onlinelibrary.wiley.com/doi/abs/10.1002/aur.2244
20. Hong, H., Yarosh, S., Kim, J.G., Abowd, G.D., Arriaga, R.I.: Investigating the use of circles in social networks to support independence of individuals with autism. In: Proceedings of the SIGCHI Conference on Human Factors in Computing Systems, CHI 2013, pp. 3207–3216. ACM, New York, NY, USA (2013). https://doi.org/10.1145/2470654.2466439
21. Horowitz, D., Contreras, D., Salamó, M.: EventAware: a mobile recommender system for events. Pattern Recogn. Lett. **105**, 121–134 (2018). https://doi.org/10.1016/j.patrec.2017.07.003, https://www.sciencedirect.com/science/article/pii/S0167865517302350, machine Learning and Applications in Artificial Intelligence
22. Hymas, R., Badcock, J., Milne, E.: Loneliness in autism and its association with anxiety and depression: a systematic review with meta-analyses. Review J. Autism Dev. Disord. **11**, 121–156 (2024). https://doi.org/10.1007/s40489-022-00330-w
23. John, O., Srivastava, S.: The Big-Five trait taxonomy: history, measurement, and theoretical perspectives. Handbook Pers. Theor. Res. **2**, 102–138 (1999)
24. Locke, J., Ishijima, E.H., Kasari, C., London, N.: Loneliness, friendship quality and the social networks of adolescents with high-functioning autism in an inclusive

school setting. J. Res. Special Educ. Needs **10**(2), 74–81 (2010). https://doi.org/10.1111/j.1471-3802.2010.01148.x

25. Macedo, A.Q., Marinho, L.B., Santos, R.L.: Context-aware event recommendation in event-based social networks. In: Proceedings of the 9th ACM Conference on Recommender Systems, RecSys 2015, pp. 123–130. ACM, New York, NY, USA (2015). https://doi.org/10.1145/2792838.2800187

26. Mauro, N., Ardissono, L., Cena, F.: Personalized recommendation of PoIs to people with autism. In: Proceedings of the 28th ACM Conference on User Modeling, Adaptation and Personalization, UMAP 2020, pp. 163–172. ACM, New York, NY, USA (2020). https://doi.org/10.1145/3340631.3394845

27. Mauro, N., Ardissono, L., Cena, F.: Supporting people with autism spectrum disorders in the exploration of PoIs: an inclusive recommender system. Commun. ACM **65**(2), 101–109 (2022). https://doi.org/10.1145/3505267

28. Purushotham, S., Kuo, C.C.J.: Personalized group recommender systems for location- and event-based social networks. ACM Trans. Spatial Algorithms Syst. **2**(4) (2016). https://doi.org/10.1145/2987381

29. Rathod, V.N., Goudar, R.H., Kulkarni, A., M, D.G., Hukkeri, G.S.: A survey on e-learning recommendation systems for autistic people. IEEE Access **12**, 11723–11732 (2024). https://doi.org/10.1109/ACCESS.2024.3355589

30. Ricci, F., Rokach, L., Shapira, B.: Recommender systems: techniques, applications, and challenges, pp. 1–35. Springer US, New York, NY (2022). https://doi.org/10.1007/978-1-0716-2197-4_1

31. Robinson, E., Hull, L., Petrides, K.: Big five model and trait emotional intelligence in camouflaging behaviours in autism. Person. Individ. Differ. **152**, 109565 (2020). https://doi.org/10.1016/j.paid.2019.109565, https://www.sciencedirect.com/science/article/pii/S0191886919304970

32. Russell, G., et al.: Time trends in autism diagnosis over 20 years: a UK population-based cohort study. J. Child Psychol. Psychiatry **63**(6), 674–682 (2022). https://doi.org/10.1111/jcpp.13505

33. Sevilla, J., Zapater, J.J.S., Herrera, G.: An ontology-based recommendation system for people with autism and technology apps: ontology application for helping persons with autism. In: Proceedings of the Euro American Conference on Telematics and Information Systems. EATIS 2018, ACM, New York, NY, USA (2018). https://doi.org/10.1145/3293614.3293630

34. Shinde, A.V., Patil, D.D.: A multi-classifier-based recommender system for early autism spectrum disorder detection using machine learning. Healthcare Anal. **4**, 100211 (2023). https://doi.org/10.1016/j.health.2023.100211, https://www.sciencedirect.com/science/article/pii/S2772442523000783

35. Simm, W., et al.: Anxiety and autism: towards personalized digital health. In: Proceedings of the 2016 CHI Conference on Human Factors in Computing Systems, CHI 2016, pp. 1270–1281. ACM, New York, NY, USA (2016). https://doi.org/10.1145/2858036.2858259

36. Tare, S.S., Bhute, M.M., Arage, P.: Recevent: NLP based event recommender system. In: 2023 2nd International Conference on Applied Artificial Intelligence and Computing (ICAAIC), pp. 608–614. IEEE (2023). https://doi.org/10.1109/ICAAIC56838.2023.10140251

37. Tavassoli, T., Hoekstra, R.A., Baron-Cohen, S.: The sensory perception quotient (SPQ): development and validation of a new sensory questionnaire for adults with and without autism. Molecular Autism **5**, 29 (2014). https://doi.org/10.1186/2040-2392-5-29

38. Tavassoli, T., Miller, L.J., Schoen, S.A., Nielsen, D.M., Baron-Cohen, S.: Sensory over-responsivity in adults with autism spectrum conditions. Autism **18**(4), 428–432 (2014). https://doi.org/10.1177/1362361313477246
39. Tu, W., Cheung, D.W., Mamoulis, N., Yang, M., Lu, Z.: Activity recommendation with partners. ACM Trans. Web **12**(1) (2017). https://doi.org/10.1145/3121407
40. Valencia, K., Rusu, C., Quiñones, D., Jamet, E.: The impact of technology on people with autism spectrum disorder: a systematic literature review. Sensors **19**(20) (2019). https://doi.org/10.3390/s19204485, https://www.mdpi.com/1424-8220/19/20/4485
41. Zeidan, J., et al.: Global prevalence of autism: a systematic review update. Autism Res. **15**(5), 778–790 (2022). https://doi.org/10.1002/aur.2696

# Blurred Lines: Understanding the Fit of Song Lyrics in Music Catalogs That Can Reach Children Through Recommendations

Jasper Heijne, Robin Ungruh$^{(\boxtimes)}$, and Maria Soledad Pera

Delft University of Technology, Delft, The Netherlands
`J.Heijne-1@student.tudelft.nl`, `{R.Ungruh,M.S.Pera}@tudelft.nl`

**Abstract.** Recommender systems on popular online platforms expose impressionable and easily influenced younger listeners to varied content, making it crucial to reflect on the songs children can encounter due to their interactions with recommender systems. To set a foundation, we analyze the lyrics of a catalog comprised of $\sim 30,000$ songs to gauge their suitability to children. Our multi-perspective exploration reveals a high prevalence of inappropriate lyrics in music commonly heard by children. This highlights the need for further explorations pertaining online platforms and their recommender systems that curate and ultimately present items from catalogs such as the ones we examined, highlighting the potential negative impact of such lyrics on their behavior and personality by promoting harmful language or biases. Informed by our findings, we outline research directions for the information retrieval community to consider when designing, evaluating, and deploying algorithms that serve diverse audiences.

**Keywords:** Children · Music Recommender Systems · Harmful Content

## 1 Introduction

Music consumption plays a crucial role in shaping children's[1] cultural identity [57]. From a young age, children link emotions to music, associating it with enjoyment, mood, and social relationships [17,41]. Musical activities impact their development [43], fostering improved social skills, intelligence, and creativity. However, they can also prompt adverse behaviors and attitudes, e.g., imitating

---

[1] Whenever we mention children, we refer to individuals aged up to 18, as per UNICEF's definition of a child [91]. In practice, we mean those who independently access online platforms. We recognize crucial developmental and cultural differences among children [44,92]. Nevertheless, to set a knowledge foundation, in this work, we focus on children as a broader user group.


A. Bellogin et al. (Eds.): IR4U2 2025/BIAS 2025, CCIS 2786, pp. 60–75, 2026.
https://doi.org/10.1007/978-3-032-12717-4_5

inappropriate actions, repeating unsuitable words, or experiencing negative emotions evoked by certain songs [9,61]. Today, children listen to music on digital devices via streaming platforms like Spotify or Apple Music [10,67], of which a key component is their recommender system (**RS**): Streaming services provide next-song recommendations and prominently feature recommendations for playlists, albums, and songs on their main pages [82]. Hence, children are frequently presented with music curated by RS. Despite this, research on music RS for children often focuses on algorithmic performance or song preference [31,81,84], but rarely on what is *actually* befitting for children or what is a *good* item for them.

The pervasive nature of RS calls for action to grasp how their algorithms "construct taste and its implications to our cultural experiences and cultural processes, more broadly" [39]. This is essential for children, as not all the songs they like or encounter are meant for them [87]. For example, "Blurred Lines" by Robin Thicke, T.I., and Pharrell or "Despacito" by Luis Fonsi and Daddy Yankee are popular songs (900 million and 9 billion views on YouTube, respectively) with catchy rhythms children may find appealing [84]. Yet, they convey messages unsuitable for young audiences. RS may recognize the songs' popularity and prioritize them in their suggestions, overlooking the diversity of audiences they reach. Considering these concerns, the need to further understand the interplay of RS and children is apparent. Doing so is of societal importance as children are in a forming stage with varying comprehension levels and skills and developing attitudes, behavior, and opinions [11,12]. In this vulnerable phase [80], children require content that supports their development and does not harm them.

To set a foundation on the current understanding of how well RS cater to this demographic, we start by investigating the items RS might expose children to. Specifically, we focus on song **catalogs** that form the basis for recommendations [77] and the **lyrics** of these songs, which can convey messages not always befitting children. The former as a proxy for what is recommended, since regardless of the algorithms used, if the catalog includes items unsuitable for some audiences, the algorithm may reflect those in its recommendations. The latter, as prior work on limited samples revealed the presence in popular songs of explicit lyrics [35] (including profanity, vulgarity, and epithets [6]), misogyny [3,4,26], violence [46], and references to drugs and alcohol [47]. In this work, we address the RQ: ***Do song lyrics convey content befitting children?*** We empirically explore a large dataset from the Genius website[2], covering Pop, Rock, Rap, R&B, and Country songs, which we treat as a catalog that can be utilized for an RS. Given that children often engage with platforms not specifically designed for them [22,49,59]—where safeguarding mechanisms to limit inappropriate content may be absent or inconsistently applied—this catalog serves as a proxy for analyzing the types of items they may encounter through such systems. We conduct a content analysis on the lyrics using different **lenses** to assess whether items can be deemed befitting, accounting for multiple indicators that may ultimately

---

[2] https://genius.com/.

influence song suitability: curse words, profanity, offensive speech, hate speech, text complexity, and difficult-to-articulate words.

The main contribution of this work is a comprehensive overview of the lyrical content that RS may present to children, sparking reflections about how information access systems could handle content that may not be ideal for young audiences [87]. We publish our code in a public repository[3].

Outcomes from this work have implications that extend beyond RS and music to various platforms, systems, and content types. As children's access to information and media evolves, and mindful of safety-promoting practices, the question of whether presented content 'fits' becomes a must for the information retrieval (**IR**) community.

## 2    Background

Social learning theory suggests that children learn new behaviors by observing and imitating others [12] but also by adopting behaviors observed in media consumed [11]. This theory aligns with research on the influence of music on children, indicating that certain genres are associated with negative behavior of children [9,61]. Recent studies on smaller samples of music indicate that many popular songs from recent years contain explicit lyrics [35]. Aspects such as misogyny [3] and violence [46] are frequent occurrences in popular music. Themes such as drugs, alcohol, and sex [47] are most prevalent in Rap and R&B music.

The prominence of explicit lyrics and the potential negative effects of inappropriate lyrics raise concerns about what children are exposed to online. However, RS themselves tend not to filter inappropriate content well on prominent platforms. On the contrary, children are, in fact, likely to encounter inappropriate content on online platforms due to their recommender systems [69,70,94]. Algorithms that drive online platforms can even amplify potentially harmful content online in their attempts to maximize engagement with the platform [51,76,93]. Recent work highlights that recommendation algorithms not only reflect harmful characteristics present in the training corpora, such as stereotypes, but may even amplify their presence in recommendations delivered to children [88].

Despite these risks and initial explorations on how to counteract the spread of harmful recommendations [23], RS research on how children—a particularly vulnerable user group—can be affected by inappropriate recommendations is sparse. Instead, most RS research that has children as the protagonists focuses on uncovering children's preferences [65,81,84] or improving the performance of RS [81,89]. Whether items are actually fitting to the children that use the systems is seldom explored [40,88], showcasing a critical gap. As a step toward considerations and safeguarding for children, thought has to be given to what it means for a recommendation to be truly fitting for a child.

---

[3] https://github.com/JasperHeijne/appropriate_lyrics.git.

# 3   Experimental Setup

We treat the Genius lyrics database [55,56]–GeniusDB–as a 'catalog' RS could use for recommendation purposes. GeniusDB is ideal for this study as it is sourced from the regularly updated Genius website and features a wide range of popular songs that children likely encounter when interacting with RS. It has $37,993$ songs collected between September 2019 and January 2020, each annotated with its *lyrics* and at least one of five main *genres*: Pop, Rock, Country, Rap, and R&B. Table 1 shows the distribution and overlap of songs across genres (songs can be assigned multiple tags). The prevalence of Rap is anticipated, as Genius originated as Rap-Genius [52].

**Table 1.** Song distribution and genre overlap in GeniusDB.

| Genre | Number of Songs | Overlap | | | | |
|---|---|---|---|---|---|---|
| | | *Rap* | *Pop* | *R&B* | *Rock* | *Country* |
| Rap | $30,050$ | – | $1,201$ | $2,442$ | $291$ | $28$ |
| Pop | $5,223$ | $1,201$ | – | $1,263$ | $763$ | $100$ |
| R&B | $4,537$ | $2,442$ | $1,263$ | – | $90$ | $2$ |
| Rock | $3,320$ | $291$ | $763$ | $90$ | – | $42$ |
| Country | $164$ | $28$ | $100$ | $2$ | $42$ | – |

To provide a comprehensive analysis of the words and expressions in each song lyric L in GeniusDB, we consider several lenses, each capturing a different facet that can be used to determine whether an item could be fitting for a child. We focus on identifying terms and phrases that could be considered harmful, particularly those that, if mimicked [11], may be insulting, offensive, or encourage negative attitudes toward others. We also account for *readability-related* considerations, which can be used to assess children's understanding and the intended audiences of song lyrics.

**Curse words** are expletives, insults, blasphemy, obscenities, and racial slurs, which are considered inappropriate in social contexts. To identify curse words, we refer to Google's list of banned curse words [37] that is updated monthly. As curse words indicators we use $HIT_{Curse}$, based on the HIT metric, which yields a 1 if L contains a curse word and 0 otherwise, and $P_{Curse}$, which captures the proportion of curse words in L. **Profanity** refers to hate speech, offensive language, and broader inappropriate language (e.g., toxic, obscene, threatening, and insulting) [27]. We use an SVM model [97] trained on 200k human-labeled samples of clean and profane strings to compute $L_{Profanity}$, a likelihood for L on a $[0,1]$ range—the closer to 1, the more likely the song to be profane. This model, not based on a term list, enables a dynamic estimation leveraging context.

**Offensive speech** refers to rude or insulting expressions not targeting specific vulnerable subgroups. This differs from **hate speech** that "targets the 'other' in societies" [78], i.e., minority groups like racial, ethnic, religious, or cultural minorities, women, and the LGBTQI+ community. To detect these types of speech, we use two models [1,2] that yield $L_{Offensive}$ and $L_{HS}$—likelihood scores on a $[0,1]$ range, where 1 indicates a high likelihood of offensive or hate speech. These models, based on DeBERTa [45], were trained on the `tweet_eval` dataset [13] that includes tweets annotated with offensive language [95] and hate speech [14].

**Readability** refers to "a reader's understanding, reading speed, and level of interest in the material" [25]. To infer the intended audience for L, we used widely used formulas. **Flesch-Kincaid** [34] assigns grade levels (ranging from grade 0 for Kindergarten to 13+ for graduate school) to texts based on shallow features like sentence length and syllables [5]. The **Dale-Chall** formula [21] considers familiarity with common words to assess readability. We also identify words with advanced orthographic and phonemic/phonetic patterns that we assume are **challenging** for a child to comprehend and, particularly, sing along to. For this, we use a model that accounts for phonemic decoding and educational development stages [73,74]. With $P_{Challenging}$, we reflect the proportion of challenging words in L, excluding duplicate words and stopwords (as per NLTK's English stopwords list[4]).

## 4   Results

We present the findings of our multi-lens analysis, with nuanced scrutiny of computed indicators per genre. We use a Kruskall-Wallis test ($p < .0001$) to compare indicators across genres and conduct post-Hoc Dunn's test with Bonferroni correction ($p < .0001$) to show pairwise differences between genre pairs. Results from each lense per genre can be seen in Figs. 1 and 2.

**Curse** words are frequent: $HIT_{Curse}$ ranges from 23% for Country to 88% for Rap. $P_{Curse}$ differs across genres (Fig. 1a); pairwise genre differences are significant, except for (Pop, Country) and (Rock, Country). Rap has the highest proportion of curse words—over twice as many as Pop, Rock, and Country. It is also the most likely genre to include **profanity** in its lyrics (Fig. 1b). Pairwise differences for $L_{Profanity}$ are significant for all genre pairs, except (Pop, Country) and (Rock, Country). **Offensive speech** trends are similar to those reported for curse words and profanity. Pairwise differences for $L_{Offensive}$ in Fig. 1c are significant, except for (Pop, Country) and (Rock, Country). As Fig. 1d highlights, results for **hate speech** differ from those previously reported. As per $L_{HS}$, Rock is the genre most likely to convey hate speech; pairwise differences between Rock and the other genres are significant. The only other significant differences are higher $L_{HS}$ for Rap than Pop and R&B.

As per **Flesch-Kincaid** in Fig. 2a, Rap is the most difficult genre to comprehend. Other genres yield comparable readability levels; significantly higher

---

[4] https://www.nltk.org/nltk_data/.

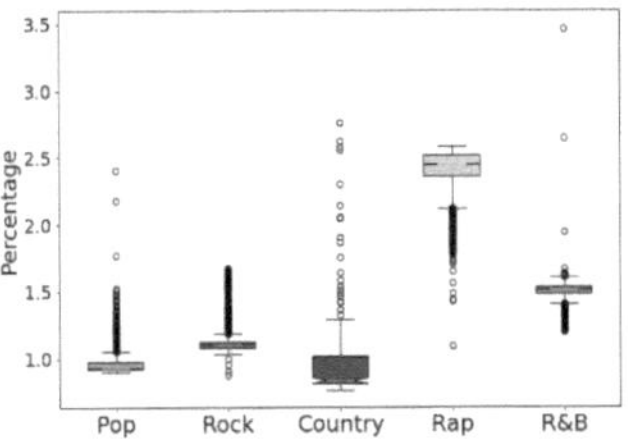
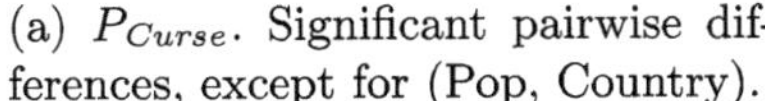

(a) $P_{Curse}$. Significant pairwise differences, except for (Pop, Country).

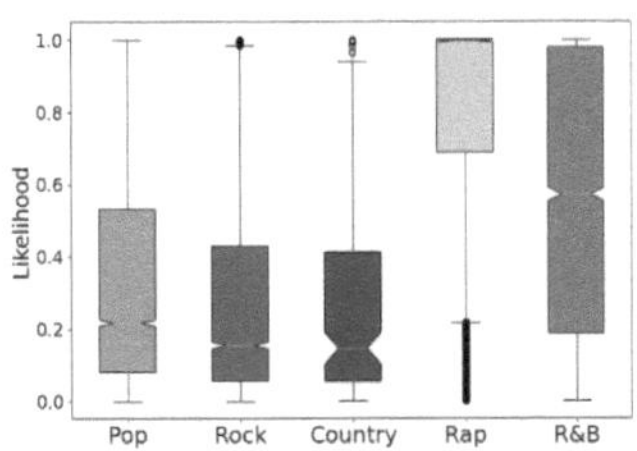

(b) $L_{Profanity}$. Pairwise differences are significant, except (Pop, Country) and (Rock, Country).

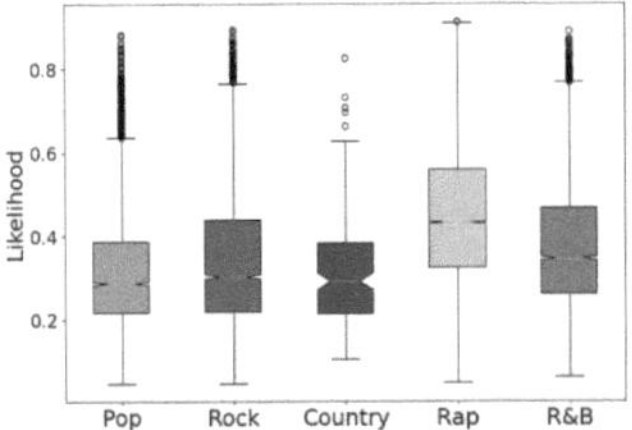

(c) $L_{Offensive}$. Pairwise differences are significant, except (Pop, Country) and (Rock, Country).

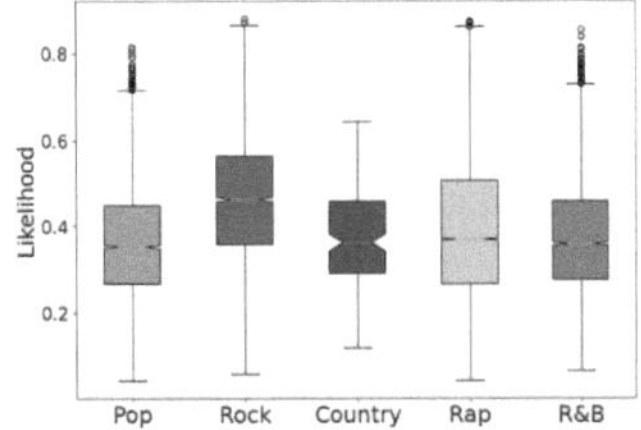

(d) $L_{HS}$. Significant pairwise differences between Rock and other genres, (Rap, Pop), and (Rap, R&B).

**Fig. 1.** Distributions of harms-related indicators for songs in GeniusDB, grouped by genre.

scores for R&B than Pop as an exception. **Dale-Chall** levels in Fig. 2b are significantly different across all genre pairs, except (Rock, Country). Regardless of genre, lyrics are relatively simple. For instance, the highest *Dale-Chall* level is $\sim 8$ which maps to 13–14 year olds. *Flesch-Kincaid* levels are even lower, ranging from $\sim 0$ to 2, i.e., 5–8 year olds would understand most lyrics according to this metric. $P_{Challenging}$ indicates that between 10 to 20% of the unique, non-stopwords in lyrics are **challenging** to utter and pronounce due to their advanced linguistic patterns [73,74]. In contrast to the readability scores, Rap is the genre with the least challenging words whereas Country songs include the most, followed by Rock.

Overall, our findings point out that Rap emerges as the most 'inappropriate' genre given the prevalence of curse words, profanity, and offensive speech. The frequent use of curse words can lead children to mimic these terms and learn improper language [11]. Lyrics with a higher percentage of bad terminology, as seen for Rap music, could negatively influence their speech behavior. Although less prominent, we see similar trends for R&B, expected due to its large overlap with Rap (Table 1). Despite lower $P_{Curse}$, $L_{Profanity}$, and $L_{Offensive}$, Rock con-

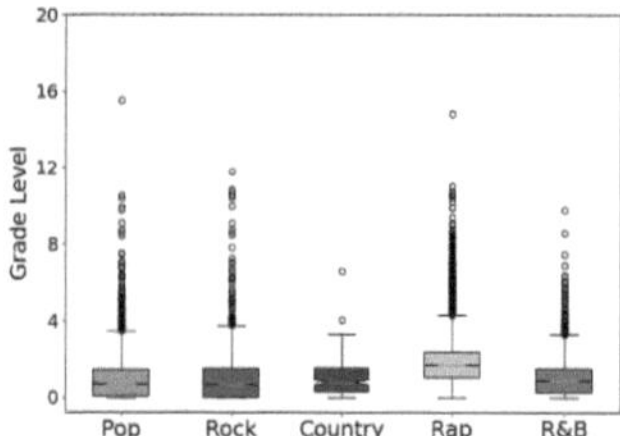

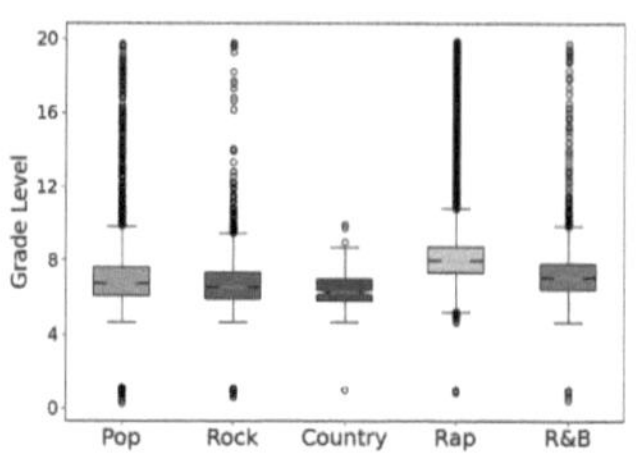

(a) *Flesch-Kincaid.* Significant pairwise differences between Rap and all other genres and (R&B, Pop).

(b) *Dale-Chall.* Pairwise differences are significant, except (Country, Rock).

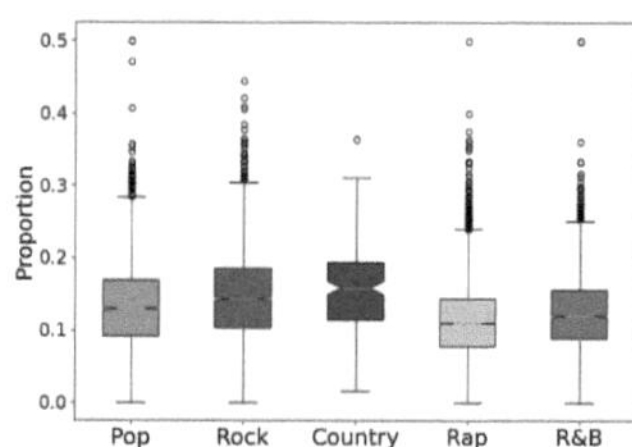

(c) $P_{Challenging}$. Pairwise differences are significant, except (Rock, Country).

**Fig. 2.** Distributions of readability-related indicators for songs in GeniusDB, grouped by genre.

veys hate speech, suggesting that this genre may contain a subtler form of undesirable content. Pop cannot be considered entirely child-friendly either; with over a third of Pop songs containing curse words, this genre requires careful screening to assess its suitability. Country, by contrast, shows few significant differences, which we attribute to a smaller sample size.

Consistently low readability levels evince that even young children could understand most lyrics in GeniusDB. Still, traditional readability formulas can be misleading [60], e.g., lyrics with short sentences lead to low levels due to the focus on shallow features like sentence length, but this does not imply these sentences are simple. Readability formulas fail to capture metaphors, euphemisms, or whether children can sing along to the songs they hear. $P_{Challenging}$ reveals a relatively low, but crucial number of challenging words in the lyrics, indicating that children can sing along to and utter many of the words in the lyrics. Lyrics from certain genres, particularly Rap, score the highest for most impropriety and reading difficulty indicators. Although more complex lyrics appear to lessen the risk of these genres influencing children, this is misleading. Despite the higher difficulty, the readability levels are quite low. This is concerning given the prevalence of inappropriate language and themes in these lyrics. The combination of accessible language and improper content may pose a risk. For instance, Rap songs, often seen as the hardest to understand, frequently use simple words children can easily repeat, unaware of the harmful content.

## 5    Discussion

Here we discuss emerging results (Sect. 4) and associated implications.

*The Fit Concept.* In addressing our RQ, we note that while songs are often deemed unsuitable by certain lenses, determining *truly* befitting songs is challenging. The '*fit*' of songs for children hinges on their content. Those promoting violence, stereotypes, or hate speech may directly impact behavior [48,75,93]. Even without explicit offensive language, some songs may subtly reinforce biases against ethnicities, religions, or social groups [12,15]. Children, however, are not a homogeneous group—they vary in developmental stages [32]. Their susceptibility to content depends on age, gender, and previous experiences [7]. Hence, a child's individual characteristics also determine the 'fit' of an item. Further, external factors play a role. For instance, "Blurred Lines" might promote problematic views on consent [11]. It can also be a vehicle for parent-child discussions on the topic [16], as discussions with parents or caretakers can mitigate potential harm [66]. Further, what may appear as hate speech, at first sight, could in reality be reclaimed language—derogatory terms, which instead of being harmful, may be used to refer positively to in-groups for de-stigmatization of negative group labels [28,38]. Appropriateness is not a stable construct: for instance, it may vary across different cultural contexts; something that is acceptable in one culture may not be in another. An item that is unsuitable for a child of a certain age may become suitable for them when they get older and gain new experiences. For example, the sexual connotation in songs like "Despacito" may be considered inappropriate for younger children or in certain cultures, but may become less problematic as children grow older and become more familiar with such themes.

Ultimately, defining 'fit' for children is complex; it requires simultaneously considering the inherent song traits, the characteristics of the listener, and the listening context. Lyrics are a relevant starting point for deepening the understanding of music characteristics [71]; however, these three pillars—*item, user*, and *context*—are also applicable to domains beyond music [90]. Thorough assessment methods of *what* is appropriate for *whom* require the involvement of experts who understand child development, cultural norms, and media effects.

*Practical Considerations for RS.* Our analysis reveals that many songs in GeniusDB contain words and phrases that could be perceived as improper. An RS leveraging this catalog may naturally suggest such songs. This issue is not limited to music; similar patterns have been noted in recommendation models across various domains [70,93]. Unfortunately, 'fit' is rarely part of *evaluation* frameworks, which typically focus on accuracy metrics [42]. Although modern evaluations increasingly account for diversity, serendipity, and fairness [30,42], assessing whether an item genuinely suits a user group is often overlooked [33]. Multistakeholder evaluation research [19,40] echoes the need to look beyond accuracy to consider other needs and requirements for assessment purposes. The lenses we considered offer a foundation for evaluation criteria beyond mere accuracy—an especially critical step for safeguarding vulnerable children as they navigate online content. With online platforms playing an increasingly influential role in shaping how young users view the world and assess right from wrong, unsuitable or inappropriate content can directly impact their development [68]. Our work emphasizes the need for safeguarding methods, parental controls, and content filtering mechanisms to consider multiple lenses and nuanced consideration of appropriateness.

To contribute to healthy media consumption, RS could remove items deemed 'unsafe,' similar to platforms using "parental advisory" labels to identify and remove explicit content [50,85]; or leverage editorial curation to offer "child-friendly" songs [36,86]. These types of *filtering*, however, are known to fall short [8], overlooking the subtleties of what makes a song unsuitable for a child in a given context. Binary classifications for fit are overly simplistic in practice. Simply 'hiding' potentially inappropriate content may not protect children [58]. Fostering media literacy [18] and a human-driven approach to design offers a better alternative. RS can optimize item selections to fulfill various roles, from providing emotional support and relaxation to entertaining [17]. Additionally, these tailored RS can facilitate positive interactions with potentially challenging content [66]. *Designing* recommendation architectures that explicitly incorporate as part of the recommendation-generation process indicators like the ones we considered to model items, alongside the child's characteristics, demographics, and contextual factors, could result in systems that promote not only enjoyable but also appropriate and beneficial content for children's specific situations.

In *real-world scenarios*, RS reach diverse audiences, including minority groups who are inevitably exposed to suggestions on these platforms. Research shows that algorithms can negatively impact minority groups, resulting in unfair outcomes for them, enabled through biases and discrimination [63]. System design should address factors relevant to minorities like personality, emotional state, or situation [83] and account for how RS decisions affect minorities. A one-size-fits-all approach will not solve this problem. Instead, designing RS with vulnerable users in mind will prioritize user well-being [29] and foster a benevolent and inclusive approach.

*Considerations for IR.* Our findings extend beyond RS to broader IR tasks, as every information access system inherently involves *content* presentation. Search engines, for example, have addressed issues like the usability and understandability of results for children, and mitigating ranking biases related to protected attributes such as gender [64,96]. Still, the lenses we introduce offer additional dimensions to scrutinize potential harms that may affect the experience of 'non-conventional' user groups [72]. Media–from informational to entertaining–is consumed in increasingly dynamic and personalized ways across search systems, RS, or conversational interfaces [24,53]. Moreover, automatically generated content is becoming more prevalent [20,98] and generative models are integrated within retrieval systems [79]. These increasingly complex dynamics exacerbate uncertainties regarding *what* content is presented to users. Information access and retrieval systems accessed by a wide range of users must be aware of the potential harms their methods may promote. Content analysis plays a key role in critically probing item corpora and informing the design of mechanisms that enable safer interactions. In our work, we leverage natural language processing methods on text as a starting point; more holistic probing must account for a wider range of media, such as images and audio, as well as gauging algorithms that curate and present content to ensure they do not expose users to what may not be suitable for them.

*Limitations and Future Work.* In GeniusDB, there is a notable imbalance in genre representation, with Rap being the most frequent genre. While we assume that observed trends for prominent genres may reflect broader patterns within those genres, this may not be true for underrepresented ones. For instance, the genre 'Country' is represented by only 164 songs. To improve the robustness and ensure the generalizability of our findings, future work should consider incorporating additional data sources with more balanced genre distributions.

Further, some lyrics mix foreign languages with English; others are mostly in foreign languages with scattered English words. We focused on English and selected text analysis models accordingly. We plan to conduct multilingual scrutiny in the future. While models from natural language processing are an effective method to detect inappropriate content, they may be disadvantaged for low-resource languages [54], emphasizing the need for complementary approaches that do not rely solely on language-specific resources. These can include metadata-based signals or analysis of visual content that often accompanies musical items.

As many factors shape lyric analysis, future work should broaden the scope to other types of inappropriate content beyond the ones we considered. This, however, must be approached with care. The perceived appropriateness of themes like violence or misogyny, is not easily mapped to specific age groups and may vary across cultural, social, and individual boundaries [62], highlighting the need for nuanced and reflexive frameworks when assessing suitability for children. Lenses should also address content not easily inferred from naive word analysis, such as metaphors or stereotypes, which may subtly convey harmful messages despite not containing explicitly inappropriate language.

Our study indicates that harmful lyrics *can* be promoted by RS when based on popular item corpora, as a large majority of lyrics include content that can be unfitting to some users. However, the degree to which RS expose children to potentially unfitting items remains unexplored. Future work should study children's exposure to such items due to RS [cf. 88] to analyze the extent to which RS can negatively impact children.

## 6  Concluding Remarks

We have provided an analysis of the content prevalent in popular music genres. Our results indicate that inappropriate content exists across all five music genres and that children can understand and articulate most lyrics. This, in turn, suggests that not all contemporary music that RS are likely to recommend may not be suitable for children, highlighting the need for caution in RS and other information access systems targeting young users, particularly considering the nuanced aspects influencing item 'fit'. With this work, we aim to raise awareness about the challenges that information access systems face when curating suggestions, particularly in contexts involving children—whether as a primary audience or indirectly impacted users [19]. We encourage reflections on the design, evaluation, and deployment of these systems. Fostering transparency and attentiveness to the content provided can contribute to a more responsible and inclusive digital music environment and beyond, ultimately supporting safer online platforms for all users.

## References


1. KoalaAI/HateSpeechDetector · Hugging Face — huggingface.co. https://huggingface.co/KoalaAI/HateSpeechDetector (2023), Accessed 12 09 2024
2. KoalaAI/OffensiveSpeechDetector · Hugging Face — huggingface.co. https://huggingface.co/KoalaAI/OffensiveSpeechDetector (3), Accessed 12 09 2024
3. Adams, T., Fuller, D.: The words have changed but the ideology remains the same: misogynistic lyrics in rap music. JBS **36**(6), 938–957 (2006)
4. Adams, T.M., Fuller, D.B.: The words have changed but the ideology remains the same: misogynistic lyrics in rap music. J. Black Stud. **36**(6), 938–957 (2006)
5. Allen, G., Milton, A., Wright, K.L., Fails, J.A., Kennington, C., Pera, M.S.: Supercalifragilisticexpialidocious: why using the "right" readability formula in children's web search matters. In: European Conference on Information Retrieval, pp. 3–18. Springer (2022)
6. Amdan, N.F.B., Shaari, A.H.: An analysis of profanity in English lyrics. J. Wacana Sarjana **1**(1) (2017)
7. Anderson, C., et al.: The influence of media violence on youth. PSPI **4**(3), 81–110 (2003)
8. Anuyah, O., Milton, A., Green, M., Pera, M.S.: An empirical analysis of search engines' response to web search queries associated with the classroom setting. Aslib **72**(1), 88–111 (2020)
9. Arnett, J.J.: Heavy metal music and reckless behavior among adolescents. J. Youth Adolesc. **20**(6), 573–592 (1991)
10. Auxier, B., Anderson, M., Perrin, A., Turner, E.: Children's engagement with digital devices, screen time. https://www.pewresearch.org/internet/2020/07/28/childrens-engagement-with-digital-devices-screen-time/ (2021), Accessed 23 Jul 24
11. Bandura, A.: Social cognitive theory of mass communication. In: Media effects, pp. 110–140. Routledge (2009)
12. Bandura, A., Walters, R.H.: Social learning theory, vol. 1. Englewood cliffs Prentice Hall (1977)

13. Barbieri, F., Camacho-Collados, J., Espinosa-Anke, L., Neves, L.: TweetEval: unified benchmark and comparative evaluation for tweet classification. In: Findings of EMNLP (2020)
14. Basile, V., et al.: SemEval-2019 task 5: multilingual detection of hate speech against immigrants and women in Twitter. In: SemEval, pp. 54–63. ACL (2019)
15. Block, K., Gonzalez, A.M., Choi, C.J., Wong, Z.C., Schmader, T., Baron, A.S.: Exposure to stereotype-relevant stories shapes children's implicit gender stereotypes. PLoS ONE **17**(8), e0271396 (2022)
16. Blossom, P.: 15 moms share the dirty, inappropriate song their kid is obsessed with. https://www.romper.com/p/15-moms-share-the-dirty-inappropriate-song-their-kid-is-obsessed-with-5467 (2016), Accessed 25 Jul 24
17. Boal-Palheiros, G.M., Hargreaves, D.J.: Listening to music at home and at school. Br. J. Music Educ. **18**(2), 103–118 (2001)
18. Buckingham, D.: Digital media literacies: rethinking media education in the age of the internet. Res. Comp. Int. Educ. **2**(1), 43–55 (2007)
19. Burke, R., et al.: De-centering the (traditional) user: multistakeholder evaluation of recommender systems. arXiv preprint arXiv:2501.05170 (2025)
20. Cao, Y., et al.: A comprehensive survey of ai-generated content (aigc): a history of generative ai from gan to chatgpt. arXiv preprint arXiv:2303.04226 (2023)
21. Chall, J.S., Dale, E.: Readability Revisited: The New Dale-Chall Readability Formula. Brookline Books (1995)
22. Charmaraman, L., Lynch, A.D., Richer, A.M., Grossman, J.M.: Associations of early social media initiation on digital behaviors and the moderating role of limiting use. Comput. Hum. Behav. **127**, 107053 (2022)
23. Chee, J., Kalyanaraman, S., Ernala, S.K., Weinsberg, U., Dean, S., Ioannidis, S.: Harm mitigation in recommender systems under user preference dynamics. In: Proceedings of the 30th ACM SIGKDD Conference on Knowledge Discovery and Data Mining, pp. 255–265 (2024)
24. Chen, J., et al.: When large language models meet personalization: perspectives of challenges and opportunities. World Wide Web **27**(4), 42 (2024)
25. Collins-Thompson, K.: Computational assessment of text readability: a survey of current and future research. ITL **165**(2), 97–135 (2014)
26. Couto, L., Hust, S.J., Rodgers, K.B., Kang, S., Li, J.: A content analysis of music lyrics exploring the co-occurrence of violence, sexual content, and degrading terms toward women. Sex. Cult. **26**(6), 1965–1980 (2022)
27. Davidson, T., Warmsley, D., Macy, M., Weber, I.: Automated hate speech detection and the problem of offensive language. In: AAAI ICWSM, pp. 512–515 (2017)
28. De Smet, B., Dhaenens, F.: Heteromasculinity and queer reappropriation in music streaming practices: exploring homonegative curation by ordinary spotify users. Fem. Media Stud. **24**(4), 695–712 (2024)
29. Ekstrand, M., Beattie, L., Pera, M.S., Cramer, H.: Not just algorithms: strategically addressing consumer impacts in information retrieval. In: ECIR, pp. 314–335. Springer (2024)
30. Ekstrand, M., Das, A., Burke, R., Diaz, F.: Fairness in recommender systems. In: Recommender Systems Handbook, pp. 679–707. Springer (2012)
31. Ekstrand, M., et al.: All the cool kids, how do they fit in?: Popularity and demographic biases in recommender evaluation and effectiveness. In: ACM FAccT Conference, pp. 172–186. PMLR (2018)
32. Feldman, D.: Piaget's stages: the unfinished symphony of cognitive development. New Ideas Psychol. **22**(3), 175–231 (2004)

33. Ferraro, A., Ferreira, G., Diaz, F., Born, G.: Measuring commonality in recommendation of cultural content: recommender systems to enhance cultural citizenship. In: ACM RecSys, pp. 567–572 (2022)

34. Flesch, R.: A new readability yardstick. J. Appl. Psychol. **32**(3), 221 (1948)

35. Frisby, C.M., Behm-Morawitz, E.: Undressing the words: prevalence of profanity, misogyny, violence, and gender role references in popular music from 2006-2016. Media Watch **10**(1) (01 2019)

36. Gabb Wireless Inc.: Gabb Music — gabb.com. https://gabb.com/gabb-music (2024), Accessed 12 Sep 2024

37. Gabriel, R.J.: Full list of bad words and top swear words banned by Google. https://github.com/coffee-and-fun/google-profanity-words (2024), Accessed 23 May 24

38. Galinsky, A.D., Wang, C.S., Whitson, J.A., Anicich, E.M., Hugenberg, K., Bodenhausen, G.V.: The reappropriation of stigmatizing labels: the reciprocal relationship between power and self-labeling. Psychol. Sci. **24**(10), 2020–2029 (2013)

39. Gaw, F.: Algorithmic logics and the construction of cultural taste of the netflix recommender system. Media Cult. Soc. **44**(4), 706–725 (2022)

40. Gómez, E., Charisi, V., Chaudron, S.: Evaluating recommender systems with and for children: towards a multi-perspective framework. In: Perspectives@ RecSys (2021)

41. Gregory, A.H., Worrall, L., Sarge, A.: The development of emotional responses to music in young children. Motiv. Emot. **20**, 341–348 (1996)

42. Gunawardana, A., Shani, G., Yogev, S.: Evaluating recommender systems. In: Recommender Systems Handbook, pp. 547–601. Springer (2012)

43. Hallam, S.: The power of music: its impact on the intellectual, social and personal development of children and young people. IJME **28**(3), 269–289 (2010)

44. Hargreaves, D.J., North, A.C., Tarrant, M.: How and why do musical preferences change in childhood and adolescence. The child as musician: A handbook of musical development, pp. 303–322 (2015)

45. He, P., Liu, X., Gao, J., Chen, W.: Deberta: decoding-enhanced bert with disentangled attention. arXiv:2006.03654 (2020)

46. Herd, D.: Changing images of violence in rap music lyrics: 1979–1997. J. Public Health Policy **30**(4), 395–406 (2009)

47. Holody, K., Anderson, C., Craig, C., Flynn, M.: "Drunk in love": the portrayal of risk behavior in music lyrics. J. Health Commun. **21**(10), 1098–1106 (2016)

48. Huesmann, L.R., Moise-Titus, J., Podolski, C.L., Eron, L.: Longitudinal relations between children's exposure to tv violence and their aggressive and violent behavior in young adulthood: 1977–1992. Dev. Psychol. **39**(2), 201–221 (2003)

49. Huk, T., et al.: Use of facebook by children aged 10–12. presence in social media despite the prohibition. New Educ. Rev. **46**(1), 17–28 (2016)

50. Jackson, A.: Parental advisory: the story of a warning label (09 2020), https://daily.jstor.org/parental-advisory-the-story-of-a-warning-label/

51. Kasirzadeh, A., Evans, C.: User tampering in reinforcement learning recommender systems. In: Proceedings of the 2023 AAAI/ACM Conference on AI, Ethics, and Society, pp. 58–69 (2023)

52. Kehrer, L.: Genius (formerly rap genius). genius media group, inc. genius. com. J. Soc. Am. Music **10**(4), 518–520 (2016)

53. Klopfenstein, L.C., Delpriori, S., Malatini, S., Bogliolo, A.: The rise of bots: a survey of conversational interfaces, patterns, and paradigms. In: Proceedings of the 2017 Conference on Designing Interactive Systems, pp. 555–565 (2017)

54. Li, Z., Shi, Y., Liu, Z., Yang, F., Payani, A., Liu, N., Du, M.: Language ranker: a metric for quantifying llm performance across high and low-resource languages. In: Proceedings of the AAAI Conference on Artificial Intelligence, vol. 39, pp. 28186–28194 (2025)

55. Lim, D., Benson, A.: Expertise and dynamics within crowdsourced musical knowledge curation: a case study of the genius platform. In: AAAI ICWSM, vol. 15, pp. 373–384 (2021)

56. Lim, D., Benson, A.R.: Genius - expertise dataset — cs.cornell.edu. https://www.cs.cornell.edu/~arb/data/genius-expertise/ (2021), Accessed 12 Sep 2024

57. Lincoln, S.: Feeling the noise: teenagers, bedrooms and music. Leis. Stud. **24**(4), 399–414 (2005)

58. Livingstone, S., Helsper, E.J.: Parental mediation of children's internet use. J. Broadcast. Electr. Media **52**(4), 581–599 (2008)

59. Livingstone, S., Ólafsson, K., Staksrud, E.: Social networking, age and privacy (2011)

60. Madrazo Azpiazu, I., Pera, M.S.: Multiattentive recurrent neural network architecture for multilingual readability assessment. TACL **7**, 421–436 (2019)

61. Martin, G., Clarke, M., Pearce, C.: Adolescent suicide: music preference as an indicator of vulnerability. J. Am. Acad. Child Adolesc. Psychiatry **32**(3), 530–535 (1993)

62. McClelland, S.I., Hunter, L.: Bodies that are always out of line: a closer look at "age appropriate sexuality". In: The Moral Panics of Sexuality, pp. 59–76. Springer (2013)

63. Mehrabi, N., Morstatter, F., Saxena, N., Lerman, K., Galstyan, A.: A survey on bias and fairness in machine learning. ACM CSUR **54**(6), 1–35 (2021)

64. Milton, A., Anuya, O., Spear, L., Wright, K.L., Pera, M.S.: A ranking strategy to promote resources supporting the classroom environment. In: 2020 IEEE/WIC/ACM International Joint Conference on Web Intelligence and Intelligent Agent Technology (WI-IAT), pp. 121–128. IEEE (2020)

65. Milton, A., Batista, L., Allen, G., Gao, S., Ng, Y.K.D., Pera, M.S.: "Don't judge a book by its cover": Exploring book traits children favor. In: Proceedings of the 14th ACM Conference on Recommender Systems, pp. 669–674 (2020)

66. Nathanson, A.: Identifying and explaining the relationship between parental mediation and children's aggression. CR **26**(2), 124–143 (1999)

67. OfCom, U.: Children and Parents: Media use and Attitudes Report 2022. Office of Communications London, London (2022)

68. O'Keeffe, G.S., Clarke-Pearson, K., et al.: The impact of social media on children, adolescents, and families. Pediatrics **127**(4), 800–804 (2011)

69. Papadamou, K., et al.: Disturbed youtube for kids: characterizing and detecting inappropriate videos targeting young children. AAAI ICWSM **14**(1), 522–533 (2020)

70. Papadamou, K., et al.: Disturbed youtube for kids: characterizing and detecting inappropriate videos targeting young children. In: AAAI ICWSM, vol. 14, pp. 522–533 (2020)

71. Parada-Cabaleiro, E., et al.: Song lyrics have become simpler and more repetitive over the last five decades. Sci. Rep. **14**(1), 5531 (2024)

72. Pera, M.S., Cena, F., Huibers, T., Landoni, M., Mauro, N., Murgia, E.: 1st workshop on information retrieval for understudied users (ir4u2). In: European Conference on Information Retrieval, pp. 409–414. Springer (2024)

73. Pinney, C., Bettencourt, B.J., Fails, J.A., Kennington, C., Wright, K.L., Pera, M.S.: How readability cues affect children's navigation of search engine result pages. In: ACM IDC, pp. 62–69 (2024)

74. Pinney, C., Kennington, C., Pera, M.S., Wright, K.L., Fails, J.A.: Incorporating word-level phonemic decoding into readability assessment. In: LREC-COLING, pp. 8998–9009 (2024)

75. Raj, A., Milton, A., Ekstrand, M.D.: Pink for princesses, blue for superheroes: The need to examine gender stereotypes in kid's products in search and recommendations. In: 5th International and Interdisciplinary Perspectives on Children & Recommender and Information Retrieval Systems (KidRec 2021), in Conjunction with ACM IDC 2021, https://doi.org/10.48550/arXiv.2105.09296 (2021)

76. Ribeiro, M.H., Ottoni, R., West, R., Almeida, V.A., Meira Jr, W.: Auditing radicalization pathways on youtube. In: Proceedings of the 2020 Conference on Fairness, Accountability, and Transparency, pp. 131–141 (2020)

77. Ricci, F., Rokach, L., Shapira, B.: Recommender systems: techniques, applications, and challenges. In: Recommender Systems Handbook, pp. 1–35 (2021)

78. Rights for Peace: what is hate speech? https://www.rightsforpeace.org/hatespeech#:~:text=Speech%20that%20is%20simply%20offensive (2024), Accessed 23 Jul 24

79. Salemi, A., Zamani, H.: Evaluating retrieval quality in retrieval-augmented generation. In: Proceedings of the 47th International ACM SIGIR Conference on Research and Development in Information Retrieval, pp. 2395–2400 (2024)

80. Scharfe, E.: Development of emotional expression, understanding, and regulation in infants and young children. In: The Handbook of Emotional Intelligence: Theory, Development, Assessment, and Application at Home, School, and in the Workplace, pp. 244–262 (2000)

81. Schedl, M., Bauer, C.: Online music listening culture of kids and adolescents: Listening analysis and music recommendation tailored to the young. In: KidRec Workshop (2017). https://doi.org/10.48550/arXiv.1912.11564

82. Schedl, M., Knees, P., McFee, B., Bogdanov, D.: Music recommendation systems: techniques, use cases, and challenges. In: Recommender Systems Handbook, pp. 927–971. Springer (2021)

83. Schedl, M., Zamani, H., Chen, C.W., Deldjoo, Y., Elahi, M.: Current challenges and visions in music recommender systems research. Int. J. Multimedia Inf. Retrieval 7, 95–116 (2018)

84. Spear, L., et al.: Baby shark to barracuda: analyzing children's music listening behavior. In: ACM RecSys, pp. 639–644 (2021)

85. Spotify AB: explicit content - Spotify — support.spotify.com. https://support.spotify.com/us/article/explicit-content/ (2024), Accessed 12 Sep 2024

86. Spotify AB: spotify kids - spotify (US) — spotify.com. https://www.spotify.com/us/kids/ (2024), Accessed 12 Sep 2024

87. Tang, T.Y., Winoto, P.: I should not recommend it to you even if you will like it: the ethics of recommender systems. NRHM 22(1–2), 111–138 (2016)

88. Ungruh, R., Al Nahadi, M., Pera, M.S.: Mirror, mirror: exploring stereotype presence among top-n recommendations that may reach children. ACM Trans. Recommender Syst. (2025)

89. Ungruh, R., Bellogín, A., Pera, M.S.: The impact of mainstream-driven algorithms on recommendations for children. In: European Conference on Information Retrieval, pp. 67–84. Springer (2025)

90. Ungruh, R., Pera, M.S.: Ah, that's the great puzzle: on the quest of a holistic understanding of the harms of recommender systems on children. In: DCDW co-located with ACM IDC 2024. https://doi.org/10.48550/arXiv.2405.02050 (2024)
91. UNICEF: The convention on the rights of the child: the children's version (2019), https://www.unicef.org/child-rights-convention/convention-text-childrens-version#:~:text=A%20child%20is%20any%20person%20under%20the%20age%20of%2018
92. Valkenburg, P.M., Cantor, J.: The development of a child into a consumer. J. Appl. Dev. Psychol. **22**(1), 61–72 (2001)
93. Whittaker, J., Looney, S., Reed, A., Votta, F.: Recommender systems and the amplification of extremist content. Internet Policy Rev. **10**(2) (2021)
94. Yesilada, M., Lewandowsky, S.: Systematic review: Youtube recommendations and problematic content. Internet Policy Rev. **11**(1), 1652 (2022)
95. Zampieri, M., Malmasi, S., Nakov, P., Rosenthal, S., Farra, N., Kumar, R.: Semeval-2019 task 6: identifying and categorizing offensive language in social media (offenseval). In: SemEval, pp. 75–86 (2019)
96. Zerveas, G., Rekabsaz, N., Cohen, D., Eickhoff, C.: Mitigating bias in search results through contextual document reranking and neutrality regularization. In: Proceedings of the 45th International ACM SIGIR Conference on Research and Development in Information Retrieval, pp. 2532–2538 (2022)
97. Zhou, V.: Building a better profanity detection library with scikit-learn, February 2019, https://victorzhou.com/blog/better-profanity-detection-with-scikit-learn/
98. Zhu, Y., et al.: Large language models for information retrieval: a survey. arXiv preprint arXiv:2308.07107 (2023)

# Can You Feel It? Exploring the Emotional Profile of LLM Responses to Children's Queries

Hrishita Chakrabarti[✉][iD] and Maria Soledad Pera[iD]

Delft University of Technology, Delft, The Netherlands
{h.chakrabarti,M.S.Pera}@tudelft.nl

**Abstract.** Agents based on Large Language Models (LLM) have introduced a new way of information seeking that could simplify the search process to suit children's cognitive skills, as these agents often respond to natural language inquiries with easy-to-read and plausible answers. Still, with emotions playing a crucial role in children's information seeking and consumption behaviours, it is important to consider whether these agents suit children's **emotional intelligence**. With that in mind, in this work, we examine the emotional undertones of LLM agent responses for children's inquiries. Considering the known impact of prompt engineering on an agent's response, we investigate whether explicitly informing an agent that the user is a child influences the emotions conveyed in its response. Outcomes from this empirical study reveal the limitations of LLM agents to fit children's emotional intelligence, with agents tending to over-amplify any underlying emotion in a child's inquiry. With our findings, we advance knowledge in the role of emotions in children's online search and offer insights that could be used to improve children's online information access.

**Keywords:** Children · Search · LLM · Emotions · Information Access Systems

## 1 Introduction

In their quest for information, children increasingly turn to general-purpose information access systems (**IAS**) like commercial search engines (**SE**) such as Google and Bing as their initial point of information discovery [14,38]. These systems, however, are not necessarily designed with the abilities of these young searchers in mind. In fact, children are known to face several barriers when searching for information using a mainstream SE, such as struggles with query formulation, difficulty with understanding search results due to the retrieved content often being too complex for their reading skill, and vulnerability to misleading information due to limited critical thinking and digital literacy [3,7,19,20].

Agents based on Large Language Models (**LLM**), like ChatGPT and Gemini, have introduced new opportunities for information access [47]. Particularly for


A. Bellogin et al. (Eds.): IR4U2 2025/BIAS 2025, CCIS 2786, pp. 76–92, 2026.
https://doi.org/10.1007/978-3-032-12717-4_6

children, these agents show potential in simplifying the information seeking process. For instance, LLM agents can handle long natural language queries, which is how children usually pose their inquiries [5,11]. Moreover, the agents respond to inquiries in a conversational manner, offering direct answers that could be less taxing for a child to extract information from, compared to browsing through the numerous results provided by an SE. Still, existing literature highlights that when it comes to children's information access, their in-development cognitive ability is only *one* factor influencing their search experience and overall development [18,41].

Children are at a stage in their life where they are developing several essential life skills pertaining not only to their motor and cognitive abilities, but also their **Emotional Intelligence** [28]. Emotional intelligence pertains to an individual's ability to sense and distinguish their emotions and those of others, use the information to guide their thinking, and regulate their emotions to achieve a certain goal [28]. The role of emotions in the information seeking process has long been recognised as significant for users of all ages [e.g., 15,22,25,29]. Previous studies exploring the emotional charge conveyed on Search Engine Result Pages (**SERP**) generated in response to user inquiries find that the user queries themselves heavily influence the emotional charge of SERP responses and play an important role in the overall search experience [15], more so for children [21]. Explicitly focused on young searchers and extending these works, Chakrabarti et al. [6] instead analyse the emotional charge of LLM agent responses to children's inquiries. Findings from this recent work reveal that, much like SE, LLM agents also tend to be influenced by the emotions conveyed in a query when generating their responses. This further serves as evidence of the prevalence of emotions in children's search environment across different types of IAS. This work, however, probes responses generated if a child were to use an LLM agent "in the wild", i.e., the agent was not provided any explicit information about the user [6]. This prompts us to question whether LLM agents–known for their adaptability [12,32]–can also be adjusted to consider a child's emotional intelligence when addressing their inquiries.

Building on the discourse on the role of emotions on information seeking when children are at the center, we conduct an empirical exploration of the emotional undertones of LLM agents when responding to children's inquiries, focusing on the change in responses—from an emotional perspective—when the agent is explicitly informed that the user is a child. In our study, we probe LLM agent responses for queries formulated by Italian-speaking children, aged 9 to 11 years old, looking for information on topics commonly taught in primary school. Considering the impact of prompt engineering on LLM outcomes [27,39], we leverage different prompt variations to examine the change in emotional tone of LLM responses when the model is informed that the user is a child and explicitly instructed to be mindful of children's emotional intelligence. Using the different prompt variations, we elicit responses from ChatGPT and Gemma, and capture their emotional tone as an *emotional profile* we generate using the `InsideOut Framework` introduced in [21] and extended to LLM agents in [6]. Knowing that the affective undertone of queries (and ultimately prompts) heavily sways the emotional charge of IAS responses [15, 21], we pay particular attention to the change in emotional tone across different prompt variations when the child's query already has an underlying sentiment associated with it.

The outcomes of our analysis reveal that LLM agents do modify the emotional tone of their responses when aware that the user is a child. However, the modification entails over-amplification of a singular emotional tone – a reflection of LLM agents' sentiment bias observed in previous studies [23, 24]. This pattern is concerning, particularly for children's information access, given the strong influence of emotions on children's comprehension and decision-making [17, 41].

The primary contribution of this work is identifying LLM agents' limitations in adapting to children's emotional intelligence, thereby underscoring the need for further exploration of the role of emotions in these generative models. Our work also highlights the continued prevalence of emotions as a core component in the information seeking process and their role in biasing outcomes of popular IAS, which evinces the need to re-examine the concept of relevance to encompass emotions, particularly when it pertains to the information access for children, but also other populations vulnerable to emotions, such as those afflicted by mental health conditions. To facilitate future work in this direction and for reproducibility purposes, we share our code in a public repository: https://github.com/SOLandChildren/SIGIR2025/tree/main/CanYouFeelIt.

## 2    Data Generation and Exploration Framework

To guide data generation and empirical exploration of the emotional undertone of LLM agent responses to children's queries when an agent is informed that the user is a child, we turn to the `InsideOut Framework` introduced in [21] to examine SE and extended to LLM agents in [6]. This framework consists of five components: a *scope compass* and *IAS*, which dictate the data (*log*) to be examined—a snapshot of user-system interactions during information seeking—, the *emotional detection* component that defines the strategy and perspective for affect analysis, and the *emotional profile*, which quantifies the emotional undertone of different text samples (e.g., a query, SERP snippets, etc.).

The **scope compass** is comprised of four dimensions proposed by Landoni et al. [19] to guide the design and evaluation of IAS: (1) user group, (2) task, (3) environment, and (4) search strategy. In our case, Italian-speaking children, aged 9 to 11, undertaking information discovery tasks in the classroom context on topics common to the primary five curriculum using a text-based search strategy. For our exploration, we consider task variations characterised by the underlying sentiment inherent to (or lacking in) the task as categorised in [21]: **General** tasks related to inquiries on topics with no inherent sentiment, such as queries on tornadoes and their formation (e.g., *Cosa sono e come nascono i* *tornadi?*[1]); and **Positive** or **Negative** tasks referring to inquiries that reflect the corresponding sentiment, for example, *Perchè gli orsi polari sono a rischio di estinzione?*[2] relates to a distressing topic of extinction of polar bears and is categorised as a Negative task, whereas *Quali sono le regole per tenere le spiagge polite?*[3] is about rules for keeping beaches clean, and thus categorised as a Positive task.

Regarding *IAS*, we focus on LLM agents. Specifically, we probe two types of LLM: one proprietary and one open-source. For the former, we turn to OpenAI's **ChatGPT** due to its popularity [8,44]. Specifically, we scrutinise responses generated by `chatgpt-4o-latest`[4], denoted as `GPT`, as it is the LLM driving Chat-GPT's response generation at the time of the study [35]. For the latter, we use Google's **Gemma**, particularly `gemma-2-2b-it`[5]–which is a lightweight open model built using the same technology as that of Google's flagship LLM agent, Gemini [10].

An instantiation of the scope compass and IAS components determines the data used for analysis purposes: a *log* capturing user-IAS interactions. Considering our focus on a vulnerable user group, for our exploration, we rely on a synthetic log that we create following common practices from existing literature [e.g., 6,21,29]. We use the queries introduced in [21] (provided by the authors), which abide by the requirements of the scope compass as adapted for our study. We use these queries to elicit responses from `GPT` and `GEM`. Each query is associated with a search task type, resulting in three distinct query sets: $Q_G$ consisting of General queries (211), $Q_P$ Positive queries (39), and $Q_N$ Negative queries (43).

Given how a prompt is formulated greatly influences the LLM response [27, 39], we use several prompt variations for log generation, each consisting of a query—from either $Q_G$, $Q_P$, or $Q_N$—and a pre-defined set of instructions dictating response generation.

As the **Baseline** (B) prompt for our explorations, we use the prompt introduced in [6], which instructs the model to generate text in Italian, but does not provide information about the user formulating the query.

```
#Baseline#
#Gemma
{"role":"user", "content":""},
{"role": "assistant", "content": "Follow these instructions in all your responses:
 1. Use Italian language only;
 2. Do not use English except in programming language if any."},
{"role": "user", "content": query}

#ChatGPT
{"role": "system",
 "content": "Follow these instructions in all your responses:
```

---

[1] English translation based on Google Translate: What are tornadoes and how do they form?

[2] English translation based on Google Translate: Why are polar bears at risk of extinction?

[3] English translation based on Google Translate: What are the rules for keeping beaches clean?

[4] https://platform.openai.com/docs/models#current-model-aliases.

[5] https://huggingface.co/google/gemma-2b-it as `GEM`.

```
 1. Use Italian language only;
 2. Do not use English except in programming language if any."},
{"role": "user", "content": query }
```

The **Child-Aware (C)** prompt used to investigate whether the emotional tone of an LLM alters when it becomes aware that the user formulating the query is a child, extends the list of instructions from the baseline prompt to modify the response to suit a child who is 9–11 years old.

```
#Child-Aware#
#Gemma
{"role":"user", "content":""},
{"role": "assistant", "content": "Follow these instructions in all your responses:
 1. Use Italian language only;
 2. Do not use English except in programming language if any.;
 3. The response is meant for a child who is 9-11 years old."},
{"role": "user", "content": query}

#ChatGPT
{"role": "system",
 "content": "Follow these instructions in all your responses:
 1. Use Italian language only;
 2. Do not use English except in programming language if any.;
 3. The response is meant for a child who is 9-11 years old."},
{"role": "user", "content": query }
```

The **Emotional Intelligence-Aware** (textbttE) prompt enables probing of the extent to which an LLM adapts its responses to fit the emotional stimuli children can handle. In this case, we modify the Child-Aware prompt to explicitly require the model to be mindful of children's emotional intelligence.

```
#Emotional Intelligence Aware#
#Gemma prompt
{"role":"user", "content":""},
{"role": "assistant", "content": "Follow these instructions in all your responses:
 1. Use Italian language only;
 2. Do not use English except in programming language if any.;
 3. The response is meant for a child who is 9-11 years old.;
 4. Be mindful of the child's emotional intelligence when generating the response."},
{"role": "user", "content": query}

#ChatGPT prompt
{"role": "system",
 "content": "Follow these instructions in all your responses:
 1. Use Italian language only;
 2. Do not use English except in programming language if any.;
 3. The response is meant for a child who is 9-11 years old.;
 4. Be mindful of the child's emotional intelligence when generating the response."},
{"role": "user", "content": query }
```

Each synthetic log, denoted {GPT, GEM}-{$Q_G$, $Q_P$, $Q_N$}-{B, C, E}, consists of <prompt,response> pairs where the **response** refers to the text generated by an LLM (GPT or GPT) for a **query** (from $Q_G$, $Q_P$, or $Q_N$) based on a given **prompt** (B, C, or E).

For ***inferring emotions*** from a text sample–an LLM response in our study–we rely on `FEEL-IT` [4], a state-of-the-art strategy tailored to the Italian language which has been successfully employed for emotional analysis tasks [e.g., 6,30,37]. Specifically, `FEEL-IT` leverages two `UmBERTo`[6] models: `feel-it-italian-sentiment`[7] and `feel-it-italian-emotion`[8] to produce an **emotional vector** for a text sample as a distribution of weights across two sentiments: *Positive* and *Negative*, and four emotions, i.e., *Anger, Fear, Joy,* and *Sadness*.

The ***emotional profile*** of a `log`, i.e., **EP**(`log`), is a vector representation of the overall intensity distribution across six components based on the sentiments and emotions captured by `FEEL-IT`, which are `Positive`, `Negative`, `Anger`, `Fear`, `Joy`, and `Sadness`, computed by taking an element-wise average of the emotional vectors of each response in the `log`.

## 3 Results and Discussion

We anchor our analysis on the sentiment and emotions LLM convey in their responses to children's inquiries on the emotional profiles of the logs generated using the LLM, queries and prompts discussed in Sect. 2, which we outline in Table 1. All reported results are tested for significance using an independent T-test, $p < 0.05$.

*The Change in LLM Agents' Emotional Tone for a Child.* In a classroom setting, children, unless provided emotionally evocative search tasks, tend to formulate queries that are objective and neutral in tone [21]. Therefore, we first examine the degree to which different prompts lead to a change in the emotional tone of LLM responses to children's inquiries related to General search tasks ($Q_G$). Comparing EP(`GEM`-$Q_G$-B) with EP(`GEM`-$Q_G$-C), there is a significant increase in the `Positive` and a significant decrease in `Negative` when `GEM` is made aware that the user is a child. The overall increase in the positive undertone is also reflected in the significant rise in `Joy`, while `Fear` significantly decreases. We also observe a notable–but not significant–decrease in the intensity of `Anger`. When `GEM` is instructed to be specifically mindful of children's emotional intelligence, we find similar trends; responses are more positive overall, which is evident from significantly higher intensities of `Positive` and `Joy`, and significantly lower intensity of `Negative`, `Fear` and `Anger` in EP(`GEM`-$Q_G$-E) compared to EP(`GEM`-$Q_G$-B). Based on these results, we find that just by informing that the user is a child, `GEM` shifts its tone to a strongly positive tone, but further instructing the model to be mindful of children's emotional intelligence does not lead to prominent changes.

When examining GPT-based logs, we observe the same trend of an overall increase in the positive tone of responses, with significant increase in `Positive`

---

[6] https://huggingface.co/Musixmatch/umberto-commoncrawl-cased-v1.

[7] https://huggingface.co/MilaNLProc/feel-it-italian-sentiment.

[8] https://huggingface.co/MilaNLProc/feel-it-italian-emotion.

**Table 1.** Emotional profiles based on **FEEL-IT**; sentiment/emotion vectors sum up to 100%. '*' implies significant differences (independent T-test, $p < 0.05$) with respect to the counterpart component in the corresponding baseline.

| LLM | Query Set | Prompt Variation | Sentiment | | Emotion | | | |
|---|---|---|---|---|---|---|---|---|
| | | | Positive | Negative | Joy | Sadness | Anger | Fear |
| GEM | $Q_G$ | B | 51.17 | 48.83 | 41.63 | 26.41 | 3.66 | 28.3 |
| | | C | 62.05* | 37.95* | 53.09* | 25.49 | 1.61 | 19.81* |
| | | E | 61.83* | 38.17* | 55.58* | 25.18 | 0.75* | 18.5* |
| | $Q_P$ | B | 57.06 | 42.94 | 57.46 | 22.84 | 17.13 | 2.58 |
| | | C | 48.91 | 51.09 | 58.73 | 18.52 | 20.98 | 1.78 |
| | | E | 50.46 | 49.54 | 51.52 | 21.68 | 23.22 | 3.58 |
| | $Q_N$ | B | 2.35 | 97.65 | 2.09 | 49.36 | 10.79 | 37.75 |
| | | C | 7.39 | 92.61 | 15.6* | 66.99 | 7.05 | 10.36* |
| | | E | 25.51* | 74.49* | 26.54* | 56.74 | 4.79 | 11.93* |
| GPT | $Q_G$ | B | 41.22 | 58.78 | 27.09 | 22.63 | 1.34 | 48.94 |
| | | C | 62.09* | 37.91* | 58.24* | 18.12 | 0.33 | 23.31* |
| | | E | 67.92* | 32.08* | 62.04* | 16.17 | 0.42 | 21.37* |
| | $Q_P$ | B | 53.89 | 46.11 | 37.67 | 42.61 | 8.41 | 11.31 |
| | | C | 79.72* | 20.28* | 64.8* | 18.44* | 12.32 | 4.44 |
| | | E | 87.37* | 12.63* | 76.73* | 12.34* | 1.19 | 9.73 |
| | $Q_N$ | B | 0.04 | 99.96 | 0.16 | 46.98 | 5.55 | 47.31 |
| | | C | 0.03 | 99.97 | 2.45 | 62.59 | 3.33 | 31.63 |
| | | E | 3.7 | 96.3 | 2.32 | 82.98* | 2.05 | 12.64* |

and Joy, and significant decrease in Negative and Fear when comparing both EP(GPT-$Q_G$-C) and EP(GPT-$Q_G$-E) with EP(GPT-$Q_G$-B) respectively, but unlike in GEM responses, the margin of difference across all components is higher between EP(GPT-$Q_G$-B) and EP(GPT-$Q_G$-E) than the difference in counterpart components between EP(GPT-$Q_G$-B) and EP(GPT-$Q_G$-C), implying that GPT responses overall become consistently more positive in tone the more information we provide about the child user, while GEM tends to temper the overall intensities of sentiments when instructed to be mindful of a child's emotional intelligence, compared to when it is only informed that the user is a child.

*The Impact of Query's Sentiment on LLM's Emotional Tone.* Previous studies exploring the emotional undertone of IAS responses find that when for inquiries on "controversial" or "emotionally-charged" topics, the underlying emotion in a user's query significantly biases the response an IAS generates, particularly from an emotional perspective [15,21,29]. With this in mind, and considering children's tendency to reflect the emotional tone of a search topic in the query they formulate [21], we investigate the degree to which the different prompt variations described previously change the emotional profile of GPT and GPT responses when the query the LLM is responding is associated with a task with an implicit sentiment, which in our case is either a positive or negative connotation.

Based on the emotional profiles reported in Table 1 for GEM responses to positively-charged tasks ($Q_P$), i.e., EP(GEM-$Q_P$-B), EP(GEM-$Q_P$-C), and EP(GEM-$Q_P$-E), we find that when the LLM is informed that the user is a child, the responses are overall *less* positive, as observed from the lower intensity for Positive and higher intensity of Negative and Anger in EP(GEM-$Q_P$-C) compared to EP(GEM-$Q_P$-B). Similarly, when GEM is instructed to be mindful of children's emotional intelligence, the responses are overall less positive as inferred from the lower intensity of Positive and Joy, and the higher intensity of Negative, Anger, and Fear in EP(GEM-$Q_P$-E) compared to in EP(GEM-$Q_P$-B). The only exception to this trend is the higher intensity of Joy and lower intensities of Sadness and Fear in EP(GEM-$Q_P$-C) than in EP(GEM-$Q_P$-B). However, none of the differences are statistically significant.

Comparing GPT's emotional profiles based on different prompts for the same positively-charged tasks from Table 1, we find that overall GPT responses are *more* positive in tone when the model is informed that the user is a child, and even more so when the model is instructed to be mindful of children's emotional intelligence. This we infer based on significantly higher intensity of Positive and Joy, along with significantly lower intensity of Negative and Sadness in both EP(GPT-$Q_P$-C) and EP(GPT-$Q_P$-E) when compared to EP(GEM-$Q_P$-B) respectively. Our findings imply that for tasks with an implicit positive tone, GEM responds positively but does not modify its response in a significant manner for children, whereas GPT becomes overly positive while tuning out any negative tones when responding to children.

Turning to the emotional profiles in Table 1 for GEM and GPT responses for tasks with a negative connotation ($Q_N$), which are EP(GEM-$Q_N$-B), EP(GEM-$Q_N$-C), EP(GEM-$Q_N$-E), EP(GPT-$Q_N$-B), EP(GPT-$Q_N$-C), and EP(GPT-$Q_N$-E), we observe more significant changes in the overall emotional tone of GEM responses than in GPT responses. Comparing EP(GEM-$Q_N$-B) with EP(GEM-$Q_N$-C), we find the latter profile to have significantly higher intensity of Joy and significantly lower intensity of Fear, implying GEM tempers the negative tone of its response for negatively-charged inquiries when aware that the user is a child. When the LLM is instructed to be mindful of children's emotional intelligence, we observe further moderation as inferred from the significantly higher intensity of Positive and Joy and significantly lower intensity of Negative and Fear in EP(GEM-$Q_N$-E) compared to EP(GEM-$Q_N$-B). These findings indicate that GEM indeed can moderate its emotional tone—up to a certain extent—for children inquiring about potentially distressing topics, but only when specifically instructed to consider children's emotional intelligence.

In the case of GPT responses, informing the LLM that the user is a child leads to responses with generally *higher* intensity of Negative and Sadness and lower intensity of Positive, but also a higher intensity of Joy along with lower intensity of Fear in EP(GPT-$Q_N$-C) than in EP(GPT-$Q_N$-B), however none of the differences hold true in practice. When the LLM is instructed to be mindful of children's emotional intelligence, we observe significant changes only across **Sadness** and **Fear**, but the intensity of **Sadness** is higher while that of **Fear** is lower in EP(GPT-$\mathbf{Q}_N$-E) than in EP(GPT-$\mathbf{Q}_N$-B). The contrasting results along with non-significant change in **Negative** component suggest that when it comes to potentially distressing topics of inquiry, **GPT** is not capable of adjusting its tone to align with children's emotional needs.

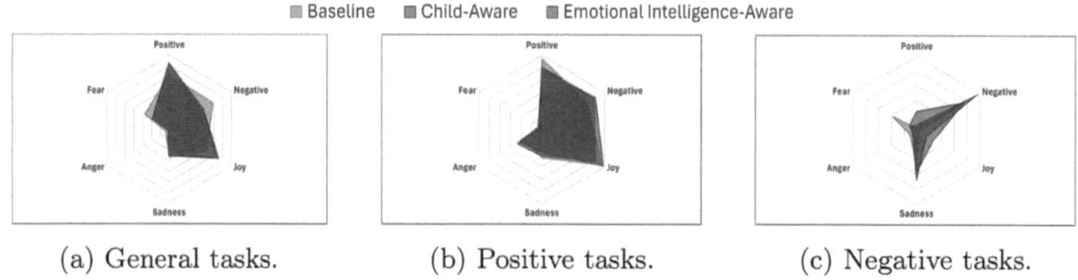


(a) General tasks.     (b) Positive tasks.     (c) Negative tasks.

**Fig. 1.** Emotional profiles of Gemma using **FEEL-IT** across different search tasks.

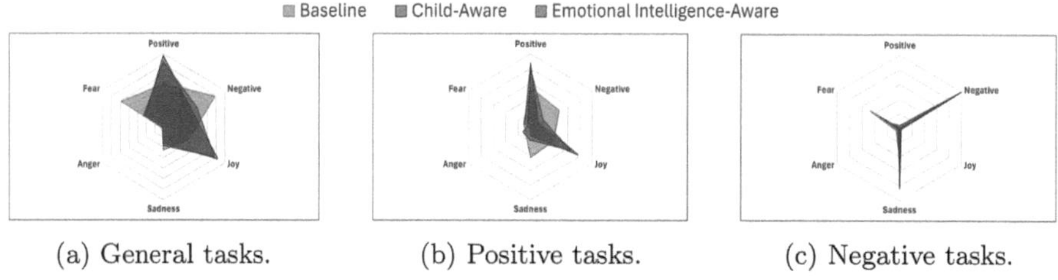


(a) General tasks.     (b) Positive tasks.     (c) Negative tasks.

**Fig. 2.** Emotional profiles of ChatGPT using **FEEL-IT** across different search tasks.

*The Emotional Tone of LLM responses to Children.* The outcomes of our experiments reveal that for General search tasks, i.e., search tasks with no inherent emotional undertone, both ChatGPT and Gemma, when aware that the user is a child, respond with a significantly stronger positive tone, with considerable moderation in the projection of fear in their responses, as illustrated in Figs. 1a and 2a. Instructing the models to be mindful of children's emotional intelligence leads to even more positive responses, but the shift in tone is not prominent. For instance, consider ChatGPT's responses to a question related to the classification of snow leopards based on different prompt variations presented in Fig. 3. Without any information about the user's identity (Baseline prompt), the salient tones conveyed in the response are **Negative** and **Fear**. We attribute this to the statement about snow leopards being a vulnerable species. When ChatGPT is informed that the user is a child (Child-Aware prompt), the response contains more exclamation points and does not mention that snow leopards are at risk of extinction, resulting in higher intensities for `Positive` and `Joy` components in its response. Directing ChatGPT to consider children's emotional intelligence (Emotional Intelligence Aware Prompt) resulted in a more verbose response and the agent personifying itself, but the overall emotional tone does not prominently change.

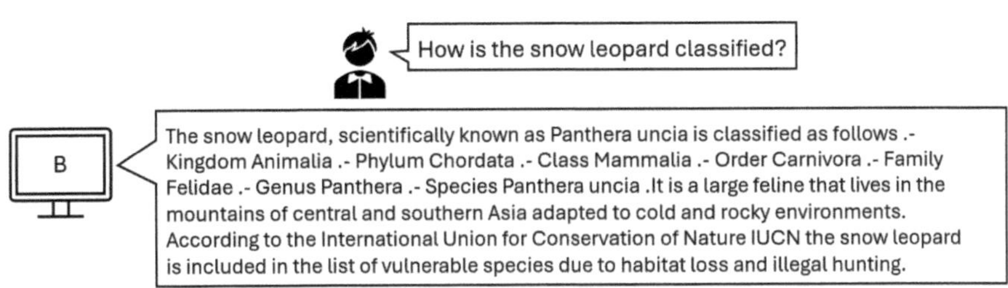


Emotional Vector: 0.048 (Positive), **99.952 (Negative),** 0.111 (Joy), 1.437 (Sadness), 0.0558 (Anger), **98.397 (Fear)**

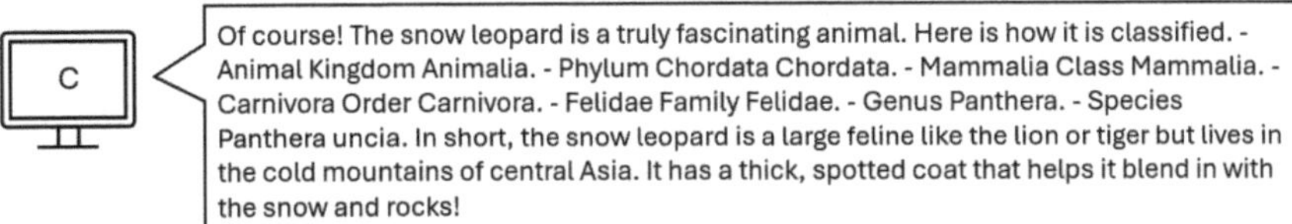


Emotional Vector: **99.972 (Positive)**, 0.028 (Negative), **99.936 (Joy)**, 0.0271 (Sadness), 0.011 (Anger), 0.026 (Fear)

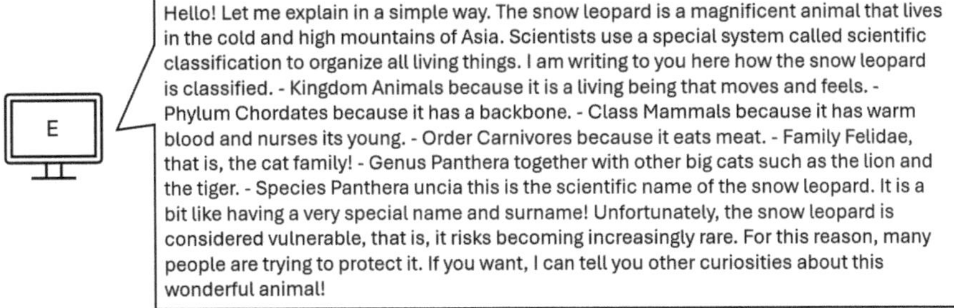


Emotional Vector: **99.974 (Positive)**, 0.026 (Negative), **99.632 (Joy)**, 0.261 (Sadness), 0.005 (Anger), 0.102 (Fear)

**Fig. 3.** ChatGPT responses for a General query generated using different prompts. Note that all text here has been translated to English, but emotional vectors are computed based on the original Italian text.

In case of search tasks with an implicit emotional tone, the two agents under scrutiny respond differently across prompt variations. For positively-charged tasks, Gemma oddly responds more negatively when informed that the user is a child, although the shift in tone is by a small margin and also does not hold in practice. ChatGPT, on the other hand, when aware that the user is a child, shifts to a significantly more positive tone as illustrated in Fig. 2b. It is evident from this figure that when instructed to be mindful of children's emotional intelligence, ChatGPT appears to amplify its positive tone almost to an extreme while tuning out all negative emotional signals as much as possible, compared to the responses produced by Gemma. Turning to inquiries on topics with a negative connotation, in which case emotional moderation would generally be beneficial for children due to their sensitivity to negative emotions, both our prompt variations fail to shift ChatGPT's emotional tone. Regardless of whether we inform the agent that the user is a child or specifically instruct it to be mindful of children's emotional intelligence, the responses at large remain strongly negative with notably stronger sad tone (Fig. 2c). We do, however, observe that, like for other types of search tasks, instructing ChatGPT to be mindful of children's emotional intelligence leads to a significant drop in the intensity of fear projected in its response. Gemma, in contrast, generated more emotionally moderated responses, particularly when instructed to consider children's emotional intelligence as illustrated in Fig. 1c. An example of Gemma's emotional moderation is presented in Fig. 4 wherein the question is related to an inherently negative topic of glaciers melting. When provided no information about the user, Gemma states the glaciers "going extinct" as a climate emergency, which can be a frightening topic for a young child. However, when informed that the user is a child and instructed to be mindful of children's emotional intelligence, Gemma doesn't disagree that glaciers are disappearing, instead explaining it with imagery like "fading dream" or "little jewel crumbling" but avoids amplifying the negative connotation by describing the situation to be an emergency.

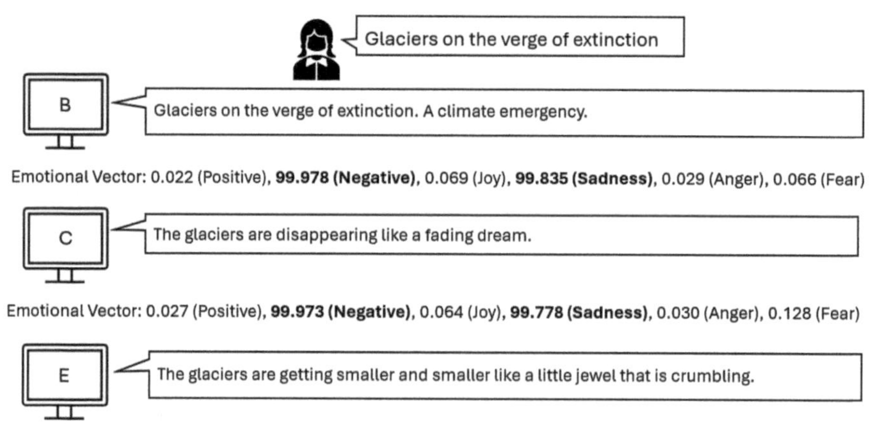


**Fig. 4.** Gemma responses for a Negative query generated using different prompts. Note that all text here has been translated to English, but emotional vectors are computed based on the original Italian text.

Overall, our results indicate that when it comes to children's inquiries, LLM are "aware" of children's emotional needs and capable of emotional moderation during response generation, but only to a certain extent. For emotionally-charged inquiries, the models end up reflecting the sentiment inherent to the topic of inquiry, implying that LLM continue to depict a sentiment bias already noted in previous studies [6,23,24], with the bias being *stronger* when the model is responding to a child specifically. The sentiment bias is not unique to LLM agents, previous studies have also highlighted the bias to be present in mainstream SE [15,46]. However, unlike an SE in which the multiple results provide a more emotionally diverse environment for a child to explore, the direct response generated by an LLM agent provides a singular voice, which, with its amplified sentiment bias, could have a much stronger impact on the emotional development of a child.

## 4  Conclusion

Back in 1993, Kuhlthau studied the role of affect and cognition in the information seeking process model [16]. Since then, the research community has continued to explore the role and influence of emotions during the online information seeking process. The conducted studies have examined the interplay of emotions and information seeking focusing on different aspects that comprise a search scenario: contexts (e.g., users conducting everyday information inquiry tasks [1,25], users searching for information on "controversial" topics [15]); domains such as education [21] and public health [22]; user groups including mainstream users [15,25] and users from vulnerable populations like children [6,21] and individuals with mental health conditions [29]. The impact of emotions is also not limited to the searchers, but has been known to bias how different IAS, including SE and conversational agents, generate content [15,21] and present it to the user [1,33].

With the growing prevalence of LLM in the Information Retrieval (**IR**) area, the affect component of search continues to be of interest for the IR community, as evidenced in works focused on the emotional tone of RAG-based and LLM-based systems, which include the use of emotions to improve the response generation [13,43] and explainability [33] of such generative AI systems, as well as examining the impact of emotions expressed by these systems on the user's information processing [48]. With this work, we have added to this discourse. Focused on children, we have built upon the work of Yi and Rieh [49] where the authors examine the potential and limitations of voice-based conversational agents (**VCA**) in facilitating children's search and learning. Inspired from the authors' suggestion of integrating emotional intelligence in child-centred voice search systems, we examine the capability of LLM—the generative AI models that generally drive VCA response generation—in modifying their responses to fit children's in-development emotional intelligence. LLM have shown great potential in modifying their responses to suit different audiences based on pre-defined characteristics [12,31,45], and yet, with this preliminary work, we showed that fitting the emotional intelligence of young searchers is something these generative models still find challenging. Worth noting that our results are based on LLM responding to Italian inquiries, and these generative models are still lacking in their multilingual capabilities [34,50], particularly from a content safety perspective [40,42]. This underscores the need to examine LLM's emotional moderation—which we posit to be an important factor in content safety for vulnerable populations like children—in a multilingual setting.

Considering children are drawn to emotionally evocative tools [21], the prominent emotional tone of LLM agent responses could foster engagement amongst these young users. Still, based on our observations of the agents reflecting the emotional tone of a child's query, there could be scenarios wherein a child remains engaged with an LLM agent but ends up being exposed to emotional stimuli that the child is not equipped to handle, impacting the child's overall development. Therefore, when designing IR solutions for children that leverage LLM, the affective component of the response generation strategy requires careful calibration to ensure that the emotional undertone conveyed by such models is suitable for the child's search experience.

The core goal of any IR strategy is to improve the retrieval of resources that are relevant *for* a target user. In general, relevance has been associated with the topical similarity of candidate resources with a user's query. Existing works on Children IR have extended the concept of relevance by focusing on aligning the content complexity to a child's readability level [2,26,36]. Motivated by our results, we argue that the emotional tone conveyed in the content should also be considered as another dimension when determining relevance as it pertains to children.

Considering children's limited emotional intelligence, they may struggle with identifying the emotional signals that influence their search behaviour and also regulating their reaction to any intense emotional stimuli. Addressing this issue by adapting IAS to respond to children's inquiries—whether in the form of a SERP or direct response produced by an LLM—with an impartial tone would be counterproductive, as emotions are a driving force for children's motivation and cognition [41]. Instead, it may be beneficial to adjust the emotional undertone of IAS responses based on the capacity of the child interacting with the IAS. This would require designing computational models and detection strategies that can effectively capture the emotional state and capacity of a child in the context of online search.

Our work adds further evidence that no existing IAS—from mainstream SE to now popular LLM agents—is fully equipped to handle all the diverse needs and expectations of children. This is not a recent issue, and yet it has long-lasting impacts on this user group. Children are at a stage where they are developing their perception of themselves and the world around them, and the information they consume at this stage plays a key role in their development [9]. In this digital era, children are increasingly relying on the web for information, with IAS serving as the bridge between these impressionable minds and the World Wide Web [18]. Moving forward, we advocate for targeted research efforts that bring children and other underserved user groups to the forefront to ensure that any future advancement in IR benefits all users, and not just the "mainstream".

**Declaration on Generative AI**

During the preparation of this work, the author(s) used ChatGPT and Grammarly to correct any grammatical or phrasing errors. No sections in the experimental code or manuscript have been created using Generative AI tool(s)/service(s).

**Acknowledgments.** Supported by SNSF Award #[IC00I0-227887 project n.10000973 SOL]

**Disclosure of Interests.** The authors have no competing interests to declare that are relevant to the content of this article.

# References


1. Abegaz, T.T.: Design with emotion: improving web search experience for older adults. Ph.D. thesis, Clemson University (2014)
2. Amendum, S.J., Conradi, K., Hiebert, E.: Does text complexity matter in the elementary grades? A research synthesis of text difficulty and elementary students' reading fluency and comprehension. Educ. Psychol. Rev. **30**, 121–151 (2018)
3. Azpiazu, I.M., Dragovic, N., Pera, M.S., Fails, J.A.: Online searching and learning: Yum and other search tools for children and teachers. Inform. Retriev. J. **20**, 524–545 (2017)
4. Bianchi, F., Nozza, D., Hovy, D.: "FEEL-IT: emotion and sentiment classification for the Italian language. In: Proceedings of the 11th Workshop on Computational Approaches to Subjectivity, Sentiment and Social Media Analysis. Association for Computational Linguistics (2021)
5. Bilal, D., Kirby, J.: Differences and similarities in information seeking: children and adults as web users. Inform. Process. Manage. **38**(5), 649–670 (2002)
6. Chakrabarti, H., Tobia, D.M., Landoni, M., Pera, M.S.: Inside out 2: make room for new emotions & LLM: a reproducibility study of the emotional side of search in the classroom, pp. 3244–3254. SIGIR 2025. Association for Computing Machinery, New York (2025). https://doi.org/10.1145/3726302.3730315
7. Chakrabarti, H., Tobia, D.M., Landoni, M., Pera, M.S.: Online information disorder & children. In: The 5th Workshop on Reducing Online Misinformation through Credible Information Retrieval (held as part of ECIR 2025: the 47th European Conference on Information Retrieval), ROMCIR 2025, p. ns (2025)
8. Chowdhury, G., Chowdhury, S.: AI- and LLM-driven search tools: a paradigm shift in information access for education and research. J. Inform. Sci. (2024). https://doi.org/10.1177/01655515241284046
9. Danovitch, J.H.: Growing up with Google: how children's understanding and use of internet-based devices relates to cognitive development. Hum. Behav. Emerg. Technol. **1**(2), 81–90 (2019)
10. Google AI for Developers: Gemma models overview, August 2024. https://ai.google.dev/gemma/docs
11. Duarte Torres, S., Hiemstra, D., Serdyukov, P.: Query log analysis in the context of information retrieval for children. In: Proceedings of the 33rd International ACM SIGIR Conference on Research and Development in Information Retrieval, SIGIR '10, pp. 847–848. Association for Computing Machinery, New York (2010). https://doi.org/10.1145/1835449.1835646

12. Eapen, J., Adhithyan, V.: Personalization and customization of LLM responses. Int. J. Res. Publ. Rev. **4**(12), 2617–2627 (2023)
13. Huang, L., Lan, H., Sun, Z., Shi, C., Bai, T.: Emotional RAG: enhancing role-playing agents through emotional retrieval. In: 2024 IEEE International Conference on Knowledge Graph (ICKG), pp. 120–127 (2024). https://doi.org/10.1109/ICKG63256.2024.00023
14. Jochmann-Mannak, H., Huibers, T.W., Lentz, L., Sanders, T.: Children searching information on the internet: performance on children's interfaces compared to Google. In: Workshop on Accessible Search Systems 2010 (2010)
15. Kazai, G., Thomas, P., Craswell, N.: The emotion profile of web search. In: SIGIR'19, pp. 1097–1100. Association for Computing Machinery, New York (2019). https://doi.org/10.1145/3331184.3331314
16. Kuhlthau, C.C.: A principle of uncertainty for information seeking. J. Doc. **49**(4), 339–355 (1993)
17. Landoni, M., Huibers, T., Murgia, E., Aliannejadi, M., Pera, M.S.: Somewhere over the rainbow: exploring the sense for relevance in children. In: Proceedings of the 32nd European Conference on Cognitive Ergonomics, ECCE '21. Association for Computing Machinery, New York (2021). https://doi.org/10.1145/3452853.3452885
18. Landoni, M., Huibers, T., Murgia, E., Pera, M.S.: Good for children, good for all? In: European Conference on Information Retrieval, pp. 302–313. Springer (2024)
19. Landoni, M., Matteri, D., Murgia, E., Huibers, T., Pera, M.S.: Sonny, Cerca! evaluating the impact of using a vocal assistant to search at school. In: Crestani, F., et al. (eds.) CLEF 2019. LNCS, vol. 11696, pp. 101–113. Springer, Cham (2019). https://doi.org/10.1007/978-3-030-28577-7_6
20. Landoni, M., Murgia, E., Huibers, T., Pera, M.S.: How does information pollution challenge children's right to information access? In: CEUR Workshop Proceedings, vol. 3406, pp. 17–29. CEUR-WS (2023)
21. Landoni, M., Pera, M.S., Murgia, E., Huibers, T.: Inside out: exploring the emotional side of search engines in the classroom. In: Proceedings of the 28th ACM Conference on User Modeling, Adaptation and Personalization, UMAP '20, pp. 136–144. Association for Computing Machinery, New York (2020). https://doi.org/10.1145/3340631.3394847
22. Lauckner, C., Hsieh, G.: The presentation of health-related search results and its impact on negative emotional outcomes. In: Proceedings of the SIGCHI Conference on Human Factors in Computing Systems, pp. 333–342 (2013)
23. Li, A., Sinnamon, L.: Examining query sentiment bias effects on search results in large language models. In: The Symposium on Future Directions in Information Access (FDIA) co-located with the 2023 European Summer School on Information Retrieval (ESSIR) (2023)
24. Li, A., Sinnamon, L.: Generative AI search engines as arbiters of public knowledge: an audit of bias and authority. Proc. Assoc. Inf. Sci. Technol. **61**(1), 205–217 (2024)
25. Lopatovska, I.: Toward a model of emotions and mood in the online information search process. J. Am. Soc. Inf. Sci. **65**(9), 1775–1793 (2014)
26. Madrazo Azpiazu, I., Pera, M.S.: An analysis of transfer learning methods for multilingual readability assessment. In: Adjunct Publication of the 28th ACM Conference on User Modeling, Adaptation and Personalization, pp. 95–100 (2020)
27. Marvin, G., Hellen, N., Jjingo, D., Nakatumba-Nabende, J.: Prompt engineering in large language models. In: International Conference on Data Intelligence and Cognitive Informatics, pp. 387–402. Springer (2023)

28. Mayer, J.D.: What is emotional intelligence. In: Salovey, P., Sluyter, D. (eds.) Emotional Development and Emotional Intelligence: Implications for Educators, pp. 3–31 (1997)
29. Milton, A., Pera, M.S.: Into the unknown: exploration of search engines' responses to users with depression and anxiety. ACM Trans. Web **17**(4), 1–29 (2023)
30. Muhammad, S.H., et al.: SemEval-2025 Task 11: bridging the gap in text-based emotion detection. arXiv preprint arXiv:2503.07269 (2025)
31. Murgia, E., Abbasiantaeb, Z., Aliannejadi, M., Huibers, T., Landoni, M., Pera, M.S.: ChatGPT in the classroom: a preliminary exploration on the feasibility of adapting ChatGPT to support children's information discovery. In: Adjunct Proceedings of the 31st ACM Conference on User Modeling, Adaptation and Personalization, UMAP '23 Adjunct, pp. 22–27. Association for Computing Machinery, New York (2023). https://doi.org/10.1145/3563359.3597399
32. Murgia, E., Pera, M.S., Landoni, M., Huibers, T.: Children on ChatGPT readability in an educational context: myth or opportunity? In: Adjunct Proceedings of the 31st ACM Conference on User Modeling, Adaptation and Personalization, UMAP '23 Adjunct, pp. 311–316. Association for Computing Machinery, New York (2023). https://doi.org/10.1145/3563359.3596996
33. Nguyen, L., Vu, Q., Sharma, R., et al.: Empathetic information seeking support using generative artificial intelligence (2024)
34. Ohmer, X., Bruni, E., Hupkes, D.: Evaluating task understanding through multilingual consistency: a ChatGPT case study (2023). https://api.semanticscholar.org/CorpusID:258823333
35. OpenAI: ChatGPT—release notes, April 2025. https://help.openai.com/en/articles/6825453-chatgpt-release-notes
36. Reed, D.K., Kershaw-Herrera, S.: An examination of text complexity as characterized by readability and cohesion. J. Exp. Educ. **84**(1), 75–97 (2016)
37. Roccabruna, G., Azzolin, S., Riccardi, G., et al.: Multi-source multi-domain sentiment analysis with BERT-based models. In: European Language Resources Association, pp. 581–589. European Language Resources Association (2022)
38. Rowlands, I., et al.: The google generation: the information behaviour of the researcher of the future. In: Aslib Proceedings, vol. 60, pp. 290–310. Emerald Group Publishing Limited (2008)
39. Schmidt, D.C., Spencer-Smith, J., Fu, Q., White, J.: Cataloging prompt patterns to enhance the discipline of prompt engineering (2023). https://www.dre.vanderbilt.edu/~schmidt/PDF/ADA_Europe_Position_Paper.pdf. Accessed 25 Sept 2023
40. Shen, L., et al.: The language barrier: dissecting safety challenges of LLMs in multilingual contexts. In: Ku, L.W., Martins, A., Srikumar, V. (eds.) Findings of the Association for Computational Linguistics, ACL 2024, Bangkok, Thailand, August 2024, pp. 2668–2680. Association for Computational Linguistics (2024). https://doi.org/10.18653/v1/2024.findings-acl.156. https://aclanthology.org/2024.findings-acl.156/
41. van der Sluis, F., van Dijk, B.: A closer look at children's information retrieval usage. In: 33st Annual International ACM SIGIR Conference on Research and Development in Information Retrieval, SIGIR'10 (2010)
42. Song, J., Huang, Y., Zhou, Z., Ma, L.: Multilingual blending: LLM safety alignment evaluation with language mixture. arXiv preprint arXiv:2407.07342 (2024)
43. Vologina, E., Matveeva, A., Makhnytkina, O., Matveev, Y., Burambayeva, N.: RAG and few-shot prompting in emotional text generation. In: International Conference on Speech and Computer, pp. 43–53. Springer, Heidelberg (2024)

44. Wang, X., Liu, C.: Finding the aha! moment of search: a preliminary examination of insight learning during search. Proc. Assoc. Inf. Sci. Technol. **60**(1), 421–432 (2023). https://doi.org/10.1002/pra2.800
45. White, J., et al.: A prompt pattern catalog to enhance prompt engineering with ChatGPT. arXiv preprint arXiv:2302.11382 (2023)
46. White, R.: Beliefs and biases in web search. In: Proceedings of the 36th International ACM SIGIR Conference on Research and Development in Information Retrieval, July 2013 (2013). https://doi.org/10.1145/2484028.2484053
47. White, R.W.: Advancing the search frontier with AI agents. Commun. ACM **67**(9), 54–65 (2024). https://doi.org/10.1145/3655615
48. Yan, L., Liu, Y., Liu, S.: The search for balance: the impact of LLM-based conversational search on information processing and polarization (2024)
49. Yi, S., Rieh, S.Y.: Children's conversational voice search as learning: a literature review. Inf. Learn. Sci. **126**(1/2), 8–28 (2025)
50. Zhang, X., Li, S., Hauer, B., Shi, N., Kondrak, G.: Don't trust ChatGPT when your question is not in English: a study of multilingual abilities and types of LLMs. In: Bouamor, H., Pino, J., Bali, K. (eds.) Proceedings of the 2023 Conference on Empirical Methods in Natural Language Processing, Singapore, December 2023, pp. 7915–7927. Association for Computational Linguistics (2023). https://doi.org/10.18653/v1/2023.emnlp-main.491. https://aclanthology.org/2023.emnlp-main.491/

# Finding Nemo: A Serious Game to Raise Children's Awareness of Information Pollution

Diletta Micol Tobia[(✉)] [iD], Vladyslav Kotov [iD], and Monica Landoni [iD]

Universita' della Svizzera Italiana, Lugano, Switzerland
{diletta.micol.tobia,vladyslav.kotov,monica.landoni}@usi.ch

**Abstract.** The emergence of digital platforms has provided unprecedented access to online content. A click, swipe, or scroll can lead to a continuous flow of news, articles, and social media posts competing for users' attention. However, within this *ocean* of content lies a hidden risk: the rapid (un)intentional contamination of information, also known as Information Pollution. Although much research has been conducted to study this problem among different age groups, there is limited understanding of how children, who have unique search needs and behaviours, interact with the overwhelming amount of online information. Therefore, it is essential to investigate the factors that influence children's perception of online content when they are inundated with irrelevant and redundant information. The contribution of this study is the development of a system to raise children's awareness of information overload through play. Inspired by the findings and gaps identified from the literature on the interaction between young generations and new Information Access Systems, this study aims to design and develop a digital game to illustrate the concept of Information Pollution to children aged between 9 and 11, using the metaphor of Ocean Noise Pollution. The game aims to provide valuable insights into how children perceive reliable information while at the same time making them aware of misleading content, ultimately trying to lay the groundwork for mitigating the effects of this phenomenon among the young generation.

**Keywords:** Information Pollution · Children · Serious Game · Digital Game · Information Access

## 1 Introduction

In today's digital era —often described as the age of "post-truth"— misinformation is widely spread and denial of established scientific claims is a commonplace [7]. This phenomenon is further amplified by the fact that users of all ages access an immense amount of different digital resources on the Web [17]. Among those most affected are children, who start accessing online content as early as the age of four [18]. Despite being considered as "digital natives", there is no research


A. Bellogin et al. (Eds.): IR4U2 2025/BIAS 2025, CCIS 2786, pp. 93–109, 2026.
https://doi.org/10.1007/978-3-032-12717-4_7

showing that they are better at understanding the Web than other generations [42]. Although some young people claim to be confident in distinguishing between credible and non-credible news, they still lack the skills to do so [41]. Results from various research indicate that adolescents tend to adopt overly superficial and uncritical strategies when assessing the credibility of online information [15,35]. The rise of the phenomenon known as **Information Disorder**, which refers to the intentional and unintentional spreading of misleading information in the public sphere [57], has resulted in an overload of information shared online, making it increasingly difficult to identify reliable content. According to a survey of over 1000 Germans [43], even adults find it difficult to judge information disseminated by the media as reliable [43]. This widespread dissemination of misleading but also irrelevant content has generated a phenomenon called **Information Pollution**, which refers to the way content on the web is being contaminated intentionally or unintentionally [36]. This poses serious challenges to younger users, since they are at a point in their lives when they become cognizant of the world around them. The information they encounter during this phase plays a vital role in their development [18]. Studies show that children often rely on superficial information and struggle to assess the credibility of online content, often using non-authoritative sources such as blogs, forums and images from Search Engines (**SE**) without even verifying the information [1,12]. This introduces a set of crucial challenges. When considering younger age groups, exposure to misleading content can distort their understanding of the world, affect their memory and learning processes [18], reduce their trust in the media, and even influence their social and political attitudes [21]. Despite these risks, the specific effects of Information Pollution on children remain little explored [31], particularly when dealing with the overload of misleading information. To fill this gap, we propose the envisioning and design of a serious digital game for children aged between 9 and 11 years old, using the metaphor of Ocean Noise Pollution to raise awareness of online Information Pollution. Based on existing research supporting the educational potential of digital games, this study aims to engage children by helping them to recognise and critically evaluate misleading content coming from different Information Access Systems (**IAS**). We aim to equip children with the essential skills needed to navigate the complex information landscape of the digital world. Additionally, we seek to gather insights into the factors that influence children's search-as-learning (**SAL**) experience [16] in the classroom setting.

## 2   Background and Related Work

### 2.1   Information Disorder and Information Pollution

Information Disorder is defined as the intentional and unintentional spread of misleading information in the public sphere [57]. It is usually categorised as: (1) *misinformation*, i.e., false information shared without the intention to harm, (2) *disinformation*, false information shared to harm, or (3) *malinformation*, genuine information meant to be private, shared in public spheres for malicious purposes

[14]. This phenomenon is now widespread across all forms of media, influencing consumers to purchase products they do not need. Additionally, Information Disorder can result in even more serious consequences, particularly in the political and medical contexts, where misleading online content significantly affects consumer decisions [38]. The presence of online misleading information is not the only risk consumers face when navigating the web. The presence of poor quality or irrelevant content can overwhelm users, causing confusion and leading to misinformation due to the lack of clarity surrounding the content itself. This phenomenon, known as Information Pollution, can significantly impact the accuracy and reliability of information. Information Pollution is defined as the contamination of information on the Web in either an intentional or unintentional manner. This can occur through various means such as rumours, fake news, misinformation, disinformation, clickbait, hoaxes, satire or parody, opinion spam, propaganda, and conspiracy theories [37]. These elements can negatively impact society at large, but not necessarily with the intent to cause harm. A polluted information is often defined by its virality: such content often appears in short-lived bursts, spreads rapidly, and fades just as quickly [37]. According to the Global Digital Report 2019 [39], 4.3 billion Internet users and 3.4 billion Social Media users regularly create, diffuse, and interact with huge volumes of data, all of which happens significantly fast [37]. Nevertheless, most of the mainstream trends quickly become irrelevant and softly fade out, as people promptly turn their attention to something new. These attributes, therefore, influence how information on social networks, for example, is structured and presented. These days, even official news media tend to prioritise the creation of provocative snippets to grab readers' attention [37]. Many users have limited time to engage with the actual content, as they are consistently bombarded with a stream of information and face competition from various content creators. The motivation behind the spread of polluted information can include political manipulation, financial gain, ideological promotion, entertainment, and attention-seeking [37]. Moreover, misleading content can originate from diverse sources—bots, criminal or terrorist organisations, activists, governments, journalists, conspiracy theorists, individuals who benefit from fake information, and trolls [60]. Research underscores that false information spreads more widely and rapidly than truthful content, largely due to its novelty and emotional appeal [56]. More importantly, humans, rather than bots, are primarily responsible for this diffusion.

In the context of children, Information Pollution poses specific threats. Children are exposed to unreliable content that may be outdated, hard to understand, or even harmful, such as material promoting hate, violence, or cyberbullying [31]. For young users, Information Pollution includes content that is unnecessary, incorrect, or presented by non-experts in inconsistent or misleading formats [29,31]. This exposure can distort their understanding of the world during their developmental years, underscoring the need for more tailored interventions.

## 2.2 Children as Digital Information Consumers

*Children's Online Search Behaviour.* Children extensively use the Internet from an early age, representing a unique user group with specific search behaviours that notably differ from adults [18,34]. Although born in the digital era, they are not inherently skilled in evaluating online information. Their developmental stage, limited experience, and evolving technical and social competences make them extremely vulnerable to Information Pollution [20,42]. Furthermore, their reading skills are still developing, making it harder for them to adequately assess the credibility of content [27]. Like adults, children also vary significantly in their ability to evaluate the credibility and trustworthiness of information, which affects how they manage Information Pollution [1]. This is due to factors such as family background, socio-economic context, personality, education and access to technology [31,42]. For instance, teenagers from less advantaged households may spend more time engaging in passive or entertainment-oriented online activities, which can result in poor critical evaluation practices [42]. When performing school-related or leisure tasks, such as assignments, online games or search activities, children often encounter difficulties in evaluating the credibility of biased or deceptive content [1,32,33]. Numerous studies confirm that children, even in higher educational levels, struggle to discern reliable from unreliable sources [28,44,46]. They tend to adopt simplistic strategies to evaluate information credibility and consume it in an uncritical and superficial manner, rather than relying on an in-depth analysis [5,26]. Despite these young users are aware of the risks of unreliable content and recognize the importance of using multiple resources and safeguarding online privacy [1,20,31], their search habits show a dependency on superficial cues like author expertise, document type, and source familiarity rather than content analysis [20,26,42]. Finally, children typically frame their search queries in a natural language rather than keywords (70% and 30% respectively), and approximately half of them are reformulations [10]. Moreover, when facing a difficult search task, they often input entire assignment questions rather than elaborating more strategic queries [1].

*Children and Information Access Systems.* Children seem to prefer easily accessible and familiar IAS such as SE, Google Images, Wikipedia, and blog platforms [1]. Among these, SE remain the most commonly used, often seen as more credible due to their authoritative presentation and popularity [9,23,52]. This perception contributes to a strong reliance on top-ranked results of the Search Engine Result Pages (SERP), where children frequently accept the first returned link without exploring or comparing alternatives [1]. Their trust in source credibility is heavily influenced by contextual and visual cues [20,26]. However, IAS are evolving beyond traditional SE. Children are increasingly turning to search tools such as Large Language Model agents (LLM), voice-controlled assistants (e.g. Siri, Alexa), and social media platforms (e.g. YouTube, TikTok) to access online information [2]. LLM agents seem to be particularly beneficial for children, bypassing common challenges associated with SE, such as difficulty in query formulation, reliance on superficial link evaluation and tendency to search for specific answers without understanding the broader context [6,30]. Moreover, LLM can reduce cognitive load by providing more synthetic answers tailored to the proposed query, supporting children who may struggle with the cognitive overload provided by the amount of information sources listed in SERP. Although there are many positive uses for LLM, users, especially children, often depend on their responses, which can sometimes be incorrect. The phenomenon known as "hallucination" is a well-documented issue in foundation models. Additionally, these models can be influenced by biases present in their training data, leading them to favour responses that reflect the existing beliefs and values of the child [58]. Beyond LLM, social media platforms and voice-controlled assistants have become usual IAS among children. While platforms such as YouTube or TikTok offer intuitive and engaging ways to reach information, they expose these young users to content more passively, often without intentionally searching for something or verifying the content itself [19,22]. Crucially, the expansion of IAS to include generative AI, social media platforms, and voice-controlled assistants has exacerbated children's exposure to Information Pollution. Since children tend to rely on surface-level variables and have limited critical skills, the growing complexity and absence of transparency beyond these tools make it even harder for them to distinguish between reliable and deceptive information. This emphasises the importance of understanding the factors that affect how children determine the reliability of information in the vast array of online information sources, focusing on improving tools and educational solutions that support online search activities and evaluation skills tailored to these young users.

*Serious Games as Educational Tools.* Play has long been a central part of human development and engagement across all ages, valued for its rewarding, enjoyable, and motivating nature [3,49]. In recent decades, the rise of digital games has taken this activity to new dimensions. At the same time, students are showing decreasing interest in traditional teaching methods, emphasising the need for more dynamic and engaging educational approaches [3]. Given the popularity of digital games and their potential to align with students' interests and learning styles, educators have increasingly adopted serious games –digital games designed primarily for educational rather than entertainment purposes– as effective tools for learning [3,8,25,54]. This approach is commonly referred to as Digital Game-Based Learning (**DGBL**) [3]. Serious games are generally understood as interactive digital experiences that aim to educate while engaging users through game mechanics [5]. According to previous research [3], serious games offer numerous benefits to learners, including:

- Cognitive development and digital literacy
- Social-emotional growth and soft skills enhancement
- Improved decision-making, critical thinking, and problem-solving
- Encouragement of collaboration and communication
- A constructive and positively competitive environment
- Increased self-esteem and learner autonomy
- Experiential, progressive learning
- A rewarding sense of achievement and progression

– Feedback-driven, student-centred engagement

A clear example of serious games' impact is *Bad News*, a game designed to teach media literacy and combat misinformation among Swedish upper-secondary students. In the study, 516 teenagers played with the game to significantly improve their ability in identifying and resisting manipulative social media content, engaging them in critical media and information literacy practices [5]. Similarly, other research has shown how digital games can be used to teach critical thinking in the context of false or misleading information [51]. The effectiveness of serious games is driven by several interconnected factors. Research has shown that students exhibit higher levels of concentration and engagement during DGBL compared to traditional instructional methods [50]. This is largely due to the integration of educational material into an enjoyable and interactive game environment, which fosters emotional involvement and personal relevance [48]. Additionally, motivation in digital gameplay has been found to stem from three main components: *Achievement* (advancement, mechanics, competition), *Social interaction* (socializing, relationships, teamwork), and *Immersion* (discovery, role-playing, customization) [59]. These same motivational drivers can make serious games especially effective in educational contexts by keeping students engaged, motivated, and willing to invest long-term effort in learning. In summary, serious games seem to provide valuable benefits in educational settings, making them an alternative to traditional instruction. They are particularly well-suited for educating younger users about complex and evolving challenges by combining cognitive skill development with emotionally engaging and immersive learning experiences.

## 3    Concept Definition

To better understand the factors influencing how these young users assess the reliability of information, we designed an educational game for children aged 9 to 11, originally titled **Finding Nemo** (see Fig. 2a). This game is inspired by a well-known Pixar Animation Studios movie [53] and adopts the metaphor of Ocean Noise Pollution to raise awareness about Information Pollution in digital environments. According to the National Oceanic and Atmospheric Administration (NOAA), Ocean Noise Pollution refers to *"the spread of sounds made by human activities that can interfere with or obscure the ability of marine animals to hear natural sounds in the ocean"* [40]. The choice of an underwater environment is closely linked to how children perceive the sea world. Since a young age, in fact, children's cultural experiences are primarily shaped by the school and multimedia content tailored for them [47]. Animation studios, such as the Walt Disney Company, and children's television networks, like Nickelodeon, have released numerous underwater-themed cartoons, including *Finding Nemo, The Little Mermaid,* and *SpongeBob SquarePants* [4,24,53] that influence children's perception of marine ecosystems. In these productions, underwater life is often depicted as being similar to human life and showcases the mysterious nature of ocean creatures. As a result of this influence, along with related curriculum activities in educational settings, primary school children develop a strong foundational understanding of ocean science and marine species. Recently, several serious games have been created within an underwater setting to promote environmental awareness and sustainable behaviour toward marine life among younger generations [55]. Additionally, the introduction of science-related games provides a more inclusive and scalable approach, as it makes science accessible beyond the educational programs of specific countries [30]. Therefore, in our game, children are immersed in an underwater environment where human activities are causing significant harm to marine life. Their ultimate goal is to restore the ocean's ecosystem and return marine life to its natural state. Playing the role of a seahorse, they navigate the ocean overwhelmed by anthropogenic noise, the taxonomy of sounds to describe human impacts on marine species and ecosystems [45]. To win, they have to *clean* this environment by exploring the space and answering questions related to marine life. Each question offers multiple responses from various IAS –such as SE, voice-controlled assistants, and LLM– presented in different formats. Children must evaluate and select the most accurate answer based on both the content and the presentation of information. With each correct response, the underwater scene becomes clearer: human-made noise is reduced, while natural sounds begin to emerge, and marine life gradually pops up in the environment. This auditory and visual progression mirrors the process of navigating digital misinformation and restoring clarity through critical thinking. This dynamic system mirrors how learners can cut through digital clutter and recognize credible information. The goal of this game is, therefore, twofold:

- **Raise children's awareness of information pollution**: helping them identify, evaluate, and question diverse, conflicting, and potentially misleading online information sources.
- **Investigate how children perceive trustworthy information**: collecting insights into the cognitive and contextual factors that influence their choices when engaging with different IAS.

Using metaphor as a strategy in the design of this game is a deliberate choice. Metaphors help users understand new or abstract concepts by relating them to familiar experiences [13]. In the Human-Computer Interaction (**HCI**) field, metaphors are commonly used across interface design phases and are deeply rooted in human cognition. Even when not explicitly applied, users naturally draw on personal metaphors to interpret digital experiences [11]. Children in particular use metaphorical thinking as a natural way to make sense of abstract ideas, making this design approach suitable for the target age group. Therefore, adopting the metaphor of the disorientation of marine life caused by polluted waters to describe the overwhelming sensation when navigating the Web polluted with irrelevant or misleading information can help children to better understand the importance of a clear environment to find the correct direction for their answers.

## 3.1  Game Architecture and Usage Scenarios

Going deeper into the architecture of the game, we first designed the user flow (see Fig. 1) and UI elements in Figma, and developed the game with Unity Engine 2D, using Italian as the primary language.

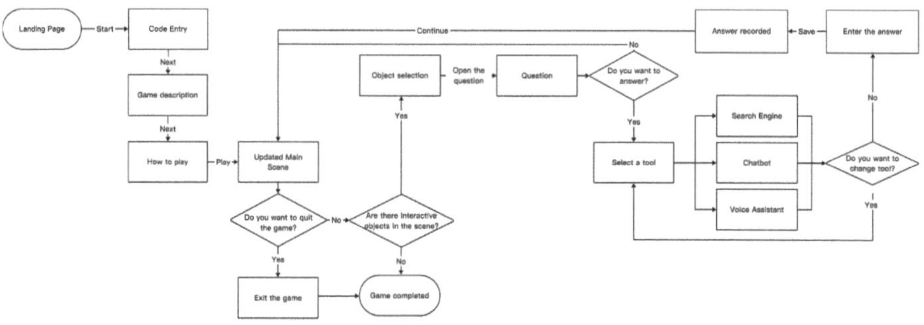

**Fig. 1.** User flow chart

*Landing and Session Code.* The game starts on the landing page (see Fig. 2a) that features the game logo and a brief introduction. After pressing "Inizia" (Start), players are directed to a session code input screen (see Fig. 2b), where they enter a unique code to anonymously track their gameplay data. A set of screens is, then, shown to the player, providing the game context and description, and giving instructions on how to play and win the game (see Fig. 3).

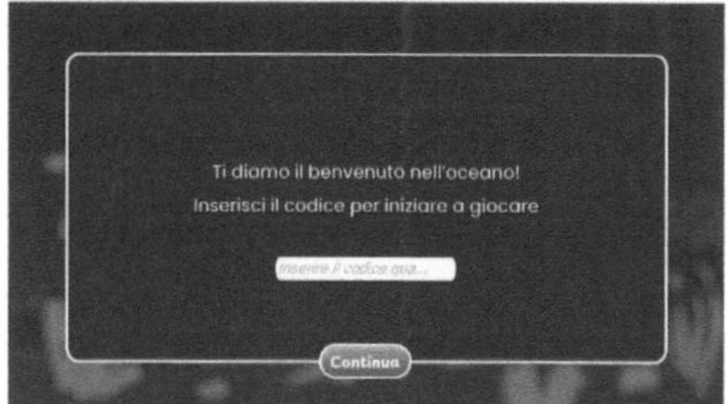


(a) Landing Page of the game                    (b) Session code input

**Fig. 2.** Finding Nemo initial screens

*Initial Scene and Controls.* Upon starting the game, players enter the underwater environment (see Fig. 4a) with minimal marine life and dominant anthropogenic sounds. They can control the seahorse Sally using the arrow keys on a computer or an on-screen joystick, designed to easily access the game on a tablet. An exit menu allows restarting or quitting the game at any time (see Fig. 4b).

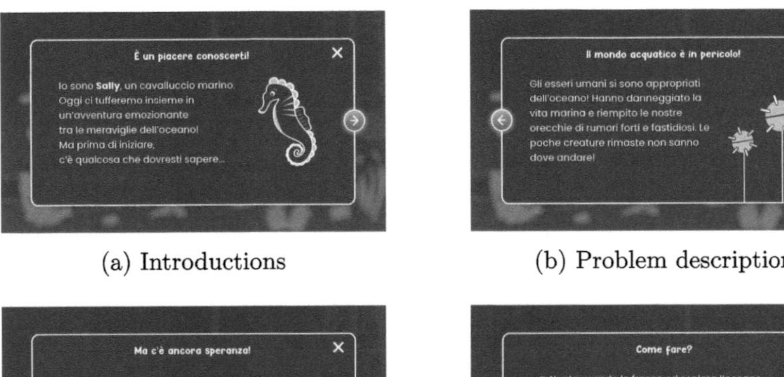


(a) Introductions                    (b) Problem description

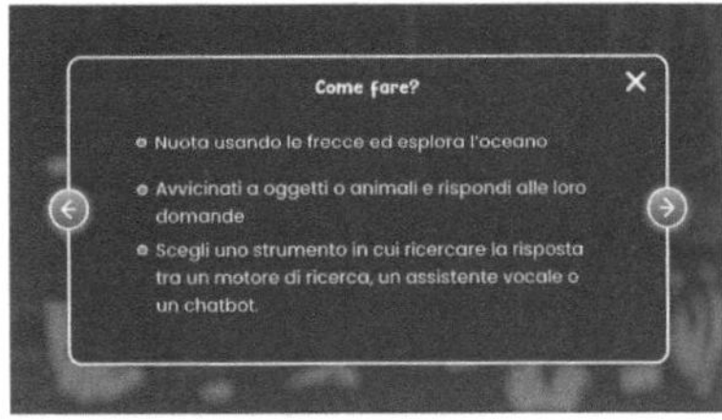


(c) Objective statement              (d) Game rules first screen

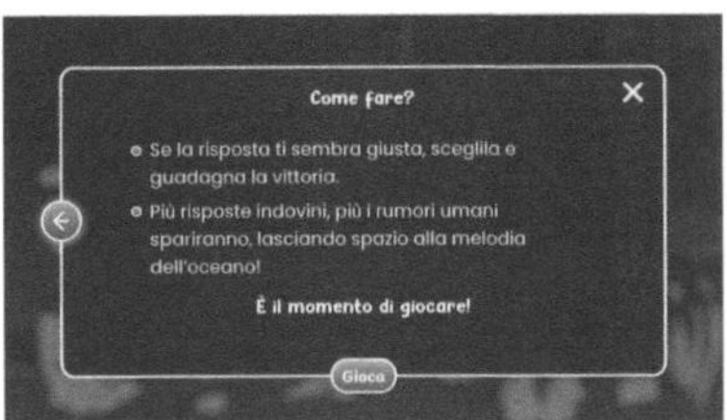


(e) Game rules second screen

**Fig. 3.** Game description and instructions

*Object Interactions and Tool Selection.* Once entering the underwater environment, players can interact with various objects. When approaching one of them, a message box appears with a related question (see Fig. 5). All questions are marine-related, tailored to the age of our target group: children between 9 and 11 years old. To answer a question, such as *"Quali sono i pericoli prodotti dall'uomo per le species animali?"* (What are the dangers posed by humans to animal species?), players can click "Rispondi" (Answer), which opens a tool selection panel offering three different IAS: a search engine, a chatbot, or a voice assistant (see Fig. 6a). Selecting, for instance, the voice assistant opens a panel (see Fig. 6b) where players can listen to a pre-recorded answer, and optionally submit their response. The chatbot panel (see Fig. 6c) presents a simulated conversation with Gemini, providing responses tailored to 9-year-old children. To ensure online safety, interactive input was deliberately restricted, so children can only submit the initial question. Similarly, the search engine panel (see Fig. 6d) displayed search results for the given question using Google as the primary search

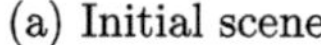

(a) Initial scene

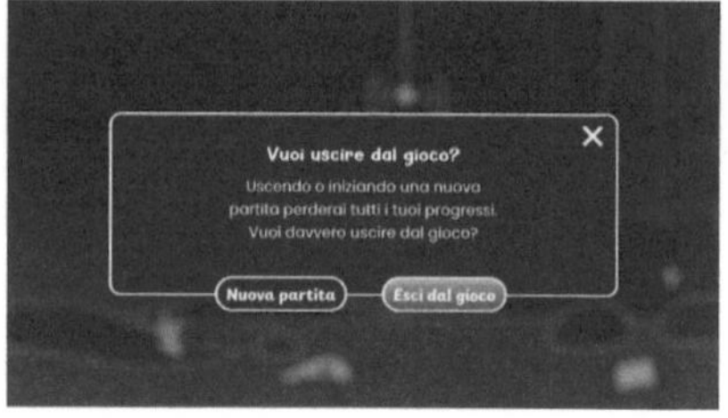


(b) Exit game pop-up

**Fig. 4.** Starting the game

engine. However, players can interact with the various results displayed in the Search Engine Result Page **(SERP)** to identify the most accurate answers. Once players select an IAS, they are always able to go back and switch the tool based on their assessment of the information, granting them complete control over their interaction with the game.

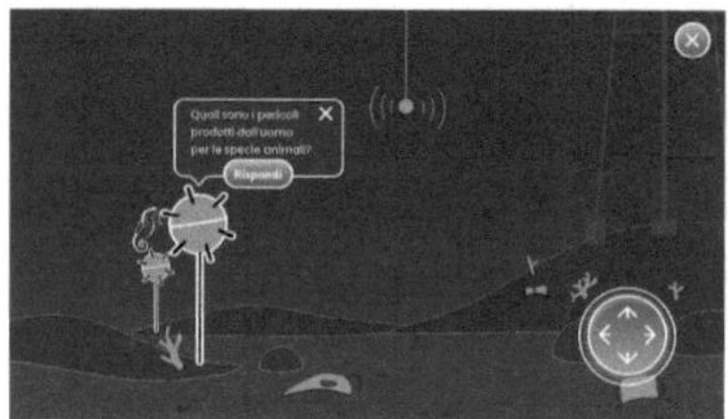


(a) Interaction with a bomb

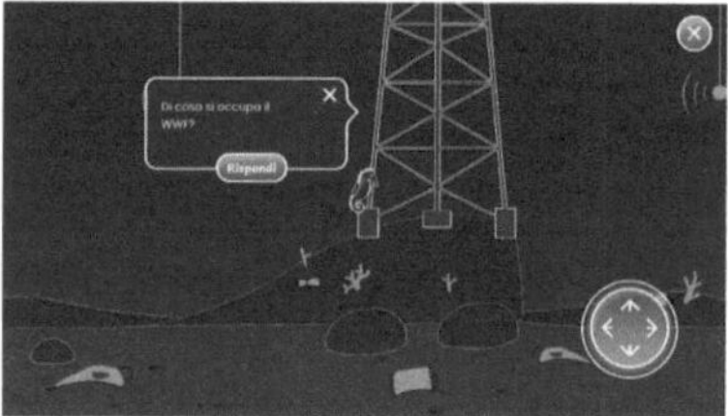


(b) Interaction with a metal structure

**Fig. 5.** Interactions with different objects in the scene

*Feedback and Scene Update.* After submitting an answer, a feedback screen confirms that the response was saved. If more questions remain, the game resumes with an updated environment, with more natural elements appearing and ambient sounds shifting accordingly. Alternatively, if the last question is answered, the final screen is shown, signifying the end of the game.

*Final Interactions.* The more questions have been answered, the more the scene is densely filled with various natural objects, and marine sounds can be clearly heard (see Fig. 7a). After answering the final question, the game transitions to a closing screen (see Fig. 7b), where researchers can download the players' responses and activity logs, while the players can start a new session or exit the game.

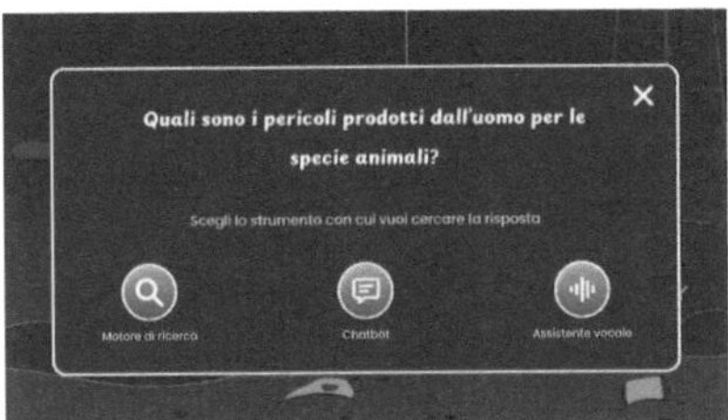

(a) Tool selection panel

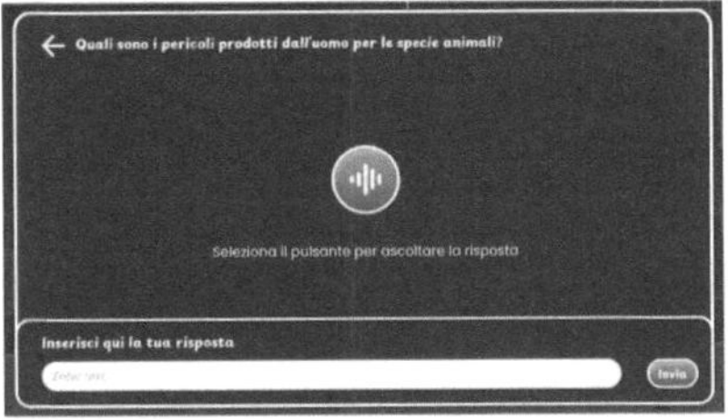

(b) Voice Assistant answer panel

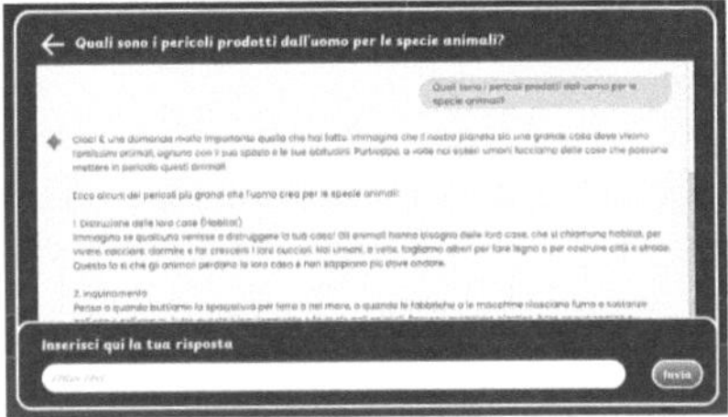

(c) Chatbot answer panel

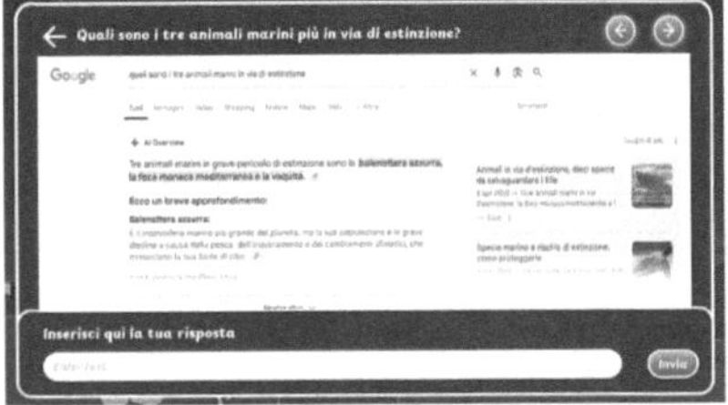

(d) Search Engine answer panel

**Fig. 6.** Available tools

(a) Final natural scene

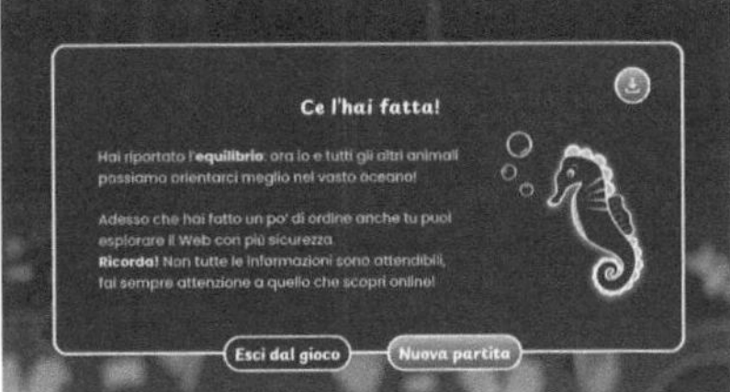

(b) Final screen

**Fig. 7.** End of the game

## 3.2   Game Development

*Scene Structure.* The development of the game was heavily influenced by Unity's scene-based architecture. Unity operates with a scene structure, where each game level or interface is a distinct *scene* within the project. Our game consists of a single scene that combines multiple functional areas, including the starting screen, the game area where players move and interact with various objects, the interaction panels where they answer questions, and the final screen to display game results and enable data downloads. The game itself is built around GameObjects, which are fundamental to Unity's system. These GameObjects represent the different interactive elements in the game, such as the player avatar, marine creatures, and objects that players can interact with. The game's logic is implemented using custom scripts written in C#, controlling the player's movement based on input from either an on-screen joystick or a keyboard, or tracking and storing player interactions, answers to questions, and tool usage.

*Embedded Information Access Systems.* Each IAS presented in the game is integrated within the game interface, allowing players to choose their preferred method for searching for the correct answers. The integration of these tools is accomplished using Unity's built-in UI system and external plugins. For example, to integrate the Google Search Engine, we used the unity-webview plugin, which allowed us to overlay a web view directly onto the game screen. This enables players to access the web directly without leaving the game environment. For both the chatbot and the voice assistant, we simulated the tool using the same GUI while adapting the output for a 9-year-old child. As players answer questions and progress through the game, their interactions and choices are tracked. All the selected queries pertain to a marine context and consist of fact-based, straightforward questions that require direct and precise answers. To ensure this, we utilized questions chosen by teachers from a previous study conducted by Landoni et al. [30] involving primary school children.

*Data Collection System.* The data collected during gameplay is stored in a session JSON file, uniquely identified by the session code entered at the beginning of the game. This data includes information such as the questions answered, tools used, the number of clicks, the list of clicked results, and the player's final responses. Importantly, this file can be downloaded at the end of the game or at any time if players choose to restart or exit before completing the session. The collection of data is not only vital for assessing player progress but also for research purposes, providing insights into the cognitive and contextual factors that influence children's choices when engaging with different IAS.

## 4   Conclusion and Future Work

By immersing players in a noisy underwater world and challenging them to restore clarity through informed decision-making, the goal of this serious game *Finding Nemo* is to promote critical thinking and digital literacy of children aged 9 to 11 years old about Information Pollution. The integration of various IAS encourages children to actively compare sources, fostering an understanding of how information is presented and perceived in the digital environment. The use of the metaphor not only enhances engagement but also serves as a cognitive bridge, helping children relate abstract concepts, such as Information Pollution, to more tangible experiences. While the current prototype establishes a promising starting point, several future directions are planned. A first step will involve expert reviews with teachers to ensure that the IAS tools embedded in the game are both safe and appropriate for our target group. Building on this, an empirical study with children will assess their engagement with the game and provide insights into how they interact with and evaluate the different information sources presented. In parallel, in-game data such as tool selection, response accuracy, and timing will be analyzed to gain a deeper understanding of children's information-seeking behaviours and their underlying decision-making processes. These behavioural patterns can help us identify what features most influence their perception of source credibility and how they navigate conflicting or misleading information. An important future improvement involves incorporating scaffolding mechanisms to support children in making informed choices. Currently, the game offers no embedded guidance on how to interpret or evaluate the information presented. Exploring how different types and levels of scaffolding impact learning outcomes –particularly in terms of credibility assessment and source comparison– can be a valuable area of research. Iterative design and testing with both children and educators can help us develop age-appropriate and effective scaffolding strategies that seamlessly integrate into the game flow. In conclusion, this work contributes to the growing field of educational serious games, showing how metaphor and narrative can support complex learning goals. Through playful interaction, Finding Nemo not only encourages children to search but also equips them with the critical skills to search for learning [16], preparing them for the challenges of an increasingly complex digital information environment.

**Declaration on Generative AI** During the preparation of this work, the author(s) used Grammarly to correct any grammatical or phrasing errors. No sections in the manuscript have been created using Generative AI tool(s)/service(s).

**Acknowledgments.** Supported by SNSF Award #[IC00I0-227887 project n.10000973 SOL]

**Disclosure of Interests.** The authors have no competing interests to declare that are relevant to the content of this article.

# References


1. Abdullah, N., Basar, S.: How children gauge information trustworthiness in online search: credible or convenience searcher? Pakistan J. Inf. Manage. Libr. **21** (2020). http://111.68.103.26/journals/index.php/pjiml/article/view/1468
2. Anandhan, A., Shuib, L., Ismail, M.A., Mujtaba, G.: Social media recommender systems: review and open research issues. IEEE Access **6**, 15608–15628 (2018). https://doi.org/10.1109/ACCESS.2018.2810062
3. Anastasiadis, T., Lampropoulos, G., Siakas, K.: Digital game-based learning and serious games in education. Int. J. Adv. Sci. Res. Eng. (IJASRE) **4**(12), 139–144 (2018). ISSN2454-8006. https://doi.org/10.31695/IJASRE. https://ijasre.net/index.php/ijasre/article/view/814
4. Walt Disney Feature Animation: The Little Mermaid (1989). https://en.wikipedia.org/wiki/The_Little_Mermaid_(1989_film)
5. Axelsson, C.A.W., Nygren, T., Roozenbeek, J., van der Linden, S.: Bad news in the civics classroom: how serious gameplay fosters teenagers' ability to discern misinformation techniques. J. Res. Technol. Educ., 1–27 (2024). https://doi.org/10.1080/15391523.2024.2338451

6. Azpiazu, I.M., Dragovic, N., Pera, M.S., Fails, J.A.: Online searching and learning: Yum and other search tools for children and teachers. Inf. Retriev. J. **20**, 524–545 (2017)

7. Barzilai, S., Chinn, C.A.: A review of educational responses to the "post-truth" condition: four lenses on "post-truth" problems. Educ. Psychol. **55**(3), 107–119 (2020). https://doi.org/10.1080/00461520.2020.1786388

8. Beck, J., Wade, M.: The Kids are Alright: How the Gamer Generation is Changing the Workplace, January 2006

9. Biddix, J.P., Chung, C.J., Park, H.W.: Convenience or credibility? A study of college student online research behaviors. Internet High. Educ. **14**(3), 175–182 (2011). https://doi.org/10.1016/j.iheduc.2011.01.003. https://www.sciencedirect.com/science/article/pii/S1096751611000042

10. Bilal, D., Gwizdka, J.: Children's query types and reformulations in Google search. Inf. Process. Manage. **54**(6), 1022–1041 (2018). https://doi.org/10.1016/j.ipm.2018.06.008. https://www.sciencedirect.com/science/article/pii/S0306457317308889

11. Blackwell, A.F.: The reification of metaphor as a design tool. ACM Trans. Comput. Hum. Interact. **13**(4), 490–530 (2006). https://doi.org/10.1145/1188816.1188820

12. Breakstone, J., et al.: Students' civic online reasoning: a national portrait. Educ. Res. **50**(8), 505–515 (2021). https://doi.org/10.3102/0013189X211017495

13. Casakin, H.P.: Assessing the use of metaphors in the design process. Environ. Plan. B Plan. Des. **33**(2), 253–268 (2006). https://doi.org/10.1068/b3196

14. Chakrabarti, H., Micol, T.D., Landoni, M., Pera, M.S.: Online information disorder & children (2025)

15. Coiro, J., Coscarelli, C., Maykel, C., Forzani, E.: Investigating criteria that seventh graders use to evaluate the quality of online information. J. Adolesc. Adult Literacy **59**(3), 287–297 (2015). https://doi.org/10.1002/jaal.448. https://ila.onlinelibrary.wiley.com/doi/abs/10.1002/jaal.448

16. Collins-Thompson, K., Hansen, P., Hauff, C.: Search as learning (Dagstuhl Seminar 17092) (2017)

17. Directorate-General for Communications Networks, Content and Technology: Better internet for kids - bik portal - bik community (2022). https://better-internet-for-kids.europa.eu/en

18. Danovitch, J.H.: Growing up with Google: how children's understanding and use of internet-based devices relates to cognitive development. Hum. Behav. Emerg. Technol. **1**(2), 81–90 (2019). https://doi.org/10.1002/hbe2.142. https://onlinelibrary.wiley.com/doi/abs/10.1002/hbe2.142

19. Adobe Express: Using TikTok as a search engine | adobe express, March 2024. https://www.adobe.com/express/learn/blog/using-tiktok-as-a-search-engine

20. Flanagin, A., Metzger, M.: The perceived credibility of online encyclopedias among children, January 2010

21. Gunther, R., Beck, P.A., Nisbet, E.C.: "fake news" and the defection of 2012 Obama voters in the 2016 presidential election. Electoral Stud. **61**, 102030 (2019). https://doi.org/10.1016/j.electstud.2019.03.006. https://www.sciencedirect.com/science/article/pii/S0261379418303019

22. Haan, K.: Is social media the new Google? Gen Z turn to Google 25% less than Gen X when searching, June 2024. https://www.forbes.com/advisor/business/software/social-media-new-google/

23. Hargittai, E., Fullerton, L., Menchen-Trevino, E., Thomas, K.: Trust online: young adults' evaluation of web content. Int. J. Commun. **4**, 468–494 (2010)

24. Hillenburg, S.: SpongeBob SquarePants (1999). https://en.wikipedia.org/wiki/SpongeBob_SquarePants
25. Huizenga, J., Admiraal, W., Akkerman, S., Dam, G.: Mobile game-based learning in secondary education: engagement, motivation and learning in a mobile city game. J. Comp. Assist. Learn. **25**, 332–344 (2009). https://doi.org/10.1111/j.1365-2729.2009.00316.x
26. Hämäläinen, E.K., Kiili, C., Marttunen, M., Räikkönen, E., González-Ibáñez, R., Leppänen, P.H.: Promoting sixth graders' credibility evaluation of web pages: an intervention study. Comput. Hum. Behav. **110**, 106372 (2020). https://doi.org/10.1016/j.chb.2020.106372. https://www.sciencedirect.com/science/article/pii/S0747563220301254
27. Kanniainen, L., Kiili, C., Tolvanen, A., Aro, M., Leppänen, P.H.T.: Literacy skills and online research and comprehension: struggling readers face difficulties online. Read. Writ. **32**(9), 2201–2222 (2019). https://doi.org/10.1007/s11145-019-09944-9
28. Kiili, C., Räikkönen, E., Bråten, I., Strømsø, H.I., Hagerman, M.S.: Examining the structure of credibility evaluation when sixth graders read online texts. J. Comput. Assist. Learn. **39**(3), 954–969 (2023). https://doi.org/10.1111/jcal.12779. https://onlinelibrary.wiley.com/doi/abs/10.1111/jcal.12779
29. Kurt, A.A., Emiroğlu, B.G.: Analysis of students' online information searching strategies, exposure to internet information pollution and cognitive absorption levels based on various variables. Malays. Online J. Educ. Technol. **6**(1), 18–29 (2018). https://mojet.net/index.php/mojet/article/view/118
30. Landoni, M., Matteri, D., Murgia, E., Huibers, T., Pera, M.S.: Sonny, Cerca! evaluating the impact of using a vocal assistant to search at school. In: Experimental IR Meets Multilinguality, Multimodality, and Interaction: Proceedings of the 10th International Conference of the CLEF Association, CLEF 2019, Lugano, Switzerland, 9–12 September 2019, pp. 101–113. Springer, Heidelberg (2019). https://doi.org/10.1007/978-3-030-28577-7_6
31. Landoni, M., Murgia, E., Huibers, T., Pera, M.S.: How does information pollution challenge children's right to information access? In: CEUR Workshop Proceedings, vol. 3406, pp. 17–29 (2023)
32. Large, A., Nesset, V., Beheshti, J.: Children as information seekers: what researchers tell us. New Rev. Child. Lit. Librarianship **14**(2), 121–140 (2008). https://doi.org/10.1080/13614540902812631
33. Livingstone, S., Helsper, E.: Parental mediation of children's internet use. J. Broadcast. Electron. Media **52**, 581–599 (2008). https://doi.org/10.1080/08838150802437396
34. Livingstone, S., Mascheroni, G., Staksrud, E.: European research on children's internet use: assessing the past and anticipating the future. New Media Soc. **20**(3), 1103–1122 (2018). https://doi.org/10.1177/1461444816685930
35. Macedo-Rouet, M., et al.: How good is this page? Benefits and limits of prompting on adolescents' evaluation of web information quality. Reading Res. Q. **54**(3), 299–321 (2019). https://doi.org/10.1002/rrq.241. https://ila.onlinelibrary.wiley.com/doi/abs/10.1002/rrq.241
36. Meel, P., Vishwakarma, D.K.: Fake news, rumor, information pollution in social media and web: a contemporary survey of state-of-the-arts, challenges and opportunities. Exp. Syst. Appl. **153**, 112986 (2020). https://doi.org/10.1016/j.eswa.2019.112986. https://www.sciencedirect.com/science/article/pii/S0957417419307043

37. Meel, P., Vishwakarma, D.K.: Fake news, rumor, information pollution in social media and web: a contemporary survey of state-of-the-arts, challenges and opportunities. Exp. Syst. Appl. **153**, 112986 (2020). https://doi.org/10.1016/j.eswa.2019.112986. https://www.sciencedirect.com/science/article/pii/S0957417419307043

38. Munger, K., Egan, P.J., Nagler, J., Ronen, J., Tucker, J.: Political knowledge and misinformation in the era of social media: evidence from the 2015 UK election. Brit. J. Polit. Sci. **52**(1), 107–127 (2022)

39. Newman, N., Fletcher, R., Kalogeropoulos, A., Levy, D., Nielsen, R.K.: Reuters Institute Digital News Report 2018 (2018). https://ssrn.com/abstract=3245355

40. NOAA: What is ocean noise? (2024). https://oceanservice.noaa.gov/facts/oceannoise.html#:~:text=Ocean%20noise%20refers%20to%20sounds,to%20hear%20for%20their%20survival

41. Nygren, T., Guath, M.: Swedish teenagers' difficulties and abilities to determine digital news credibility. Nordicom Rev. **40**, 23–42 (2019). https://doi.org/10.2478/nor-2019-0002

42. Nygren, T., Guath, M., Axelsson, C.A.W., Frau-Meigs, D.: Combatting visual fake news with a professional fact-checking tool in education in France, Romania, Spain and Sweden. Information **12**(5) (2021). https://doi.org/10.3390/info12050201. https://www.mdpi.com/2078-2489/12/5/201

43. Okan, O., Bollweg, T.M., Berens, E.M., Hurrelmann, K., Bauer, U., Schaeffer, D.: Coronavirus-related health literacy: a cross-sectional study in adults during the Covid-19 infodemic in Germany. Int. J. Environ. Res. Public Health **17**(15) (2020). https://doi.org/10.3390/ijerph17155503. https://www.mdpi.com/1660-4601/17/15/5503

44. Pieschl, S., Sivyer, D.: Secondary students' epistemic thinking and year as predictors of critical source evaluation of internet blogs. Comput. Educ. **160**, 104038 (2021). https://doi.org/10.1016/j.compedu.2020.104038. https://www.sciencedirect.com/science/article/pii/S0360131520302360

45. Pijanowski, B.C., et al.: Soundscape ecology: the science of sound in the landscape. BioScience **61**(3), 203–216 (2011). https://doi.org/10.1525/bio.2011.61.3.6

46. Potocki, A., et al.: The development of source evaluation skills during adolescence: exploring different levels of source processing and their relationships (el desarrollo de las habilidades de evaluación de las fuentes durante la adolescencia: una exploración de los distintos niveles de procesamiento de las fuentes y sus relaciones). J. Study Educ. Dev. **43**(1), 19–59 (2020). https://doi.org/10.1080/02103702.2019.1690848. https://journals.sagepub.com/doi/abs/10.1080/02103702.2019.1690848

47. Poyntz, S., Hoechsmann, M.: Children's media culture in a digital age. Sociol. Compass **5**, 488–498 (2011). https://doi.org/10.1111/j.1751-9020.2011.00393.x

48. Protopsaltis, A., Pannese, L., Pappa, D., Hetzner, S.: Serious games and formal and informal learning. E-Learning Papers (2011)

49. Rieber, L.P., Smith, L., Noah, D.: The value of serious play. Educ. Technol. **38**(6), 29–37 (1998)

50. Ronimus, M., Kujala, J., Tolvanen, A., Lyytinen, H.: Children's engagement during digital game-based learning of reading: the effects of time, rewards, and challenge. Comput. Educat. **71**, 237–246 (2014). https://doi.org/10.1016/j.compedu.2013.10.008

51. Schrier, K.: We the Gamers: How Games Teach Ethics and Civics, May 2021. https://doi.org/10.1093/oso/9780190926106.001.0001

52. Shuib, L., Noorhidawati, A.: How graduate students seek for information: convenience or guaranteed result? Malaysian J. Libr. Inf. Sci. **19**, 1–15 (2014)

53. Studios, P.A.: Finding Nemo (2003). https://www.pixar.com/finding-nemo
54. Tsai, F.H., Yu, K.C., Hsiao, H.S.: Exploring the factors influencing learning effectiveness in digital game- based learning. Educ. Technol. Soc. **15** (2012)
55. Veronica, R., Calvano, G.: Promoting sustainable behavior using serious games: seadventure for ocean literacy. IEEE Access **8**, 196931–196939 (2020). https://doi.org/10.1109/ACCESS.2020.3034438
56. Vosoughi, S., Roy, D., Aral, S.: The spread of true and false news online. Science **359**(6380), 1146–1151 (2018). https://doi.org/10.1126/science.aap9559. https://www.science.org/doi/abs/10.1126/science.aap9559
57. Wardle, C., Derakhshan, H.: Information disorder: toward an interdisciplinary framework for research and policymaking, vol. 27. Council of Europe Strasbourg (2017)
58. White, R.W.: Advancing the search frontier with AI agents (2024). https://arxiv.org/abs/2311.01235
59. Yee, N.: Motivations for play in online games. CyberPsychol. Behav. **9**(6), 772–775 (2006). https://doi.org/10.1089/cpb.2006.9.772
60. Zannettou, S., Sirivianos, M., Blackburn, J., Kourtellis, N.: The web of false information: rumors, fake news, hoaxes, clickbait, and various other shenanigans. J. Data Inf. Q. **11**(3), 1–37 (2019). https://doi.org/10.1145/3309699

# Sign Language Based Conversational Product Search

Ruichong Peng[✉], Haojie Liu, Daniel Braghis, and Haiming Liu[✉]

Electronics and Computer Science, University of Southampton, University Road,
Southampton SO17 1BJ, UK
`{rp10g22,hl15n21,h.liu}@soton.ac.uk.it, ddb1u20@southamptonalumni.ac.uk`

**Abstract.** Though accessibility is one of the fundamental principles of inclusive design, the majority of product search systems are not sign language input-friendly, while sign language is an important means of communication for individuals with hearing or speaking disabilities. However, it is rarely used in search systems. In this work, we introduce a sign language translation module that strives to fill this gap by incorporating gesture-based interaction in DoodleShoper, a conversational product search assistant [5]. The system captures hand gestures using vision-based recognition [4] and converts them into textual output. These sentences are often incomplete or follow non-standard word order due to the structural nature of sign language. To address this, a large language model (ChatGPT) is employed to reconstruct coherent, contextually appropriate sentences by reordering and completing the recognized text. The refined result is then passed to DoodleShoper, enabling users to perform visual searches through conversational queries. This integration makes it possible for sign language users to access online visual information, such as products or related concepts, through gestures alone. By bridging gesture-based input with natural language and visual search, the system expands the usability of DoodleShoper and demonstrates a practical pathway for multimodal, AI-driven accessibility tools.

**Keywords:** Sign Language Translation · Gesture Recognition · Conversational Search · Accessibility

## 1 Introduction

According to a report by the World Health Organization (WHO), over 430 million people worldwide live with disabling hearing loss [20]. While not all of them use sign language, many individuals who have profound or early-onset hearing loss rely on sign language as their primary means of communication. In the UK, the British Deaf Association (BDA) estimates that there are 151,000 people who use British Sign Language (BSL), among whom 87,000 are Deaf [6]. However, digital tools and interfaces remain largely optimized for users of spoken and written languages, making them less accessible for those who rely on BSL.


A. Bellogin et al. (Eds.): IR4U2 2025/BIAS 2025, CCIS 2786, pp. 110–126, 2026.
https://doi.org/10.1007/978-3-032-12717-4_8

Even with the increased provision of broadband internet and multimedia media, deaf users continue to experience notable obstacles in accessing internet information. Previous research [10] identified that deaf users tend to experience difficulties with text-based information, which can be attributed to lower literacy levels or inherent structural differences between written and sign languages. Hence, conventional websites may still remain a challenge for these users to access meaningfully. Such challenges emphasize the necessity of developing web systems that directly provide sign language input and output, for example, via gesture recognition or inline video translation.

Meanwhile, the recent development of deep learning re-energized the research area of Sign Language Recognition (SLR). Al-Qurishi et al. [1] observed that although different SLR models showed encouraging performances in static or isolated gestures, they continue to face challenges in real-time continuous translation and are still limited in generalization across various distinct vocabularies and sign languages. Furthermore, most models are dependent to a large extent on big annotated datasets, which are particularly lacking in regional sign languages such as BSL. These constraints indicate substantial research gaps, especially in building systems that integrate sign language recognition and natural language comprehension and facilitate conversational tasks such as product search.

The platform used in this project, Doodleshoper (Braghis and Liu, 2024) [5], is a sketch-based product search tool that allows users to find products through natural language dialogue and product sketches. While DoodleShoper supported only text and sketch input, which made it less accessible for users who rely on sign language. To improve accessibility, this study integrates an SLR module into DoodleShoper, allowing users to search for products by signing. The recognized gestures are translated into text and sent to the backend for retrieving relevant product websites. In doing so, the project addresses critical gaps in accessibility, contributes to applied research on deep learning-based SLR, and explores the feasibility of combining gesture input with conversational search systems.

While recent advances in Sign Language Production (SLP) have focused on generating photo-realistic videos from spoken or written input, such as SIGN-GAN [19], which translates text into continuous sign language videos using a pose-conditioned GAN architecture. Their aim is to improve the delivery of spoken content to Deaf users through synthetic signers. However, comparatively little research has explored the reverse direction, where sign language serves as the input modality for digital interaction. This gap is particularly evident in the domain of information retrieval and dialogue-based interfaces, where users initiate queries through gesture-based input. In contrast to production-focused systems, this project investigates how British Sign Language (BSL) can be used as a primary interaction mechanism for a conversational image search platform. By integrating a deep learning-based SLR module into DoodleShoper, the system allows BSL users to issue queries by signing, thereby contributing to the underexplored area of sign language-driven search and addressing a significant accessibility gap in interactive web systems.

This leads to the core research question of this study: *How can a Sign Language Recognition (SLR) module be integrated into a conversational search system and used to generate relevant search queries that support gesture-based product retrieval for British Sign Language (BSL) users?* The aim of this research is to further answer this questions based on the existing work through designing, prototyping and evaluating a sign language based product search tool.

## 2 Literature Review

This section reviews the related literatures and methods of the project, which includes Mediapipe, DoodleShoper, Convolutional Neural Network and insights into the syntactic structure of sign language. Each of which will be detailed in the following sections.

### 2.1 Mediapipe

Mediapipe is an open-source library developed by Google for pose tracking and gesture recognition. It is used in this project for obtaining 21 hand key points (see Fig. 1) from captured video frames [21]. The key points are the wrist and major parts of the hand, including fingertips and joints [15].

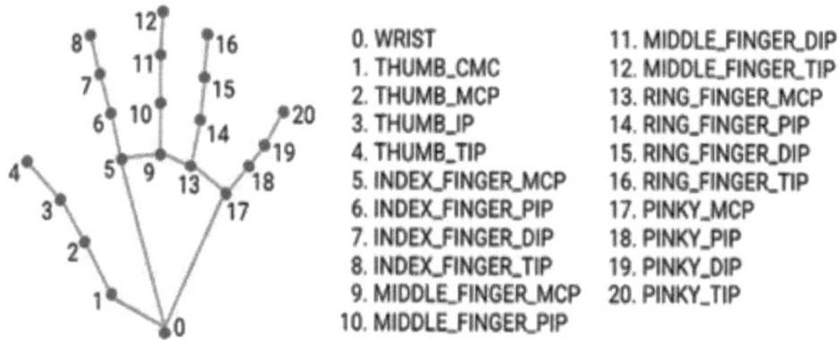


**Fig. 1.** Mediapipe Landmarks.

The spatial coordinates of these significant points are then analyzed to determine the location and configuration of the hand. All of this information is provided as input for the gesture recognition algorithm. This method yields more precise and consistent results in recognizing different hand gestures than traditional computer vision methods that operate on full images.

### 2.2 DoodleShoper

DoodleShoper [5] is a sketch-based product search tool, that is developed to enable more effective product search with the help of text along with sketch input. This project extends the DoodleShoper tool by adding sign language input for more accessible product search.

To enable the transformation of visual inputs into search queries, DoodleShoper, an assistant originally designed for sketch-based interactions, was extended to support sign language gestures as well. It allows users to search for product images on the web with the help of text along with sketch input. The system integrates Large Language Models (LLMs), such as GPT Assistants, with ControlNet-based Stable Diffusion. Then, it creates intermediary images from user-sketches and conducts reverse image searches through Google Lens. The system is characterized by modularity, permitting the flexible use of various search engines and picture-making tools. The inherent modularity in this system facilitates multimodal interaction and overcomes the limitations of solely text-based requests.

DoodleShoper demonstrates the potential of visual engagement and multimodal retrieval techniques within the context of this project. This is similar to the goal of interacting with an image search engine using sign language movements, which are a naturally visual communication tool. While DoodleShoper relies on hand-drawn sketches, our prototype aims to extend this by translating sign language gestures into search intents. This translation may occur either directly or through the generation of supplemental visual cues, thereby enriching the input modality landscape in conversational image search.

### 2.3  Convolutional Neural Network

Convolutional Neural Networks (CNNs) is applied to classify different sign gestures in the project.

Convolutional Neural Networks (CNNs) is a well-known deep learning model. As opposed to the original fully connected neural networks used in Sign Language Recognition system, CNNs are able to identify patterns within the data by reading localized regions in a sequential manner. CNNs employ convolutional layers to emphasize local features within the input data. In addition, pooling layers are used to reduce the dimensionality of the feature maps and to improve the model's robustness to variations in the input [17].

The basic architecture of a CNN typically consists of convolutional layers, activation functions such as ReLU, pooling layers, and fully connected layers. These components work together to extract features from the input data and perform classification tasks. In visual tasks, CNNs can learn simple patterns such as edges and motion, as well as more complex structures like gestures.

In this project, the input is not a normal image but a set of hand landmark points from MediaPipe. These points are turned into one-dimensional sequences Such sequences can be processed by 1D CNN layers to learn how joints move and relate to each other over time and space. Although O'Shea and Nash [17] mainly describe how CNNs work with 2D images, the key ideas—such as using shared weights, focusing on small local areas, and learning features layer by layer—can still be used in 1D CNNs [13]. This makes 1D CNNs a good choice for recognizing hand gestures in this project.

## 2.4   Challenges in Syntax of Sign Language

Since sign language is going to be applied to improve the accessibility and interaction, this section reviews the challenges of sign language translation.

Unlike spoken languages that typically rely on fixed word order—such as Subject-Verb-Object (SVO) in English—British Sign Language (BSL) demonstrates a more flexible syntactic structure. Studies have shown that BSL accepts variable word orders, especially those influenced by discourse formality and communicative context [8]. One commonly used sentence structure in BSL is the topic-comment format, where the main topic is introduced first, often accompanied by pauses or facial expressions to highlight it. In more formal contexts, signers may use word order similar to English (Subject-Verb-Object), but in daily conversations, topic-first constructions are more commonly used [8,11].

Sign languages often use space and movement at the same time to show grammar. Signers move their hands, face, and body to express who is doing what, the direction of the action, or how people are related. Because many parts of the body are used together, sign language grammar is more complicated to understand compared to spoken languages [8].

In addition, verbs in British Sign Language (BSL) possess the ability to indicate temporal aspects, quantity, and the relationship between people or entities. BSL verbs are generally classified into three types: plain verbs, agreement verbs, and spatial verbs. Each type alters its structure based on how the hands are placed and moved. There is evidence from some recent research that BSL verbs are becoming more flexible in actual use, with certain signs deviating from set forms. Although this allows signers greater liberty to express concepts in a natural way, it can also cause identification to be more problematic for computer systems [8].

In brief, British Sign Language possesses a complex grammatical structure. It employs spatial attributes, manual signs, facial expressions, and body orientation to impart meaning. These attributes distinguish it drastically from spoken languages that adhere to a rigid syntactic ordering. Thus, BSL presents more challenges to computational analysis and understanding. This situation presents challenges for linguists as much as for designers who seek to deploy systems capable of communicating in sign language [8].

## 2.5   Previous Work of Sign Language Based Interaction

Previous research in gesture-based systems has looked at different methods for helping machines understand visual input. Recent work by Deb et al. [9] explored a keypoint-based Transformer model for BSL recognition, but our project instead opts for a lightweight 1D CNN for simplicity due to the small dataset.

To understand this choice, it is helpful to revisit how CNNs have evolved as effective tools for pattern recognition. O'Shea and Nash introduced Convolutional Neural Networks (CNNs), demonstrating their ability to learn different levels of features. They also showed the success of CNNs in recognizing patterns in image and signal data [17]. Although their work mainly focused on 2D CNNs, the underlying architectural principles are equally applicable to 1D CNNs. Such 1D CNNs are often used for sequential or temporal inputs [13].

Building on these foundations, more recent studies have applied CNNs to sign language recognition tasks. Kumar, Singh, Bajpai, and Sinha developed a real-time recognition system for American Sign Language (ASL) that combined MediaPipe for hand landmark detection with a CNN-based classifier [14]. They achieved a high accuracy of 99.95% across 26 ASL letters by normalizing the landmark coordinates and turning them into 1D feature vectors. Their work demonstrated the effectiveness of pairing lightweight hand tracking with deep learning for gesture classification.

As an early attempt to apply sign language recognition in a web-based demonstration, one related study proposed a sign language translator web application based on deep learning [2]. Their system converts isolated hand gestures into voice output using a webcam and a CNN classifier. While this work demonstrates the feasibility of sign language input on the web, it does not support real-time interaction or integrate with any task-oriented application such as search or dialogue systems. The system operates in a standalone manner, lacking feedback or further interaction with the user.

This project extends Kumar et al.'s methodology in several key ways. Firstly, the system changes from ASL to British Sign Language (BSL), which comes with distinct syntactic and lexical challenges. Secondly, it refines the CNN-classified gesture outputs into coherent English phrases using a large language model (GPT), thus ensuring compatibility with conversational search flows. Finally, sign-based input has been directly integrated into DoodleShoper as a new method alternative to sketch- and text-based interaction. It allows users to search for images using sign language instead of drawing or typing. These improvements work together to make the system more inclusive and easier to use for people who prefer sign language.

### 2.6  Inclusive Design and Accessibility

Inclusive design emphasizes removing barriers, following the social model of disability, to enable individuals with impairments to achieve their goals independently [16]. A key principle is the deliberate attention to needs often neglected in conventional design, avoiding assumptions that may unintentionally marginalize users with disabilities [18]. Scholars argue that design should not focus solely on "typical" users or treat assistive technologies as mere addons but rather embrace the dynamic diversity of user capabilities through user-centered inclusive design practices [12]. This includes participatory design approaches where users with disabilities actively co-create systems to ensure that their lived experiences shape functionality and usability [3]. For example, while multimodal systems incorporating sign language have shown promise in improving accessibility for users with hearing or speech impairments, most search interfaces still lack support for gesture-based input [5]. Zheng et al. demonstrated that combining visual and textual input in conversational search interfaces enhances user engagement and may offer benefits for users with cognitive disabilities [22]. These findings highlight the value of inclusive design principles in building accessible, adaptive, and user-friendly interactive systems.

# 3   Methodology

This section describes the workflow of the sign language-based product search module, which is integrated into the existing DoodleShoper system (see Sect. 2.2). It also presents the design of the user experiment and evaluation.

## 3.1   Workflow of Sign Language Based Search Module

This section states the pipeline of the sign language based search module (See Fig. 2) that is added to the DoodleShoper system.

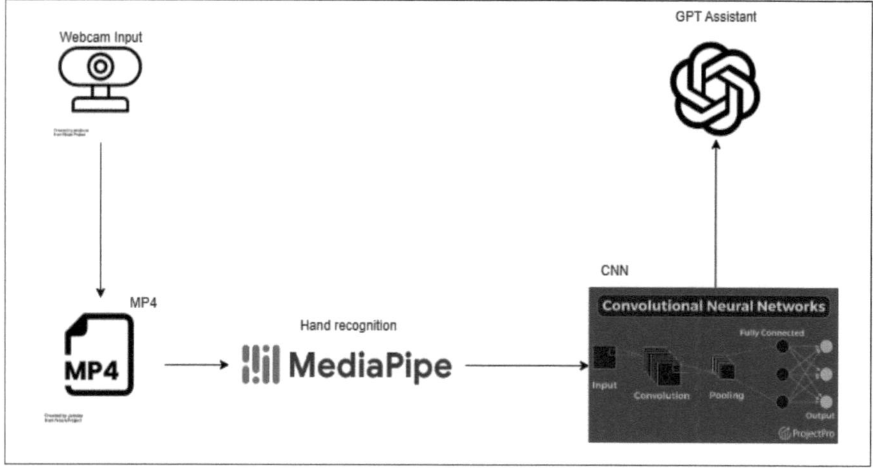


**Fig. 2.** Pipeline of the gesture classification module based on MediaPipe and CNN.

This project connects gesture recognition with natural language processing and image search. The process begins with the user performing sign language gestures in front of a camera. Instead of processing the live stream directly, the system saves the recording as a .mp4 file instead of .webm file. This is necessary because OpenCV, which helps extracting frames from videos in Sign Language Recognition system, cannot access pre-recorded .webm files in the current Docker environment. This conversion step ensures compatibility with the processing workflow and allows the system to proceed with frame-by-frame analysis.

Each frame is taken from a recorded video using OpenCV and sent to a hand landmark detection module. The 21 points in the hand are then detected from each frame by using MediaPipe. The coordinates are then converted to 1D vectors by flattening and normalizing them, in order to use them as input for the model.

The model is a 1D convolutional neural network (CNN), trained to recognize a set of hand points as a sign of a British Sign Language (BSL) word. This kind of neural network is better than fully connected networks used in the original recognition system because it can understand patterns in sequences and works faster.

However, because of the grammar of BSL, the model's output is often not complete or is in the wrong order. This reflects a broader challenge in sign language translation noted by Camgoz et al. [7], To address this, our system uses a large language model (ChatGPT) to transform incomplete SLR output into grammatically coherent and semantically accurate English queries. These queries are then used by DoodleShoper to find the right images based on what the user meant.

During development, many important choices are made. Instead of using live camera input, the system uses .mp4 video files. This makes testing easier and more stable, especially when running the system in Docker, where OpenCV cannot use live cameras easily. MediaPipe was chosen because it is fast, easy to use, and doesn't need extra training to detect hand landmarks.

**Fig. 3.** User Prompt.

To convert the output into meaningful search queries, ChatGPT is used in a post-processing stage. It takes the recognized words and restructures them into complete English phrases. To enhance contextual relevance, the system also includes the previous user prompt from DoodleShoper as part of GPT's input (see Fig. 3), helping the model produce more accurate and coherent queries that align with the ongoing conversation.

This design also makes the system flexible and maintainable and also allows components to easily be updated or swapped out without impacting the overall prototype. By encapsulating all of gesture recognition and text smoothing within DoodleShoper, the system is able to handle gesture-based multimodal search in a more accessible way for sign language users.

## 3.2  User Experiment Design

This section details the user experiment design preparation, task design and experiment procedure.

**User Experiment Preparation.** To see how well the system could handle real-world use, we invited eight students from the University of Southampton to take part in a hands on experiment. Each person was given a simple but meaningful task: to search for three everyday items, "a red cotton hat," "a black leather jacket," and "a red T-shirt" but instead of typing or drawing, they had to use British Sign Language (BSL).

The idea was straightforward: could the system understand people signing naturally, just as they would in real life? And more importantly, what would happen when those signs varied slightly from person to person? We weren't just looking for perfect results, we were curious about the messy moments too, when the system might struggle to keep up with different signing styles. This experiment gave us a chance to watch the system perform outside of perfect lab conditions, with all the unpredictability that real users bring.

**Task Design.** To maintain a fair and consistent testing environment, the vocabulary used in the experiment was limited to a set of 13 familiar words. These included common terms such as "red," "cotton," "hat," "leather," "jacket," and "T-shirt", all of which had already been used during the system's training. These words were chosen due to the limitations of the recognition system, which only supports static and single-handed signs. Keeping the queries within this known set ensured that the results reflected the system's actual recognition ability, rather than its response to unfamiliar gestures. This approach allowed the evaluation to stay focused on accuracy and stability, avoiding the noise that might come from untrained or unexpected signs.

**User Experiment Procedure.** Prior to trial onset, participants were briefly told that they would have to search for the three product objects: a red cotton cap, a black jacket, and a red T-shirt. In contrast to signing just the target item names, participants were asked to convey search intentions in terms of whole, natural BSL sentences. This meant that participants would, for instance, signal concepts like 'I' and 'want' as well as the target item. Signing single nouns would not communicate effectively.

For this, participants were provided with samples of potential sentence forms, and an opportunity to practice with the real-time recognition system before taking the official test. Participants with an interest in rehearsing were able to preview how their complete sentences were recognized by the system and fine-tune accordingly. The others went on to take part directly in the trial.

During the experiment, every participant signed the three product-based questions separately at a laptop containing an integrated camera. Each signing activity was captured and processed by the backend recognition module and provided a textual result. This result was then passed to the DoodleShoper platform in order to get image-based search results back (See Fig. 4). The outcomes were subsequently recorded and summarized in a results table (see Table 1).

This enabled more realistic use of language and made sure that the system was subjected to conditions that were nearer to real-life interaction scenarios.

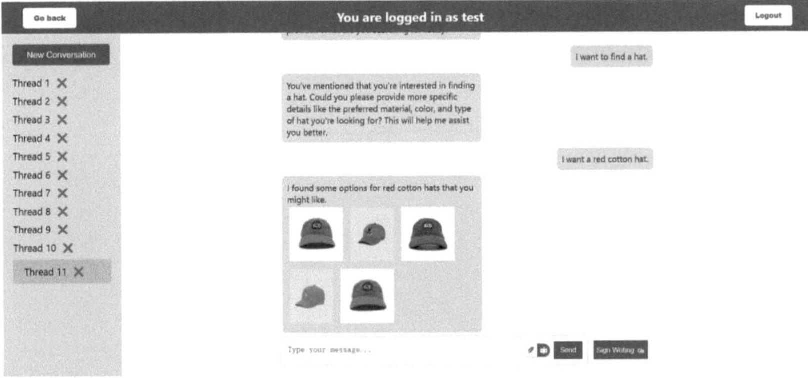

**Fig. 4.** Red Cotton Hat. (Color figure online)

## 4   User Experiment Results

The data was collected from eight participants, who are undergraduate university students with no experience of sign language communication, because the project team did have access to users who has sign language communication experience. This section will report the quantitative and qualitative data that are collected through interaction attempt counting and questionnaire that include multi choice questions and open questions.

### 4.1   Initial Sign Language Recognition Result

**Table 1.** Recognition Attempts (before the correct recognition)

| Participant | Red Cotton Hat | Black Leather T-shirt | Red T-shirt |
| --- | --- | --- | --- |
| 1 | 3 | 1 | failed (5) |
| 2 | 2 | 3 | 6 |
| 3 | 1 | 2 | 6 |
| 4 | 2 | 1 | 2 |
| 5 | 1 | 1 | 2 |
| 6 | 4 | 1 | 3 |
| 7 | 2 | 2 | 1 |
| 8 | 1 | 1 | 4 |

The outcome revealed significant variation in recognition success across different gestures. For 'red cotton hat' and 'black leather jacket' gestures, participants were mostly successful with one or three attempts. The most difficult was 'red

T-shirt' gesture: one participant (P1) failed to achieve any recognition and others (P2 and P3) took as much as six attempts. The initial success in this gesture was with only one participant (P7) on one attempt. The results reveal that the 'T-shirt' gesture is more difficult for the system to recognize reliably.

The difficulty can also stem from visual aspects of the gesture—close, flat hands against the body—and variation in camera angle that can result in landmark occlusion or deformation. One participant also had difficulty with 'red' containing gestures. Differences in finger lengths caused bent fingers to be misinterpreted as a closed fist, demonstrating how physical variation among users can influence recognition.

## 4.2   Search Performance Through Sign Language Interaction

For these discrepancies to be resolved, a confidence threshold was added to the classifier strategy. The model now uses a SoftMax probability distribution and only accepts predictions greater than a predetermined value. Although this adjustment didn't solve the problem of T-shirt recognition, it decreased errors and made the entire system more resilient.

Table 2 presents the recognition performance for each of the three product-based queries. For "red cotton hat" and "black leather jacket," the system achieved a 100% recognition success rate. The average number of attempts required were 2.0 and 1.5 respectively, with maximum attempts of 4 and 3 (see Table 2).

In contrast, the "red T-shirt" gesture proved more challenging. Its recognition rate was 87.5%, with an average of 3.43 attempts and a maximum of 6 attempts. One participant failed to obtain any valid recognition after multiple attempts, while two others required six tries before receiving a correct result. These results indicate that while the system performs reliably for gestures involving distinctive and structured movements (e.g., hats or jackets), it struggles with flatter or body-adjacent gestures such as "T-shirt."

The difficulty likely stems from visual ambiguity in the gesture shape, potential occlusion due to camera angles, and physiological differences such as finger length, which affected model interpretation.

**Table 2.** Query Accuracy

| Query | Recognition Rate | Average Attempts | Maximum Attempts |
| --- | --- | --- | --- |
| Red Cotton Hat | 100% | 2.0 | 4 |
| Black Leather Jacket | 100% | 1.5 | 3 |
| Red T-Shirt | 87.5% | 3.43 | 6 |

## 4.3   Questionnaire Results

Following the task, participants were asked to rate the system in terms of usability, recognition accuracy, responsiveness, and clarity of input capture. The purpose of this questionnaire was to gather user feedback regarding their experience and perception of the system across these key dimensions. Although seven out of eight participants reported having no prior experience with sign-language interfaces, six found the system to be either "very easy" or "somewhat easy" to use. One participant reported difficulty (Figs. 5 and 6).

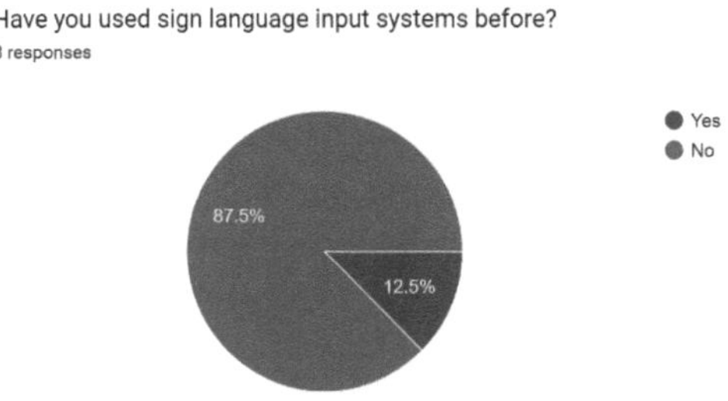

Fig. 5. Question about prior experience.

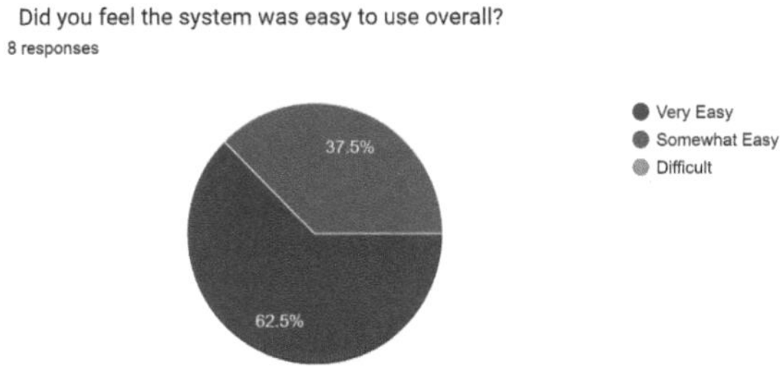

Fig. 6. Question about usability.

In terms of recognition accuracy, two participants rated the system as "very accurate," four as "mostly accurate," and one as "sometimes inaccurate." The T-shirt gesture was specifically mentioned as problematic by one participant, confirming quantitative findings (Fig. 7).

System response time was generally well received. While two participants considered it slow, the remaining six rated it as "acceptable" or "very fast." All participants found gesture capture through the camera to be "very clear" (Fig. 8).

When asked whether the recognized signs led to meaningful image search results, five answered "yes," two "partially," and one "no." This suggests that while the system generally retrieved relevant content, occasional mismatches remain a

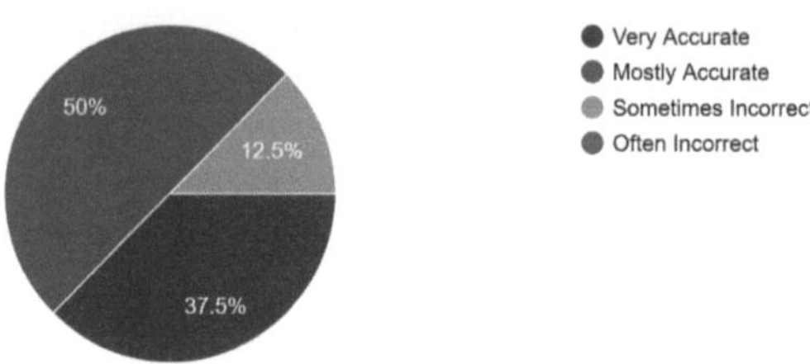

Fig. 7. Question about accuracy.

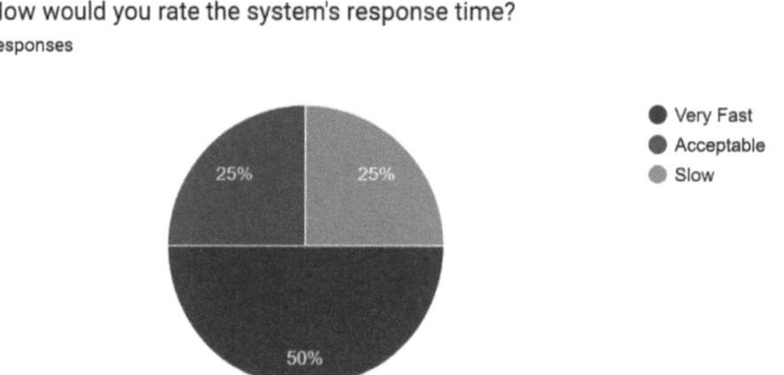

Fig. 8. Question about response time.

concern. Participants highlighted the responsive interface and ease of interaction as strengths while recommending improvements in recognition accuracy and the addition of alternative input methods (e.g., text input) (Fig. 9).

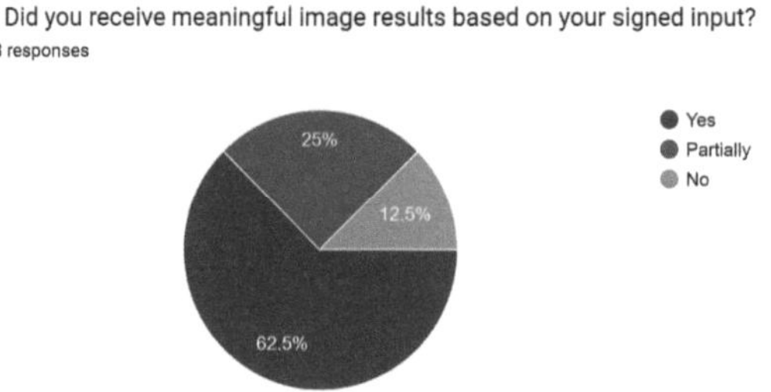

Fig. 9. Question about meaningful results.

Nevertheless, in response to the question *"Did any specific sign(s) fail to be recognized correctly?"*, one participant mentioned the sign "T-shirt", which corresponds with the observation in the experimental results (see Sect. 4.1) (Fig. 10).

Lastly, participants were asked about their willingness to use such a gesture-based system in real-world settings. Most responded positively, indicating inter-

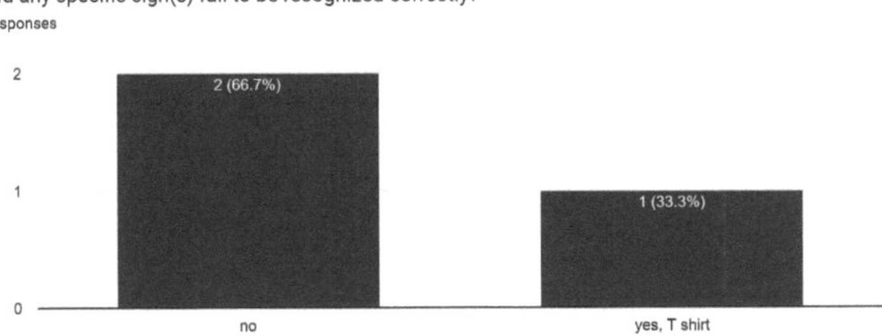



**Fig. 10.** Question about failed sign.

est under suitable circumstances. Only one user explicitly preferred traditional text-based search systems.

### 4.4   Discussion and System Improvement

Early testing revealed that the system sometimes struggled to confidently distinguish between similar gestures. To improve recognition stability, a confidence-based threshold was introduced into the classification process. In earlier versions, the system would simply choose the gesture with the highest score, even if that score wasn't particularly strong. This often led to mistakes when multiple gestures had nearly identical confidence levels.

With the new approach, the system calculates a probability distribution across all gesture classes using a SoftMax function. A prediction is only accepted if its confidence score surpasses a set threshold. This added layer of caution helps the system avoid low-confidence guesses and reduces the risk of misclassification, particularly when the input is ambiguous or unclear.

While the adjustment didn't fully resolve certain issues, like the ongoing difficulty with recognizing the "T-shirt" gesture, it led to noticeably more consistent results. Common gestures such as "red cotton hat" were recognized more reliably, and false positives became less frequent. The improvement highlights the value of post-processing in small-scale gesture recognition, where even minor refinements can make a meaningful difference. For future versions, smarter thresholding methods that account for gesture dynamics or timing could further enhance performance.

## 5   Conclusion and Future Work

The present study investigated incorporating sign language recognition into a multimodal conversational image retrieval system. The proposed system enables the use of British Sign Language (BSL) by users of DoodleShoper through gesture interaction by incorporating MediaPipe real-time hand landmark detection, a 1D CNN classifier for recognizing gestures, and a large language model (Chat-GPT) for textual enrichment.

Through design and experimentation, the prototype successfully demonstrated the feasibility of gesture-based query input for image search. While most common signs could be recognized reliably, the evaluation revealed several important limitations. First, the system currently supports only single-hand gesture recognition, even though many BSL signs require the use of both hands. For two-handed signs, only the landmarks of the first hand that enters the camera view are processed, which leads to incomplete understanding of the full sign. In addition, the system does not capture facial expressions, which are an essential part of BSL grammar and meaning. Without this information, some signs may lose important context or be misinterpreted.

Another major limitation is that the system recognizes static gestures rather than dynamic sequences. Since sign language is dynamic, with meaning conveyed through movement paths, speed changes, and direction changes, the current static-frame approach severely restricts the system's ability to interpret natural signing. This limitation was shown in the experiment, that users had to hold precise hand positions rather than sign naturally.

MediaPipe hand tracking had technical limitations which limits the performance, and especially with mostly flat palm gestures. As can be seen in my analysis, signs such as "T-shirt" were problematic signs. In the experiment, some participants were unable to achieve correct recognition in multiple attempts. This demonstrates the limitation that still exists in the hand landmark detection technique and machine learning progress today.

Although our normalization strategy helps to mitigate individual differences in hand size and proportions, differences in finger length ratios, gesture execution style and personal signing characteristic are likely to continue to impact the recognition performance across different users. A number of those such variations are caused by the above conditions and therefore the system would benefit from being trained on a more diverse training dataset that can accommodate for them.

Nevertheless, the work demonstrates that by integrating vision-based recognition with language models, it is possible to bridge the gap between sign-based input and text-based retrieval. This project presents an early but promising attempt to integrate sign language input into conversational image retrieval, thereby expanding accessibility beyond traditional text and sketch modalities. Furthermore, the use of confidence-based modification in the classification stage allowed for increased robustness by reducing false positives and improving the overall applicability of the model.

In addition, the project proposes a simplified yet effective classification pipeline based on 1D convolution over coordinate features, avoiding reliance on image-based inputs or more complex architectures such as Transformer. This makes the system easier to implement, extend, and debug, particularly in research or prototype environments.

In the future work, more BSL gestures could be supported, and dual-hand tracking could be included. Since sign language is temporally dependent, incorporating temporal information to model dynamic sequences would more accurately capture the signing dynamics. Sensing technologies, such as wearable sensor gloves, could help improve the detection of palm orientation and fine-grained hand movements, thereby enhancing the system's recognition performance. Furthermore, it would enhance the ability of the system to generalise by increasing the training sets through obtaining recordings of similar gestures performed by different people. This is due to the fact that this would offer more standardised performance across a wide range of hand shapes, signing styles, and body types. In addition, further user studies would be beneficial to perform. Feedbacks from sign language users may reflect the actual effectiveness of the system in everyday situations. Problems would be easily identified and solved through these feedbacks. Eventually, such improvements could lead to the development of a more inclusive and reliable recognition system that is more capable for meeting practical application needs.

**Declaration on Generative AI**

During the development of the system presented in this paper, the authors used OpenAI's GPT-4 to transform incomplete or grammatically incorrect BSL gesture recognition outputs into fluent English sentences. This was part of the system's post-processing pipeline to enable accurate image retrieval. The authors reviewed the model outputs and take full responsibility for the system's behavior.

# References


1. Al-Qurishi, M., Saeed, R.A., El-Tazi, N., Anwar, S., Jain, R.: Deep learning for sign language recognition: current techniques, benchmarks, and open issues. IEEE Access **9**, 67840–67865 (2021). https://doi.org/10.1109/ACCESS.2021.3090833
2. Baktash, A., Mohammed, S., Yahya, A.: Sign language translator: web application based deep learning. AIP Conf. Proceed. **2398**, 050020 (2022). https://doi.org/10.1063/5.0093367
3. Bennett, C.L., Rosner, D.K.: The promise of empathy: design, disability, and knowing the "other". In: Proceedings of the 2019 CHI Conference on Human Factors in Computing Systems, pp. 1–13 (2019). https://doi.org/10.1145/3290605.3300528
4. Bilibili: Sign language recognition based on mediapipe [video] (n.d.). https://www.bilibili.com/video/BV1rr4y1t7nx/?spm_id_from=333.999.0.0&vd_source=646c9f284584a24eb65c354f340dd01d. Accessed 6 Dec 2024
5. Braghis, D.D., Liu, H.: Conversational image search: a sketch-based approach. In: Proceedings of the 2024 International Conference on Multimedia Retrieval, ICMR 2024, pp. 1265–1269. Association for Computing Machinery (2024). https://doi.org/10.1145/3652583.3657594
6. British Deaf Association: Help & resources (2022). https://bda.org.uk/help-resources/#statistics
7. Camgoz, N.C., Koller, O., Hadfield, S., Bowden, R.: Sign language transformers: joint end-to-end sign language recognition and translation. In: Proceedings of the IEEE/CVF Conference on Computer Vision and Pattern Recognition (CVPR), pp. 10023–10033 (2020)
8. Caudrelier, G.: The syntax of British sign language: an overview (2014). https://clok.uclan.ac.uk/11260/2/Caudrelier%20Gail%20Final%20e-Thesis%20%28Master%20Copy%29.pdf

9. Deb, O., Prajwal, K., Zisserman, A.: New keypoint-based approach for recognising British sign language (BSL) from sequences. arXiv preprint arXiv:2412.09475 (2024). https://arxiv.org/abs/2412.09475
10. Debevc, M., Kosec, P., Holzinger, H., Heričko, T.: Improving multimodal web accessibility for deaf people: sign language interpreter module. Multimedia Tools Appl. **54**(1), 181–199 (2010). https://doi.org/10.1007/s11042-010-0529-8
11. Deuchar, M.: Sign language diglossia in a British deaf community. Sign Lang. Stud. 17, 347–356 (1977). http://www.jstor.org/stable/26203280
12. Frauenberger, C., Good, J., Alcorn, A., Pain, H.: Supporting the design of technology-mediated social participation for children with autism. ACM Trans. Comput. Hum. Interact. (TOCHI) **19**(3), 1–35 (2012). https://doi.org/10.1145/2362364.2362365
13. Kiranyaz, S.: 1d convolutional neural networks and applications: a survey. Mech. Syst. Sig. Process. **151**, 107398 (2021). https://doi.org/10.1016/j.ymssp.2020.107398
14. Kumar, R., Bajpai, A., Sinha, A.: MediaPipe and CNNs for real-time ASL gesture recognition (2023). https://arxiv.org/abs/2305.05296
15. Lugaresi, C., et al.: MediaPipe: a framework for building perception pipelines (2019). https://arxiv.org/pdf/1906.08172
16. MIT Communication Lab: Thoughtful engagement with disability through inclusive design principles (2024). https://mitcommlab.mit.edu/aeroastro/2024/07/25/thoughtful-engagement-with-disability-through-inclusive-design-principles/
17. O'Shea, K., Nash, R.: An introduction to convolutional neural networks (2015). https://arxiv.org/pdf/1511.08458
18. Persson, H., Åhman, H., Yngling, A.A., Gulliksen, J.: Universal design, inclusive design, accessible design, design for all: different concepts—one goal? On the concept of accessibility—historical, methodological and philosophical aspects. Univ. Access Inf. Soc. **14**(4), 505–526 (2014). https://doi.org/10.1007/s10209-014-0358-z
19. Saunders, B., Camgöz, N.C., Bowden, R.: Everybody sign now: translating spoken language to photo realistic sign language video. CoRR abs/2011.09846 (2020). https://arxiv.org/abs/2011.09846
20. World Health Organization: Deafness and hearing loss, 26 February 2025. https://www.who.int/news-room/fact-sheets/detail/deafness-and-hearing-loss
21. Zhang, F., et al.: MediaPipe hands: on-device real-time hand tracking. arXiv preprint arXiv:2006.10214 (2020). https://arxiv.org/abs/2006.10214
22. Zheng, Y., et al.: Inclusive design insights from a preliminary image-based conversational search systems evaluation. In: IR4U2 at the 46th European Conference on Information Retrieval, ECIR 2024, Glasgow, Scotland (2024)

# Towards Accessible Information Retrieval for Children With a Mild Intellectual Disability

Ruben Weijers[1(✉)] [iD], Simone Ooms[1] [iD], Kellin Pelrine[2] [iD], and Hanna Hauptmann[1] [iD]

[1] Utrecht University, Heidelberglaan 8, 3584 CS Utrecht, The Netherlands
`rubenweijers29@gmail.com`
[2] McGill University, 845 Sherbrooke Street West, Montreal, QC H3A 0G4, Canada

**Abstract.** The ability to generate simple text is essential for Large Language Models (LLMs) to support individuals with mild intellectual disabilities (MID). This study compares GPT-4o and Llama3 on text simplification (TS) benchmarks, evaluating five metrics: FKGL, BLEU, METEOR, BERTScore, and SARI. We also conduct an LLM-based evaluation and compare all benchmarks with human judgments. Our findings show that GPT-4o consistently outperforms Llama3 across all benchmarks with statistical significance. However, the LLM-based evaluation slightly favors Llama3. Human judgments highlight that performance is more nuanced—while GPT-4o is preferred for structure, simplicity, and trust, Llama3 is valued for engagement and friendliness. In an experimental study on children with MID, we compare a chat system powered by GPT-4o to a control system using Google search in a self-exploration task. Results show that children with MID can understand GPT-4o well linguistically, but struggle to formulate inputs to the model. Additionally, we find that personalization and continuity play important roles in sustaining engagement. Our findings suggest that AI has the potential to support education and self-exploration for students with MID, but requires personalization for forming a bond.

**Keywords:** LLMs · AI in Education · Children · Mild Intellectual Disabilities · MID

## 1 Introduction

Large Language Models (LLMs) are rapidly advancing across domains [13,17]. In education, ChatGPT assists instructors in course design and helps students with personalized tutoring [23,47,82]. While students view it positively, concerns remain around hallucinations, loss of critical thinking, and academic integrity [44,55,63]. Still, its popularity persists [42]. LLMs primarily rely on text, posing challenges for individuals with intellectual disabilities (IDs), particularly those with low reading ability [50]. In the Netherlands, around 500,000 people are


A. Bellogin et al. (Eds.): IR4U2 2025/BIAS 2025, CCIS 2786, pp. 127–153, 2026.
https://doi.org/10.1007/978-3-032-12717-4_9

diagnosed with Mild Intellectual Disabilities (MID), with IQs between 50–70 [48,78]. They face difficulties in conceptual, social, and practical skills [64,72]. Some 11,000 youths with MID face compounded issues like addiction and school dropout [37]. Current support often neglects long-term development [10,36]. As AI capabilities grow rapidly [20,30], it is vital that people with MID are not left behind. Tailored AI assistants could support their independence and self-efficacy.

This study aims to make LLMs more accessible to Dutch children with MID, who often struggle with reading [9]. We built an AI assistant that communicates in simple, concise dialogue. Unlike prior work focusing on academic outcomes [4], our system supports information retrieval (IR) for self-exploration. To accomplish this, we benchmark multiple LLMs, collect human ratings on their outputs, and select the best model for a user study. Then, children interact with one of two IR systems (using the AI or a Google search) to retrieve information that can help them find new hobbies. We aim to investigate how proprietary and open-source LLMs compare on text simplification, what traits matter in AI for children with MID, and whether Dutch children with MID can effectively use an AI system for self-exploration.

## 2   Literature Review

### 2.1   Mild Intellectual Disabilities

MID is a condition that affects cognitive functions and mental ability, such as verbal working memory, resulting in challenges in daily life [51]. As a result, individuals with MID are more vulnerable to problematic behavior, such as a heightened risk of substance abuse [19]. Many with MID also experience co-occurring conditions such as ADHD or autism [2]. Compared to the general population, families that include someone with MID tend to experience poorer overall health and greater stress [68]. Approximately 6.4% of the Dutch population have MID, including those with borderline intellectual functioning (IQ up to 85) [52,61]. Individuals with MID often face cognitive, social, and practical challenges, including difficulties in communication, learning, and independent living. Despite having greater needs, they are frequently underdiagnosed and undertreated, especially in mental healthcare [61,77]. During childhood, MID is usually identified in primary school, with students transitioning into special practical education that focuses on vocational skills. Their post-school success remains limited, with few achieving competitive employment due to gaps in social skill development and lack of long-term support [10,67].

Technology is increasingly used to support independence in individuals with MID [35]. Examples include mobile apps for health education [58], self-controlled tools that teach daily skills through virtual environments, or other handheld devices [12]. For such tools to be most effective, they should be tailored to those with MID, with features like simple interfaces, large visuals, sequential tasks, predictable navigation, repeated instructions, and/or immediate feedback [6,11].

Recent work explores how AI can enhance support for those with MID. While earlier studies in the field used AI to detect behavioral patterns in individuals with MID [39,71], newer research focuses on applications of generative AI. For instance, chatbots can adjust to users' cognitive levels and offer personalized assistance [3,35]. Additionally, AI can simplify complex texts, thereby aiding in therapeutic or educational contexts [31]. A recent study found that AI-supported instruction significantly improved academic outcomes in children with MID, with effects lasting weeks after the intervention [4].

## 2.2  Text Simplification for People with MID

To retrieve information successfully, individuals must be able to comprehend the text presented. Children with an MID typically struggle with reading comprehension of both narrative text (e.g. school materials) and the more complex expository text (content beyond the classroom, e.g. news websites) [66]. Simplifying expository text using short sentences with a limited vocabulary, no abstract argumentation, and no overload of information can make written content more accessible for individuals with MID [22,53]. To do text simplification (TS), early methods used rule-based or lexical approaches [14,15], while modern techniques rely on neural networks, especially transformer-based models like BERT and GPT-4 [34,74]. These models can simplify complex text in multiple languages and outperform traditional sentence simplification systems [21,38].

LLMs can simplify Dutch text effectively, even without additional domain-specific fine-tuning. For example, readers aided by ChatGPT had a 20% increase in comprehension of Dutch government letters [62]. Furthermore, GPT-4 has been shown to improve the readability of Dutch municipality and Wikipedia texts [65,75].

Since prior work shows that general-purpose LLMs already perform well in generating Dutch text [29,65], our study focuses on using those LLMs without additional fine-tuning. To evaluate simplification quality, we apply five commonly used TS metrics that measure multiple aspects of text complexity [5,38]. Since metrics cannot capture all aspects of simplification, human evaluations remain essential [1,5]. And although LLMs are shown to be more robust evaluators of text simplicity [46], even top-performing LLMs occasionally hallucinate or distort meaning [1,18]. To address this, we include both benchmark scores and human assessments of task-specific performance in our evaluation.

## 3  Methodology

One of the target goals for children with MID enrolled in Dutch practical education is to learn how to retrieve information online to spend their leisure time meaningfully[1] This study explores whether children with MID can naturally engage with an AI system in a classroom setting to support their search for meaningful leisure time activities. Our approach, depicted in Fig. 1, is split up into

---

[1] Curriculum   Dutch   practical   education:   https://www.praktijkonderwijs.nl/kennisbank/curriculum-praktijkonderwijs/.

three parts. First, we select two datasets: source simple data from a Dutch newspaper, and complex source data from Dutch Wikipedia. We use three Llama3 models (of size 1B, 3B, and 8B), as well as GPT-4o and GPT-4o-mini to generate a total of 12,000 simplified sentences per model across the two datasets. These sentences are benchmarked (FKGL, BLEU, METEOR, BERTScore, SARI) to measure readability, meaning preservation, and simplification quality related human-written text. We also conduct an LLM-based analysis of text simplification, based on the approach of [46]. Following this, we conduct a survey that gathers human feedback on task-specific performance of the two candidate models that performed best on the simplification benchmarks. Based on the results of the survey and benchmarks, we apply the top-performing model in an IR system for a user study, where we compare it to another system using Google search. The participants in this study are children with MID, who will use both systems for IR to discover new hobbies during their citizenship lesson, in which they would normally spend time on meaningful use of leisure time.

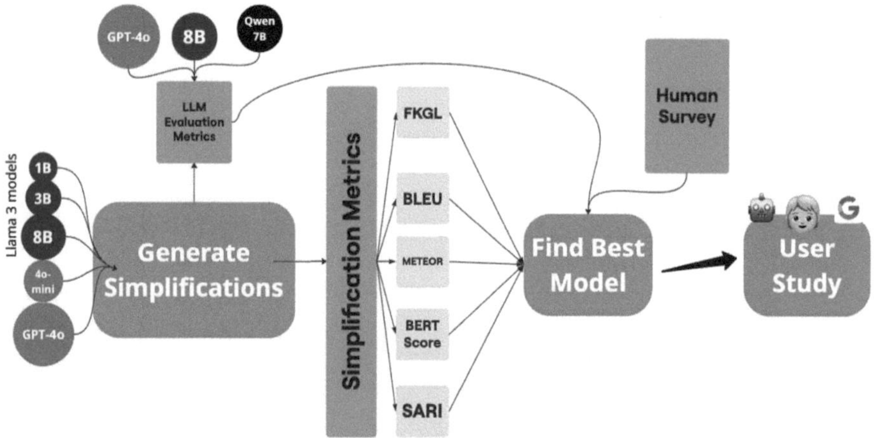


Fig. 1. Flowchart of methods.

## 4    Evaluating LLMs on Dutch Text Simplification

We evaluate OpenAI's GPT-4o, GPT-4o-mini, and Meta's Llama 3 (1B, 3B, 8B) for Dutch text simplification. These models are selected due to their top rankings on the LMSYS ChatBot Arena[2] and application in TS research [46,56]. Our goal is not an exhaustive model comparison, but rather to demonstrate a replicable evaluation process using both proprietary and open-source models.

We use two types of data for our evaluation of simplification ability: simple Dutch text for reference-based metrics, and complex Dutch text for reference-less

---

[2] https://lmarena.ai/leaderboard.

metrics. For simple source data, we use text from a Dutch newspaper (Wablieft) written for readers with lower literacy. This data was previously established as a gold standard for simple Dutch [29]. Due to the lack of Dutch human-written reference simplifications, we employ a semi-synthetic approach that follows [41]: using GPT-4o, we complexify Wablieft texts (Appendix A.1), similar to [65], then simplify those outputs with all candidate models, treating the original Wablieft texts as human references. We use synthetic data because gold-standard Dutch reference simplifications are missing. While this method introduces additional complexity and a potential loss of meaning during complexification, prior work by [41] demonstrated that synthetic data can improve TS performance even in a low-resource setting. We use simple newspaper text, rather than text written for children specifically, because the low-literacy focused newspaper text covers a wider variety of topics on a level more appropriate than text written for children.

For complex source data, we extract paragraphs from Dutch Wikipedia (2.87 million in total) via the Leesplank project[3]. Following [29], articles are split into sentences, with only the first sentence modified. To simplify these sentences, we adapt a Dutch prompt from [65], instructing models to simplify sentences for learners of Dutch with low reading proficiency (Appendix A.1).

We randomly select 2000 sentences per iteration across three iterations for both datasets. Using three Llama3 models of size 1B, 3B, and 8B, and two GPT-4o models (4o and 4o-mini) with a temperature of 0.7—generating 60,000 simplifications in total.

## 4.1   Evaluation Metrics

Models are evaluated using five text simplification metrics and one LLM-based method. We use FKGL to assess readability based on sentence length and syllable count [40]; while its correlation with human judgment is limited [5,70], it remains a popular metric [24,38] and is particularly suited to our target group that benefits from short, simple sentences. We use BLEU to measure n-gram overlap with reference texts [60]. Despite its prevalence in TS evaluation [33], it is sensitive to lexical and structural variation and may penalize desirable simplifications [5,49,69]. To address some of BLEU's limitations, we use METEOR, which incorporates stemming, synonym matching, word order, and recall [7]. We use BERTScore to evaluate semantic similarity based on contextual embeddings [80], measuring meaning preservation despite changes in wording or structure. We use SARI to capture how outputs modify source texts through n-gram additions, deletions, and retentions [79]. Finally, we apply G-eval from [46], using Llama3:8B, GPT-4o, and Qwen2:7B to evaluate five custom criteria, namely simplicity, meaning preservation, grammar, coherence, and use of Dutch (Appendix A.1); allowing us to measure aspects of output quality that are difficult to measure with benchmarks alone.

---

[3] https://huggingface.co/datasets/UWV/Leesplank_NL_wikipedia_simplifications.

**Metrics Results.** Our results, displayed in Table 1, show that GPT-4o achieves the best scores across all five simplification metrics, while the smallest model, Llama3:1B, scores the lowest. The model with the best simplification performance, GPT-4o, is also considered the most generally capable according to human rankings [16]. Llama3:8B's performance lies between these two, suggesting a relationship between model size and TS ability. When looking at individual metrics, GPT-4o obtains the best FKGL scores (4.69 grade level difference), indicating that its output text is suitable for the reading comprehension level of a 10-year-old. Thus, GPT-4o's lower scores are preferred for those with a reading disability.

Furthermore, all models score low on BLEU for word-for-word matching, suggesting that they use new words outside the reference text for simplification. Higher METEOR scores compared to BLEU imply that models use different word forms. Llama3:1B scores lowest on meaning preservation, measured by BERTScore, due to excessive simplification, while GPT-4o scores highest, followed by the other Llama models. Finally, GPT-4o performs best on SARI, but still scores low on BLEU compared to other state-of-the-art models [44], suggesting that LLMs can achieve strong simplification (high SARI), despite significant differences in word choice and sentence structure from reference simplifications (low BLEU).

**Table 1.** TS results, on a 0–1 scale, except FKGL. For FKGL, lower scores indicate simpler text (best = lowest). For BLEU, METEOR, BERTScore, and SARI higher scores are better. Bold values indicate the best performance per metric.

| Model | FKGL | BLEU | METEOR | BERTScore | SARI |
|---|---|---|---|---|---|
| Original | 9.10 | – | – | – | – |
| LLAMA 1B | 7.46 | 0.02 | 0.29 | 0.67 | 0.49 |
| LLAMA 3B | 7.78 | 0.04 | 0.40 | 0.71 | 0.51 |
| LLAMA 8B | 6.70 | 0.04 | 0.39 | 0.72 | 0.56 |
| GPT-4o | **4.41** | **0.06** | **0.47** | **0.74** | **0.57** |
| GPT-4o-mini | 4.61 | 0.05 | 0.46 | 0.74 | 0.55 |

In an LLM-evaluation, we used GPT-4o, Llama3:8B and Qwen2:7B to evaluate simplifications generated by GPT-4o and Llama3:8B respectively. We evaluate five custom criteria designed to validate and complement the TS benchmarks; simplicity, meaning preservation, grammar, coherence, and use of Dutch. As shown in Table 2, both GPT-4o and Llama3:8B achieve average scores above 80% across all metrics, without clear self-preference (Appendix A.2). Although GPT-4o is superior according to TS benchmarks, Llama3:8B is slightly preferred in LLM-based evaluations, trailing GPT-4o only in usage of Dutch (Appendix A.2). Whether these differences matter for the target audience requires confirmation by human evaluations of the model's performance.

**Table 2.** Average scores (on a 1–5 scale) assigned by GPT-4o, Llama, and Qwen to two sets of text simplifications.

| Evaluator | GPT-4o Simplifications | Llama3:8b Simplifications |
| --- | --- | --- |
| GPT-4o | 4.38 | 4.70 |
| Llama | 4.56 | 4.58 |
| Qwen | 4.13 | 4.28 |

## 5  Survey

Despite using multiple benchmarks to measure TS, we recognized their limitations and thus conducted a human survey that found preferences for task-specific model output. Our goal was to capture human-rated text quality aspects beyond what simplification metrics could measure. In the survey, we selected qualitative aspects for measurement that could not be assessed by TS benchmarks, such as trust, friendliness, and engagement. To measure this, we created a set of 10 questions that simulated a hypothetical AI-child interaction, with questions formed based on discussions with the teacher of the children. Our survey compared responses of "Model Blue" (Llama3:8B) and "Model Green" (GPT-4o) for a hypothetical 14-year-old with reading difficulties who is seeking new hobbies. Due to the survey's complexity, we studied Dutch-speaking adults (n=23) instead of children from the target group. More concretely, participants were asked to consider the following scenario:

*"You are the parent of a 14-year-old child named Robin, who struggles with reading and comprehending text. Robin's school is introducing an AI tool to support students with similar difficulties, and your role is to help decide between two AI models: Model Blue and Model Green.".*

The order in which the model outputs were displayed alternated per question. Participants were not informed which model was which, while they compared the responses of these two AI models across a series of assignments that Robin had to complete. These hypothetical assignments were based on questions that we had designed for the target group study that would follow the survey. Participants were provided with three types of information: the assignment, which was the question Robin wanted to answer, such as "Find a new hobby that you would like to do together with a friend"; the user input, which was what Robin asked the model given the assignment, for example "hobby for two people"; and the responses generated by Model Blue and Model Green to Robin's question. Although the survey instructions were in English, the assignment and model outputs were in Dutch.

Specifically, the survey included 10 single-turn questions (one input, one reply, Appendix A.3), 5 two-turn questions (follow-up input: "I want a different hobby", with an additional reply), and 4 general questions for general preference and opinions. Concluding questions asked which model participants preferred overall, preferred for their hypothetical child, or would prefer as the child in the scenario, and why.

To complement simplification metrics assessing linguistic aspects, we asked survey participants to rate six criteria: simplicity, engagement, structure, friendliness, trustworthiness, and general preference. Capturing human-rated text quality aspects beyond simplification metrics allowed us to select the best-suited model for children with MID for the self-exploration task they would complete in the user study.

## 5.1 Survey Results

This section presents the survey results from 23 Dutch-speaking adult participants, who spent an average of 24 min on the survey. GPT-4o was preferred in both single-turn and two-turn conversations. More specifically, Fig. 2 shows that GPT-4o was strongly preferred for its structure, simplicity, and trustworthiness. Conversely, both models performed similarly on engagement and friendliness. In the first 10 questions, most respondents favor GPT-4o (66.1%) over Llama3:8B (12.2%), with 21.7% having no clear preference.

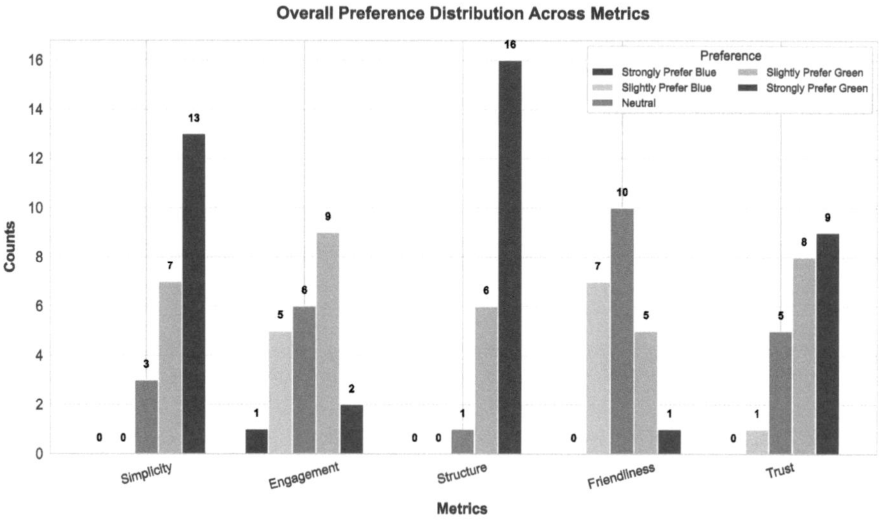



**Fig. 2.** When asked for a final preference rating per metric, GPT-4o was more strongly preferred on metrics it was already dominant in.

General preferences (Q16–18) showed stronger GPT-4o favor after exposure, especially in simplicity, structure, and trust. When asked for overall preference, 83.04% favored GPT-4o.

When participants were specifically asked which model they would prefer for their hypothetical child Robin, 52% of participants *strongly preferred* GPT-4o.

This suggests that parents place a higher value on the GPT-4o favored metrics: structure, trust, and simplicity, rather than engagement and friendliness. Conversely, when asked which model they would prefer for themselves if they were the child in the scenario, fewer participants strongly preferred GPT-4o, and more felt neutral or preferred Llama3:8B; the model that was more appreciated for its friendliness and engagement. These results suggest that parents may prioritize different qualities when selecting a model for their child compared to when they are choosing one for themselves.

Furthermore, open-ended feedback revealed that GPT-4o was favored for certain aspects, such as using bold text and bullet points more frequently, found particularly helpful for children with reading disabilities—though it lacked Llama's enthusiasm and engagement (Table 3). Additionally, GPT-4o's hobby suggestions aligned more closely with the prompt and contained fewer grammatical errors than those from Llama3:8B. However, the simplicity and consistency of GPT-4o's structure came at the expense of engagement.

## 6  Target Group User Study

At this stage in the study, we found GPT-4o to be the most suitable model for talking with Dutch children with MID. Our next step is creating an IR system that enables children to discover new hobbies using AI. Our experimental study involved six children aged 15–16 from a Dutch practical education high school. They were observed during a 75-min classroom session, which was a similar duration to that of a regular lesson. The study was conducted in a familiar environment in which the children regularly had their lessons. Each child visited a website created for the purposes of the study on their own school-provided laptop, with user data stored in a secure database for analysis. The website used two IR systems, an AI system based on GPT-4o and a search system that used Google search. Participating children were tasked with finding new hobbies. This specific task was chosen because prior interviews with teachers of the children showed that these children rarely explore new hobbies. As mentioned in Sect. 3, these children require help spending their leisure time meaningfully; for instance by exploring new hobbies that they would like to do.

To compare performance of the systems, we create a set of 10 scenario-based assignments, each tasking the children to write down three new hobbies they would enjoy doing based on the constraints of the scenario, for example: *"Find three new hobbies you would like to do that you can do inside when it rains."* (Appendix A.4). The children were able to interact with each system for as long as they wanted without needing to submit answers immediately. Knowing from prior discussions that the children worked at different paces and had varying cognitive abilities, we included 10 questions, expecting them to complete 3 to 4, to ensure the children had enough content to engage with. After submitting each answer, the children were asked for feedback by rating how easy it was to find hobbies using the system, and briefly explaining their hobby choices for us to extract their reasoning. During this interaction phase, children alternated between both systems, starting with answering the first question using the

AI system. Prior to starting the study, children chose from four predetermined avatars with unique names and pictures that would represent the AI. The avatar also appeared on the control page to reduce bias.

Three supervisors were present during the experiment to oversee the process and provide assistance: the principal researcher, who was responsible for the study; a second researcher, who had previously conducted the poster session and was familiar with the children, and the teacher. The supervisors took an active role throughout the session, moving around the classroom to check in with students and to ensure the children felt supported and remained engaged.

### 6.1   The AI System

The AI system (Fig. 3) used a chat interface powered by GPT-4o, the best model from our analysis. We implemented insights from open feedback of the survey, where respondents praised GPT-4o's use of bold text and bullet points, in order to write the system prompt (Appendix A.1). The AI's conversation history was reset after each interaction.

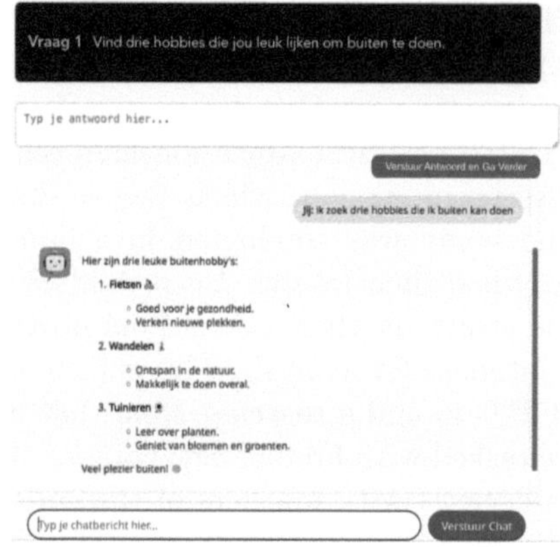

**Fig. 3.**  A sample conversation using the AI system.

**Fig. 4.**  A sample query using the search system.

### 6.2   The Search System

The control system (Fig. 4) used a Programmable Search Engine (PSE) from the Google API, adjusted to use safe search and return results from Dutch websites. Although Google's PSE is not as robust as a standard Google search in the browser, we chose it for several reasons. First, it allowed us to track behavior, such as collecting the links they clicked, without using screen capture software. Second, we anticipated that children might get confused if they had to open up Google in a separate window. Thus, this setup enabled us to contain the experiment in the dedicated website and kept user confusion to a minimum.

## 6.3   User Study Findings

At the start of the user study, the children experienced confusion navigating to the website despite the URL being displayed on a whiteboard. This suggested digital illiteracy among the children, which would further manifest throughout parts of the experiment. For example, some children were unsure of the purpose of an answer input field, while others struggled to understand how to send messages in the chat. Because multiple children encountered similar technical issues, we reinforced the instructions by displaying an example interaction on a digital teaching board present in the classroom.

Once the experiment began, we observed that the children had no issues understanding the AI's responses, but rather struggled to come up with questions to ask the AI. Many found it difficult to take initiative, formulate their thoughts into words, or think of questions to ask. For some, even copying the exact question text into the chat was not an intuitive step.

**Participant Engagement and Sentiment.** Not all children engaged in the experiment with the same interest; some appeared highly invested at all times, others were partially interested, and some were constantly disengaged. 69% of conversations with the AI consisted of only a single input before children submitted their answers (Fig. 7).

Conversely, the avatar selection activity was met with strong enthusiasm, indicated by children asking each other: "Which one are you choosing?". They appeared appreciative of the personalization made available by this choice. During the first question, one child asked the teacher if they could give the AI a new name, and if they could tell the AI their own name as well. This enthusiasm was followed by the longest conversation, consisting of 19 turns. Other children also showed high engagement during the AI interactions, displayed by conversations with peers and positive comments towards the teacher and researchers. In a post-study conversation, the teacher praised the AI, complementing its simple conversation style and natural interaction with the children.

Some participants displayed low engagement. One child, for example, consistently provided the bare minimum input and completed the experiment quickly. This child repeated unproductive answers, suggesting a lack of interest. Another child barely participated, stopping after providing just one non-constructive input and not showing interest in any form of adult assistance or motivational support. Furthermore, the children struggled to formulate questions to start and continue the conversation; "What should I ask the AI?" was asked multiple times throughout the experiment. Additionally, negative comments on the high similarity of the questions suggested that the hobby exploration task was not sufficiently varied to sustain participant interest. We suspect that the children found the questions to overlap too much, leading to them repeatedly filling in the same hobbies and losing engagement.

Another factor that may have influenced engagement was the children's preference for familiarity. Being part of a close-knit classroom and having a personal and informal relationship with their teacher, the children were accustomed to a supportive and familiar environment. In contrast, the presence of an unfamiliar researcher was met with wariness in the children. This preference for familiarity extended to the AI interaction as well. When one child, who had previously engaged in the 19-turn conversation, encountered a second interaction that restarted without context from the previous conversation, she immediately lost interest and stopped participating.

**Hobby Exploration.** Because the children found the questions repetitive, their focus shifted away from actively finding new hobbies. Instead, they listed hobbies that they already engaged in, repeating responses across multiple questions (Fig. 8). This pattern was more pronounced when using the search system, where children identified fewer hobbies overall, as well as fewer new hobbies (Fig. 9). In total, children found 28 unique hobbies using the AI system, with 46 entries in total. Using the search system, the children found 18 unique hobbies, with 36 entries in total. The AI system led to more discovered hobbies on average, although many of these hobbies were activities that the children were already doing, such as "chilling" or "walking". However, there were more one-off hobbies found using the AI system, which suggests that the AI had a mild positive effect on children's self-exploration.

**System Interaction Metrics.** Children engaged slightly more with the AI system than with the control system. On average, they initiated 2.32 chats per question with the AI, compared to 2.16 per question in the search system, where they clicked approximately one link per two conducted searches. When asked to rate how easy it was to find new hobbies, children gave the AI system an average score of 4.32 out of 5, while the search system received a slightly lower rating of 4.0. The time spent per question also varied between the systems. On average, children spent 178.3 s per question using the AI system, compared to 196.3 s with the search system. While none of the differences were statistically significant, they suggest that children slightly preferred the AI system, where interactions were marginally more efficient and intuitive.

## 7    Discussion

This study examined the necessary steps to develop an AI system that Dutch children with MID can interact with successfully. To accomplish this, we benchmarked several AI models on their ability to generate simplified Dutch text. We then identified the most suitable model based on human preference in a task-specific context. We integrated this model into an AI system and compared it to a control system that used Google search. This was followed by a target-group experiment that observed 6 children with MID tasked with exploring new hobbies using both systems in a classroom setting.

## 7.1 Benchmarks

On TS benchmarks, GPT-4o consistently outperformed Llama3:8B, with statistically significant differences across all five metrics. GPT-4o generated the most readable text, retained key content from the reference simple text more effectively, and preserved meaning better. Additionally, GPT-4o achieved the highest SARI score, indicating superior simplification ability.

However, these results were not consistent with our LLM analysis of simplification. For instance, based on LLM-evaluated simplicity and meaning preservation, Llama3:8B scored higher than GPT-4o. Despite this, the statistical significance of the benchmarks suggests that the larger proprietary GPT-4o has a slight advantage over the smaller open-sourced Llama3:8B. Given the difference in model sizes, the performance of the smaller 8B model was a notable finding that supports existing work by [26], who found a domain-specialized Llama3:8B model to perform on par with GPT-4o.

## 7.2 Survey

Our survey results indicate that an LLM's performance cannot be solely determined through TS benchmarks, thus requiring human evaluation on task-specific performance for a comprehensive understanding. Although benchmarks assessed ability to generate simple Dutch text, the survey revealed that human preference is more nuanced. Unlike the small benchmark score differences, the survey showed a clear human preference for GPT-4o.

However, the survey also highlighted different LLM strengths; Llama3:8B scored comparably in friendliness and engagement, while GPT-4o excelled in simplicity, structure, and trust. This suggests adults prioritize structure and reliability for children with MID, while believing children value engagement and friendliness more. As the survey showed, preference is individual, which encourages personalized models and prompts that are based on user needs and the specific task. This aligns with research from [32] and [16], who suggest that LLMs have distinct personalities that resonate with different users. For vulnerable populations like children with MID, we need human-centric benchmarks prioritizing trust, engagement, and usability over mathematical quantifications, measuring human *preference* rather than *reference*, and focusing on how text is suited to a user's needs.

## 7.3 User Study

Our experimental study revealed that while frontier AI models excel at meeting the linguistic needs of children with MID in Dutch, engagement relies on connection and continuity. Children's enthusiasm for personalization was highlighted during the selection of the AI avatar. This suggests that AI could evolve from a chatting tool to a continuous social assistant/companion. In this approach, the AI would maintain its conversational history, similar to the familiar student-teacher bond that is developed in schools. This resonates with existing research that shows how routine protocols reduce externalizing problem behavior in children with MID through familiarity and repetition [28]. Another suggestion we make is the implementation of gamification, shown by [54] to motivate students with MID, into the AI system. Notably, children with MID struggled to generate inputs, signaling a need for a chatting tool that supports them with drafting input prompts. Strategies that could mitigate this challenge are, for example, scaffolding or multimodal input options. Scaffolding during instruction, a strategy that structures tasks and breaks them into components to learn [8], could be applied in the form of reducing the degrees of freedom of writing the prompt. For instance, providing the beginning of a prompt sentence for the user to finish. Multimodal input options like Speech-to-Text remove the transcription task in writing. This allows for a full focus on composing one's thoughts, which can make a writing task more manageable for children with learning disabilities like this group [27].

## 7.4   Limitations

This study highlights the potential of generative AI for children with MID, but has several limitations. First, our benchmarks lacked a gold-standard human reference dataset. While generating synthetic complex text was cost-effective, it may have skewed results [57]. Additionally, we tested only a subsample of LLMs. Other models may have performed better or revealed other traits preferred by this target group, especially since model preference is subjective and context-dependent [16].

The user study involved only six children, limiting the robustness of our findings. Engagement dropped significantly after the first two questions (Fig. 10), partly due to increased familiarity with the interface and a dislike for restarting conversations, but mainly because the children found the questions repetitive, leading to rushed responses and reduced quality in comparing the systems for self-exploration. Furthermore, because the survey was conducted on a group of adults, their model-preferences might not translate to those of the children.

Children's ratings also did not always reflect system effectiveness. High scores were sometimes given when answers aligned with pre-existing interests, not because the system aided exploration. Disengaged participants skewed results by repeating hobbies, inflating completion rates and reducing data quality. In contrast, engaged children submitted fewer responses but spent more time per conversation, highlighting a drop-off pattern.

Children with severe reading difficulties often completed only one or two questions. Thus, quantitative results must be contextualized with qualitative observations. The hobby-exploration task may also have been too narrow for evaluating model suitability. Furthermore, the search system was underdeveloped compared to a regular Google search in the browser, potentially biasing results in favor of the AI system. Finally, qualitative data was limited to classroom observations and would have benefited from short follow-up interviews to capture children's preferences and suggestions.

## 7.5  Future Work

Based on our findings, we identify three potential aspects on which future work can build.

**Expansion.** This study provides a first step showing that children with MID can interact successfully with AI assistants. Future work can strengthen these findings by conducting experimental studies across multiple classrooms and schools. Additionally, the hobby-exploration task could be modified, depending on the curriculum of the school and development of the students. For example, since all students at *praktijkscholen* are required to do an internship, future research could use AI for career exploration, helping them find internships that better match with their interests and abilities. Additionally, adaptive prompting can be used to support children struggling to formulate inputs [45]. Future work should investigate whether the intellectual impairments impact critical thinking in detecting false LLM outputs or hallucinations. If children are unable to distill factuality from the LLMs outputs, the system should more strongly emphasize its limitations to the users. Finally, future work could test a wider variety of leading proprietary models and compare them to smaller open-source models that are further fine-tuned on Dutch, such as those presented by [73].

**Personalization.** Given the positive reception of the avatar selection step, future research could explore stronger personalization by applying a longer context window, allowing the AI to use data from past conversations during inference. One way to assess the effect of personalization is to compare two AI systems—one with a default AI persona, and another that allows children to choose and name their AI companion. Furthermore, aligning the LLM's personality to individual users could help sustain engagement—in a study supporting this idea, [76] showed that participants found personalizable aspects such as conversation style, personality, and avatar important. Furthermore, the authors found that features like the chatbot addressing users by their name and being transparent about what it had learned about them helped establish a stronger therapeutic bond.

**Learning.** Following the work of [4], future research could assess the AI's effectiveness in improving academic skills. For instance, the study could compare two classrooms—one using an AI system for self-study and homework alongside regular teaching methods, and the other relying on regular teaching without the AI.

Although this study focused on a self-exploration task, the lessons learned are transferable to applying AI for improved academic outcomes. When building such a system for students with MID, we recommend testing out several frontier models, such as those from Anthropic, OpenAI and Meta. When choosing a model, one should prioritize models with high EQ [59], over reasoning capabilities

[25]. For example, GPT-4.5 was recently introduced by OpenAI to have a better understanding of what humans mean, interpreting subtle cues with greater nuance and higher EQ[4]. We believe these traits to be particularly important for this target group.

Additionally, we recommend building a system that allows users to test out different models, where prompts are dynamically adapted to the user's needs. To be more personalized to the user, the AI could draw upon information from past conversations by using a longer context-window [81]. Additionally, gamification elements can help students with MID stay engaged, as shown by [54]. More specifically, the system could implement work from [43] by using the personal assistant for AI-enabled gamification in education, such as custom positive feedback and animations.

## 8   Conclusion

This study explored the development of an AI system that children with MID could effectively interact with. We benchmarked AI models for TS in Dutch, identified which traits were preferred and found important by adults, and evaluated how children engaged with the AI in a self-exploration task. Our findings show that even though proprietary models like GPT-4o outperform on TS benchmarks, human preference is more nuanced and influenced by traits such as engagement, trust, and friendliness. In an experimental study, we observed that frontier AI models can successfully interact with children with MID using a simple prompting approach. However, personalization and task design are crucially important in sustaining engagement.

These findings contribute to existing research on this vulnerable group by demonstrating that AI has the potential to facilitate meaningful interaction for children with MID. However, the study was limited by a small sample size and a lack of gold-standard reference data for TS benchmarking. Future studies on this target group should explore the role of personalization in sustaining engagement, as well as investigate the potential of AI in enhancing learning outcomes.

By demonstrating the potential of current AI in supporting children with MID, we hope to pave the way for future research to empower their development through this transformative and rapidly advancing technology.

## A   Appendices

### Declaration on Generative AI

During the preparation of this work, the author(s) used GPT-4o to help with shortening certain paragraphs from the thesis paper that was the source for this shorter version. After using these tool(s)/service(s), the author(s) reviewed and edited the content as needed and take(s) full responsibility for the publication's content.

---

[4] https://openai.com/index/introducing-gpt-4-5/.

## A.1   Prompts

**Prompt to Simplify a Complex Dutch Sentence (Translated to English).** Je bent een assistent die moeilijke Nederlandse zinnen vereenvoudigt. Je herschrijft de zinnen in korte, duidelijke zinnen met alledaagse woorden. Vermijd lange zinnen en vakjargon. Leg technische termen en culturele verwijzingen op een eenvoudige manier uit. Gebruik actieve zinnen en houd de uitleg makkelijk te begrijpen.
**User Instruction:** Vereenvoudig de volgende text voor volwassen lezers die Nederlands leren als tweede taal. Gebruik korte zinnen, alledaagse woorden en vermijd vaktaal. Leg waar nodig begrippen uit op een eenvoudige manier.
**Sentence:** [Insert complex sentence here]


**Prompt to Complexify a Simple Dutch Sentence (Translated to English).** Je bent een behulpzame assistent die eenvoudige Nederlandse zinnen complexer maakt. Je taak is om de gegeven zin te herschrijven in complexe en genuanceerde taal, terwijl je de hoofdgedachte behoudt. Geef alleen de complexe zin als antwoord, zonder extra uitleg of tekst.
**User Instruction:** Herschrijf de volgende eenvoudige Nederlandse zin tot één complexe en genuanceerde zin, geschikt voor hoogopgeleide volwassenen. Verrijk de woordenschat en gebruik een formele en academische toon. Behoud de oorspronkelijke betekenis, maar druk deze uit met geavanceerde taal en stijl. Schrijf strikt alleen de complexe zin en niets anders.
**Text:** [Insert simple sentence here]


**Prompt to Evaluate Sentence Based on LLM Metrics.** You will be given an original complex sentence and its simplified version. Your task is to rate the simplification on the following metrics:
**Evaluation Criteria:**

1. Simplicity (1–5): How much simpler is the simplified version compared to the original? (1 being not simpler, 5 being much simpler)
2. Meaning Preservation (1–5): How well does the simplified version preserve the original meaning? (1 being not preserved, 5 being fully preserved)
3. Grammaticality (1–5): How grammatically correct is the simplified version in Dutch? (1 being a lot of grammar errors, 5 being fully grammatically correct)
4. Coherence (1–5): How logically connected and well-organized is the simplified version? (1 being not coherent, 5 being very coherent)
5. Use of Dutch (1–5): To what extent does the simplified version use only Dutch words and expressions, avoiding any English? (1 being fully in English, 3 being evenly split, 4 being with one or two English words, 5 being fully Dutch)

**Evaluation Steps:**

1. Read the original complex sentence carefully.
2. Read the simplified sentence and compare it to the original.

3. Assess the simplicity, meaning preservation, grammaticality, coherence, and use of Dutch based on the criteria above.
4. Assign scores for each metric on a scale of 1 to 5, where 1 is the lowest and 5 is the highest.

Original: *original sentence*
Simplified: *simplified sentence*

**Prompt to Interact During Target Group Study.** You are an intelligent assistant helping the user find answers to their questions. Provide clear and concise responses using Markdown syntax, including bold text and bullet points where appropriate. Make your text short and extremely simple. Suitable for Dutch teenagers with a mild intellectual disorder and reading disabilities. Assume that the user gets bored of long texts and prefers short, engaging responses.

## A.2   Graphs of LLM-Evaluation

See Figs. 5 and 6.

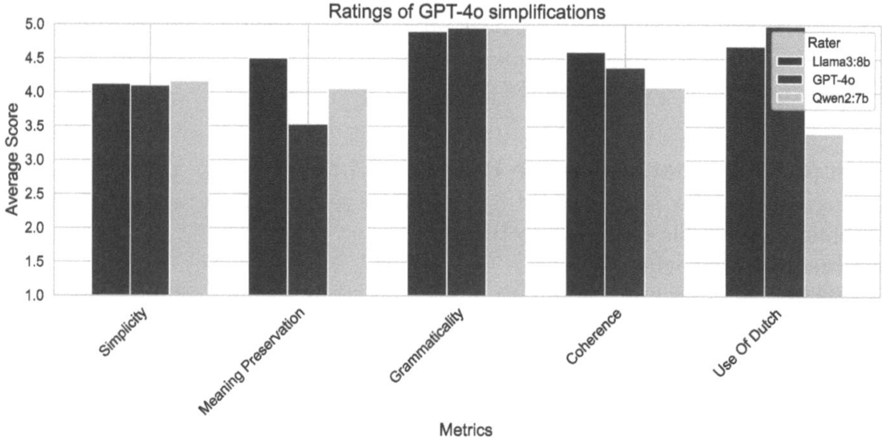


**Fig. 5.** GPT-4o simplified text rated by GPT-4o, Llama3:8B and Qwen2:7B.

## A.3   Example Survey Suestion

Please evaluate the blue and green model responses to the question: **Vind een hobby die je buiten kunt doen.**

Robin asked the model: "`buiten hobbie`"

Please rate the model replies in the table below.

## Blue Model:

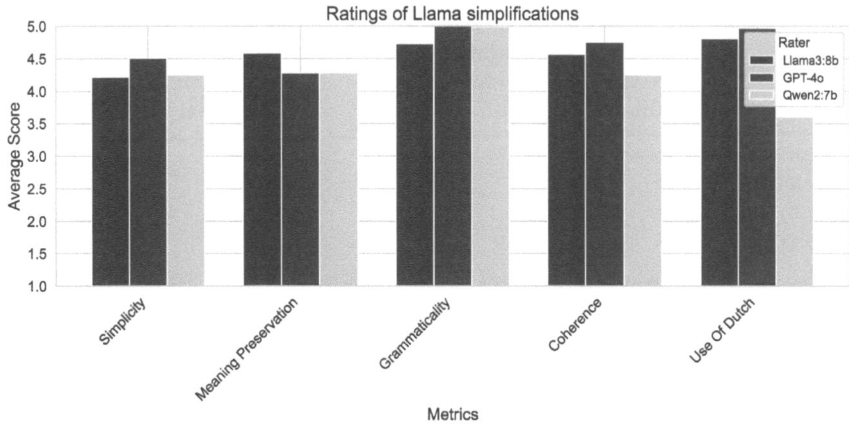


**Fig. 6.** GPT-4o was preferred for single turn conversations.

Hallo! Ik ben hier om je te helpen met het vinden van een leuke hobby. Een hobby doet zoveel goed voor je! Je wilt buiten zijn, maar je weet niet wat je precies wilt doen. Dat is oké! Er zijn veel leuke dingen die je kunt doen buiten. Een hobby kan zijn...
– Wandelen in de natuur en kijken naar vogels en bloemen.
– Fietsen door het park of door je dorp heen, zo snel mogelijk!
– Zonnebaden op een zonnige dag, met een boek of gewoon om te ontspannen.
Wat denk jij? Klinkt dit leuk voor jou?

# *Green Model:*

Hoi! Wat leuk dat je een hobby wil vinden om buiten te doen. Hier zijn er drie:
1. **Vliegeren:** Laat een vlieger vliegen in het park of op het strand. Het is leuk en je krijgt frisse lucht.
2. **Tuinen:** Planten en bloemen planten in de tuin of op een balkon. Je ziet dingen groeien.
3. **Fietsen:** Fiets door de buurt of een bos. Zo ontdek je nieuwe plekken.
Welke van deze vind jij het leukst om te proberen?

**Please Use the Rating Table Below**

|  | **Strongly Prefer Blue** | **Slightly Prefer Blue** | **Neutral** | **Slightly Prefer Green** | **Strongly Prefer Green** |
|---|---|---|---|---|---|
| Simplicity | O | O | O | O | O |
| Engagement | O | O | O | O | O |
| Structure | O | O | O | O | O |
| Friendliness | O | O | O | O | O |
| Trust | O | O | O | O | O |
| General Preference | O | O | O | O | O |

## A.4  User Study Questions

1. Vind drie hobbies die jou leuk lijken om buiten te doen.
2. Vind drie hobbies die jou leuk lijken om binnen te doen als het regent.
3. Vind drie hobbies die jou leuk lijken om samen te doen met een vriend of vriendin.
4. Vind drie hobbies die je leuk lijken on alleen te doen.
5. Vind drie hobbies die je alleen in de winter kunt doen en die jou leuk lijken.
6. Vind drie hobbies die je alleen in de zomer kunt doen en die jou leuk lijken.
7. Vind drie hobbies die jou leuk lijken waarbij je nieuwe dingen kan leren.
8. Vind drie hobbies die jou leuk lijken en weinig geld kosten.
9. Vind drie hobbies die jou leuk lijken waarbij je creatief bezig bent.
10. Vind drie hobbies die jou leuk lijken waarbij je in beweging bent.

## A.5  Annotation of Open Feedback

**Table 3.** Feedback counts per annotation category for Llama3.1-8b and GPT-4o. A higher count indicates more frequent mentions (mostly negative for Llama3:8B, positive for GPT-4o) within that category.

| **Annotation Category** | **Llama3:8B** | **GPT-4o** | **Favored Model** |
|---|---|---|---|
| Structure and Formatting | 3 | 15 | GPT-4o |
| Correctness | 3 | 6 | GPT-4o |
| Conciseness/Wordiness | 5 | 6 | GPT-4o |
| Tone, Style, and Engagement | 8 | 3 | Llama3:8B |
| Child Suitability | 2 | 4 | GPT-4o |
| Adherence to Prompt | 2 | 0 | GPT-4o |
| Grammar and Spelling | 6 | 3 | GPT-4o |
| Trustworthiness | 1 | 0 | GPT-4o |

## A.6   User Study Graphs

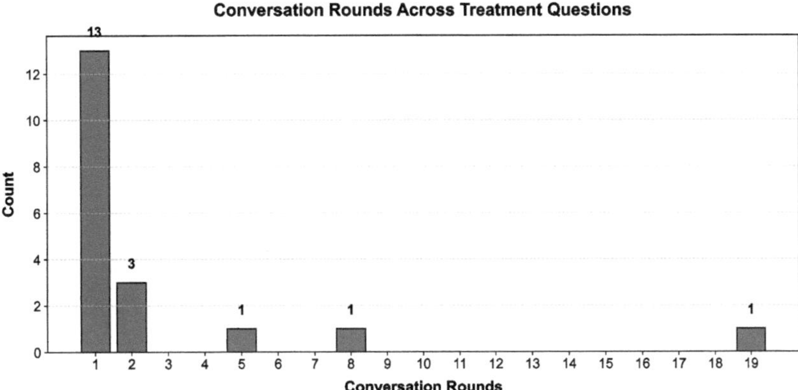


**Fig. 7.** The distribution of conversation lengths shows that most conversations lasted only a single-round.

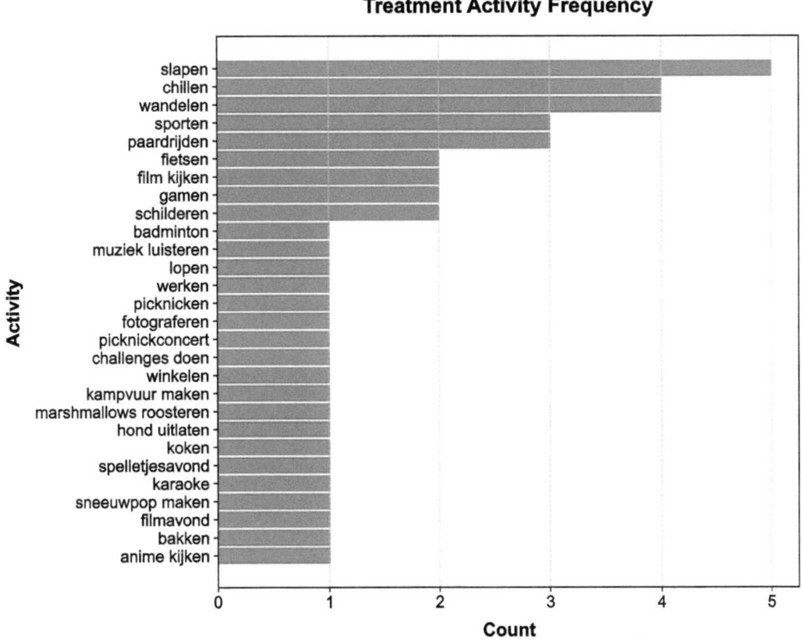


**Fig. 8.** More hobbies were found using the AI system, compared to the search system.

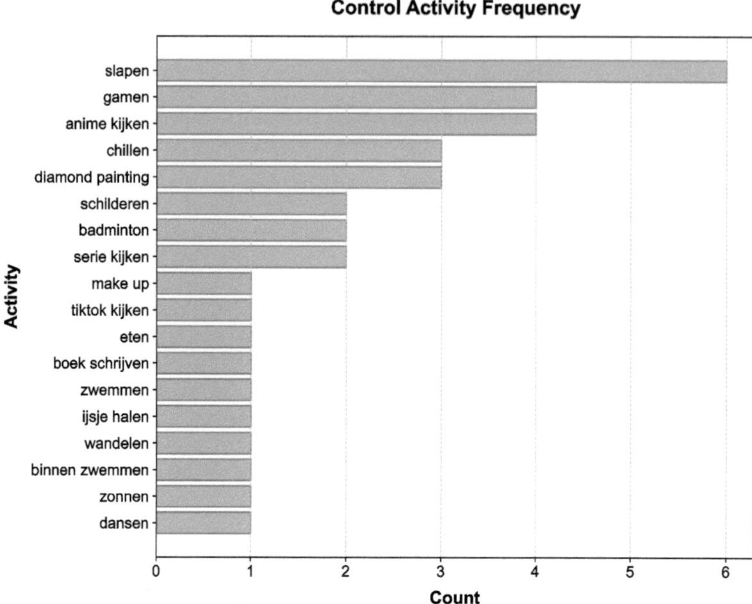

**Fig. 9.** Hobbies found with the search system show that children struggled to find new hobbies using the search system.

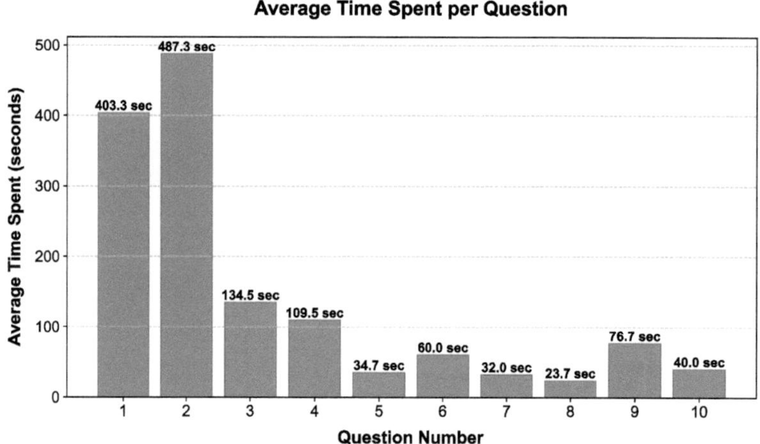

**Fig. 10.** The average time spent per question suggests that there was a sharp drop in engagement after the first two questions.

## References

1. Agrawal, S., Carpuat, M.: Do text simplification systems preserve meaning? A human evaluation via reading comprehension. Trans. Assoc. Comput. Linguist. **12**, 432–448 (2024)

2. Ahuja, A., Martin, J., Langley, K., Thapar, A.: Intellectual disability in children with attention deficit hyperactivity disorder. J. Pediatr. **163**(3), 890–895 (2013)

3. Almufareh, M.F., Tehsin, S., Humayun, M., Kausar, S.: Intellectual disability and technology: an artificial intelligence perspective and framework. J. Disabil. Res. **2**(4), 58–70 (2023)

4. Alsolami, A.S.: The effectiveness of using artificial intelligence in improving academic skills of school-aged students with mild intellectual disabilities in Saudi Arabia. Res. Dev. Disabil. **156**, 104884 (2025)

5. Alva-Manchego, F., Scarton, C., Specia, L.: The (un)suitability of automatic evaluation metrics for text simplification. Comput. Linguist. **47**(4), 861–889 (2021)

6. Balasuriya, S.S., Sitbon, L., Brereton, M.: A support worker perspective on use of new technologies by people with intellectual disabilities. ACM Trans. Accessible Comput. (TACCESS) **15**(3), 1–21 (2022)

7. Banerjee, S., Lavie, A.: METEOR: an automatic metric for MT evaluation with improved correlation with human judgments. In: Proceedings of the ACL Workshop on Intrinsic and Extrinsic Evaluation Measures for Machine Translation and/or Summarization, pp. 65–72 (2005)

8. Benko, S.L.: Scaffolding: an ongoing process to support adolescent writing development. J. Adolesc. Adult Literacy **56**(4), 291–300 (2012). https://doi.org/10.1002/JAAL.00142

9. Van den Bos, K., Nakken, H., Nicolay, P., Van Houten, E.: Adults with mild intellectual disabilities: can their reading comprehension ability be improved? J. Intellect. Disabil. Res. **51**(11), 835–849 (2007)

10. Bouck, E.: The postschool outcomes of students with mild intellectual disability: does it get better with time? J. Intellect. Disabil. Res. **58**(6), 534–548 (2014)

11. Bouck, E.C., Long, H., Jakubow, L.: Using technology to enhance learning for students with intellectual disabilities. In: Using Technology to Enhance Special Education, pp. 51–70. Emerald Publishing Limited (2023)

12. den Brok, W.L., Sterkenburg, P.: Self-controlled technologies to support skill attainment in persons with an autism spectrum disorder and/or an intellectual disability: a systematic literature review. Disabil. Rehabil. Assist. Technol. **10**(1), 1–10 (2015)

13. Brown, T., et al.: Language models are few-shot learners. Adv. Neural. Inf. Process. Syst. **33**, 1877–1901 (2020)

14. Carroll, J., Minnen, G., Canning, Y., Devlin, S., Tait, J.: Practical simplification of English newspaper text to assist aphasic readers. In: Proceedings of the AAAI-98 Workshop on Integrating Artificial Intelligence and Assistive Technology, Madison, WI, pp. 7–10 (1998)

15. Chandrasekar, R., Doran, C., Bangalore, S.: Motivations and methods for text simplification. In: COLING 1996 Volume 2: The 16th International Conference on Computational Linguistics (1996)

16. Chiang, W.L., et al.: Chatbot arena: an open platform for evaluating LLMs by human preference. In: Forty-First International Conference on Machine Learning (2024)

17. Dakhel, A.M., Majdinasab, V., Nikanjam, A., Khomh, F., Desmarais, M.C., Jiang, Z.M.J.: GitHub Copilot AI pair programmer: asset or liability? J. Syst. Softw. **203**, 111734 (2023)

18. Devaraj, A., Sheffield, W., Wallace, B.C., Li, J.J.: Evaluating factuality in text simplification. In: Proceedings of the Annual Meeting of the Association for Computational Linguistics, vol. 2022, pp. 7331. NIH Public Access (2022)

19. van Duijvenbode, N., VanDerNagel, J.E.: A systematic review of substance use (disorder) in individuals with mild to borderline intellectual disability. Eur. Addict. Res. **25**(6), 263–282 (2019)
20. EpochAI: AI trends: compute (2024). https://epoch.ai/trends/compute. Accessed 28 Feb 2025
21. Feng, Y., Qiang, J., Li, Y., Yuan, Y., Zhu, Y.: Sentence simplification via large language models. arXiv preprint arXiv:2302.11957 (2023)
22. van Financiën, M.: Interdepartementaal beleidsonderzoek mensen met een licht verstandelijke beperking, September 2019. https://www.eerstekamer.nl/overig/20191004/interdepartementaal/meta
23. Fuchs, K.: Exploring the opportunities and challenges of NLP models in higher education: is Chat GPT a blessing or a curse? Front. Educ. **8**, 1166682 (2023)
24. Goldsack, T., Scarton, C., Shardlow, M., Lin, C.: Overview of the BioLaySumm 2024 shared task on the lay summarization of biomedical research articles. arXiv preprint arXiv:2408.08566 (2024)
25. Guo, D., et al.: DeepSeek-R1: incentivizing reasoning capability in LLMs via reinforcement learning. arXiv preprint arXiv:2501.12948 (2025)
26. de Haan, T., et al.: AstroMLab 3: achieving GPT-4o level performance in astronomy with a specialized 8B-parameter large language model. arXiv preprint arXiv:2411.09012 (2024)
27. Haug, K.N., Klein, P.D.: The effect of speech-to-text technology on learning a writing strategy. Read. Writ. Q. **34**(1), 47–62 (2018). https://doi.org/10.1080/10573569.2017.1326014
28. van Herwaarden, A., Schuiringa, H., van Nieuwenhuijzen, M., de Castro, B.O., Lochman, J.E., Matthys, W.: Therapist alliance building behavior and treatment adherence for Dutch children with mild intellectual disability or borderline intellectual functioning and externalizing problem behavior. Res. Dev. Disabil. **128**, 104296 (2022)
29. Hobo, E., Pouw, C., Beinborn, L.: "geen makkie": interpretable classification and simplification of Dutch text complexity. In: Proceedings of the 18th Workshop on Innovative Use of NLP for Building Educational Applications, BEA 2023, pp. 503–517 (2023)
30. HAI Stanford University for Human-Centered: AI index report (2024). https://aiindex.stanford.edu/report/. Accessed 28 Feb 2025
31. Iyer, L.S., Chakraborty, T., Reddy, K.N., Jyothish, K., Krishnaswami, M.: AI-assisted models for Dyslexia and Dysgraphia: revolutionizing language learning for children. In: AI-Assisted Special Education for Students With Exceptional Needs, pp. 186–207. IGI Global (2023)
32. Jahan, I., Laskar, M.T.R., Peng, C., Huang, J.X.: A comprehensive evaluation of large language models on benchmark biomedical text processing tasks. Comput. Biol. Med. **171**, 108189 (2024)
33. Jamet, H., Manderlier, M., Shrestha, Y.R., Vlachos, M.: Evaluation and simplification of text difficulty using LLMs in the context of recommending texts in French to facilitate language learning. In: Proceedings of the 18th ACM Conference on Recommender Systems, pp. 987–992 (2024)
34. Jiang, C., Maddela, M., Lan, W., Zhong, Y., Xu, W.: Neural CRF model for sentence alignment in text simplification. arXiv preprint arXiv:2005.02324 (2020)
35. Johnson, K.R., Blaskowitz, M.G., Mahoney, W.J.: Technology for adults with intellectual disability: secondary analysis of a scoping review. Can. J. Occup. Ther. **90**(4), 395–404 (2023)

36. Katz, G., Lazcano-Ponce, E.: Intellectual disability: definition, etiological factors, classification, diagnosis, treatment and prognosis. Salud pública de México **50**(S2), 132–141 (2008)
37. Kenniscentrum LVB: LVB in de samenleving (2024). https://www.kenniscentrumlvb.nl/lvb-in-de-samenleving/. Accessed 03 Jun 2024
38. Kew, T., et al.: BLESS: benchmarking large language models on sentence simplification. arXiv preprint arXiv:2310.15773 (2023)
39. Kharbat, F.F., Alshawabkeh, A., Woolsey, M.L.: Identifying gaps in using artificial intelligence to support students with intellectual disabilities from education and health perspectives. Aslib J. Inf. Manag. **73**(1), 101–128 (2021)
40. Kincaid, J.P., Fishburne Jr., R.P., Rogers, R.L., Chissom, B.S.: Derivation of new readability formulas (automated readability index, fog count and flesch reading ease formula) for navy enlisted personnel (1975)
41. Klöser, L., Beele, M., Schagen, J.N., Kraft, B.: German text simplification: finetuning large language models with semi-synthetic data. arXiv preprint arXiv:2402.10675 (2024)
42. Kooli, C.: Chatbots in education and research: a critical examination of ethical implications and solutions. Sustainability **15**(7), 5614 (2023)
43. Kurni, M., Mohammed, M.S., Srinivasa, K.: AI-enabled gamification in education. In: A Beginner's Guide to Introduce Artificial Intelligence in Teaching and Learning, pp. 105–114. Springer (2023)
44. Li, L., Ma, Z., Fan, L., Lee, S., Yu, H., Hemphill, L.: ChatGPT in education: a discourse analysis of worries and concerns on social media. Educ. Inf. Technol., 1–34 (2023)
45. Liu, H., Zhang, Y., Jia, J.: The design of guiding and adaptive prompts for intelligent tutoring systems and its effect on students' mathematics learning. IEEE Trans. Learn. Technol. (2024)
46. Liu, Y., Iter, D., Xu, Y., Wang, S., Xu, R., Zhu, C.: G-Eval: NLG evaluation using GPT-4 with better human alignment. arXiv preprint arXiv:2303.16634 (2023)
47. Lo, C.K.: What is the impact of ChatGPT on education? A rapid review of the literature. Educ. Sci. **13**(4), 410 (2023)
48. Landelijk Kenniscentrum LVB: LVB in het kort (2024). https://www.kenniscentrumlvb.nl/over-lvb/. Accessed 06 Jun 2024
49. Matthews, N., Folivi, F.: Omit needless words: sentence length perception. PLoS ONE **18**(2), e0282146 (2023)
50. Milička, J., et al.: Large language models are able to downplay their cognitive abilities to fit the persona they simulate. PLoS ONE **19**(3), e0298522 (2024)
51. Van der Molen, M.J., Van Luit, J.E., Jongmans, M.J., Van der Molen, M.W.: Verbal working memory in children with mild intellectual disabilities. J. Intellect. Disabil. Res. **51**(2), 162–169 (2007)
52. Moonen, X., Festen, D., Bakker-van Gijsel, E., Vervoort-Schel, J.: A Dutch perspective on two health related issues regarding children and adolescents with intellectual disabilities. Int. J. Environ. Res. Public Health **19**(18), 11698 (2022)
53. Moonen, X.M.H.: (h)erkennen en waarderen, July 2017. https://dare.uva.nl/personal/pure/en/publications/herkennen-en-waarderen(490019d7-2191-4dfc-8456-15bb2ea3468a).html
54. Mukh, Y.A., Tarteer, S., AL-Qasim, M., Saqer, K., Daher, W.: Using gamification to motivate students with simple-moderate intellectual disabilities. Eur. J. Educ. Res. **12**(2) (2023)
55. Ngo, T.T.A.: The perception by university students of the use of ChatGPT in education. Int. J. Emerg. Technol. Learn. (Online) **18**(17), 4 (2023)

56. Nozza, D., Attanasio, G.: Is it really that simple? Prompting language models for automatic text simplification in Italian. In: Italian Conference on Computational Linguistics, p. 1 (2023)
57. Oblizanov, A., Shevskaya, N., Kazak, A., Rudenko, M., Dorofeeva, A.: Evaluation metrics research for explainable artificial intelligence global methods using synthetic data. Appl. Syst. Innov. **6**(1), 26 (2023)
58. Ownby, R.L., Acevedo, A., Waldrop-Valverde, D.: Enhancing the impact of mobile health literacy interventions to reduce health disparities. Q. Rev. Distance Educ. **20**(1), 15 (2019)
59. Paech, S.J.: EQ-Bench: an emotional intelligence benchmark for large language models. arXiv preprint arXiv:2312.06281 (2023)
60. Papineni, K., Roukos, S., Ward, T., Zhu, W.J.: BLEU: a method for automatic evaluation of machine translation. In: Proceedings of the 40th annual meeting of the Association for Computational Linguistics, pp. 311–318 (2002)
61. Pouls, K.P., et al.: Mental healthcare for adults with mild intellectual disabilities: population-based database study in Dutch mental health services. BJPsych Open **9**(2), e48 (2023)
62. van Raaij, N.B., Kolkman, D., Podoynitsyna, K.: Clearer governmental communication: text simplification with ChatGPT evaluated by quantitative and qualitative research. In: Proceedings of the Workshop on DeTermIt! Evaluating Text Difficulty in a Multilingual Context@ LREC-COLING 2024, pp. 152–178 (2024)
63. Rahman, M.M., Watanobe, Y.: ChatGPT for education and research: opportunities, threats, and strategies. Appl. Sci. **13**(9), 5783 (2023)
64. Reiss, A.L., Abrams, M.T., Singer, H.S., Ross, J.L., Denckla, M.B.: Brain development, gender and IQ in children: a volumetric imaging study. Brain **119**(5), 1763–1774 (1996)
65. Seidl, T., Vandeghinste, V.: Controllable sentence simplification in Dutch. Comput. Linguist. Neth. J. **13**, 31–61 (2024)
66. Shelton, A., Wexler, J., Silverman, R.D., Stapleton, L.M.: A synthesis of reading comprehension interventions for persons with mild intellectual disability. Rev. Educ. Res. **89**(4), 612–651 (2019). https://doi.org/10.3102/0034654319857041
67. Sigstad, H.M.H., Garrels, V.: Which success factors do young adults with mild intellectual disability highlight in their school-work transition? Eur. J. Spec. Needs Educ. **38**(4), 573–587 (2023)
68. Staunton, E., Kehoe, C., Sharkey, L.: Families under pressure: stress and quality of life in parents of children with an intellectual disability. Irish J. Psychol. Med. **40**(2), 192–199 (2023)
69. Sulem, E., Abend, O., Rappoport, A.: BLEU is not suitable for the evaluation of text simplification. arXiv preprint arXiv:1810.05995 (2018)
70. Tanprasert, T., Kauchak, D.: Flesch-Kincaid is not a text simplification evaluation metric. In: Proceedings of the 1st Workshop on Natural Language Generation, Evaluation, and Metrics, GEM 2021, pp. 1–14 (2021)
71. Tummers, H.J.M.: Health information systems in intellectual disability care: towards the re-use of routinely collected data. Ph.D. thesis, Wageningen University and Research (2022)
72. Van Ijzendoorn, M.H., Luijk, M.P., Juffer, F.: IQ of children growing up in children's homes: a meta-analysis on IQ delays in orphanages. Merrill-Palmer Q., 341–366 (2008)
73. Vanroy, B.: GEITje 7B Ultra: a conversational model for Dutch. arXiv preprint arXiv:2412.04092 (2024)

74. Vaswani, A., et al.: Attention is all you need. Adv. Neural Inf. Process. Syst. **30** (2017)
75. Vlantis, D., Gornishka, I., Wang, S.: Benchmarking the simplification of Dutch municipal text. In: Proceedings of the 2024 Joint International Conference on Computational Linguistics, Language Resources and Evaluation (LREC-COLING 2024), pp. 2217–2226 (2024)
76. Vossen, W., Szymanski, M., Verbert, K.: The effect of personalizing a psychotherapy conversational agent on therapeutic bond and usage intentions. In: Proceedings of the 29th International Conference on Intelligent User Interfaces, pp. 761–771 (2024)
77. Walton, C., Medhurst, D., Madhavan, G., Shankar, R.: The current provision of mental health services for individuals with mild intellectual disability: a scoping review. J. Mental Health Res. Intellect. Disabil. **15**(1), 49–75 (2022)
78. Woittiez, I., Eggink, E., Ras, M.: Het aantal mensen met een licht verstandelijke beperking. notitie ten behoeve van het ibo-lvb.[the number of people with a mild intellectual disability in the netherlands. note part of the interdepartmental policy research concerning intellectual disabilities.] (2019)
79. Xu, W., Napoles, C., Pavlick, E., Chen, Q., Callison-Burch, C.: Optimizing statistical machine translation for text simplification. Trans. Assoc. Computat. Linguist. **4**, 401–415 (2016)
80. Zhang, T., Kishore, V., Wu, F., Weinberger, K.Q., Artzi, Y.: BERTScore: evaluating text generation with BERT. arXiv preprint arXiv:1904.09675 (2019)
81. Zhang, Y., Sun, R., Chen, Y., Pfister, T., Zhang, R., Arik, S.: Chain of Agents: large language models collaborating on long-context tasks. Adv. Neural. Inf. Process. Syst. **37**, 132208–132237 (2025)
82. Zhu, C., Sun, M., Luo, J., Li, T., Wang, M.: How to harness the potential of ChatGPT in education? Knowl. Manage. E-Learn. **15**(2), 133–152 (2023)

# Author Index

If you have any concerns about our products,
you can contact us on
ProductSafety@springernature.com

In case Publisher is established outside the EU,
the EU authorized representative is:
Springer Nature Customer Service Center GmbH
Europaplatz 3, 69115 Heidelberg, Germany

Printed by Libri Plureos GmbH
in Hamburg, Germany